Conspiracy Investigations:
Terrorism, Drugs, and Gangs

Gregory D. Lee, M.P.A.
Supervisory Special Agent (Ret.)
U.S. Drug Enforcement Administration

D1412572

Upper Saddle River, New Jersey 07458

Library of Congress Cataloging-in-Publication Data

Lee, Gregory D.
    Conspiracy investigations : terrorism, drugs and gangs / by Gregory D. Lee. — 1st.
        p. cm.
    Includes bibliographical references and index.
    ISBN 0-13-117228-X
    1. Conspiracy—United States. 2. Criminal investigation—United States. 3. Terrorism.
4. Drug traffic. 5. Gangs. I. Title.

    KF9479.L44 2005
    363.25'0973—dc21

                                                    2004012987

Executive Editor: Frank Mortimer, Jr.
Assistant Editor: Korrine Dorsey
Production Liaison: Brian Hyland
Director of Manufacturing and Production: Bruce Johnson
Managing Editor: Mary Carnis
Manufacturing Buyer: Cathleen Petersen
Design Director: Cheryl Asherman
Senior Design Coordinator: Miguel Ortiz
Cover Designer: Carey Davies
Cover Image: Ron Sachs, CORBIS SYGMA
Director, Image Resource Center: Melinda Reo
Manager, Rights and Permissions: Zina Arabia
Interior Image Specialist: Beth Brenzel
Cover Image Specialist: Karen Sanatar
Formatting and Interior Design: Carlisle Publishers Services
Printing and Binding: Phoenix

Pearson Education LTD.   Pearson Education Australia PTY, Limited
Pearson Education Singapore, Pte. Ltd   Pearson Education North Asia Ltd
Pearson Education, Canada, Ltd   Pearson Education de Mexico, S.A. de C.V.
Pearson Education–Japan   Pearson Education Malaysia, Pte. Ltd

10 9 8 7 6 5 4 3 2 1
0-13-117228-X

This book is dedicated to my two sons, Gregory D. Lee Jr. and Christopher B. Lee, both of whom I am very proud.

It is also dedicated to the memory of Drug Enforcement Administration Special Agent Enrique "Kiki" Camarena, who was kidnapped, tortured, and murdered by drug conspirators while on assignment in Mexico.

Contents

Chapter 6. *Drug Interdiction Conspiracy Cases*   *62*

Chapter 10. *Overview of Terrorism*   *109*

Chapter 11. *Overview of Drug Trafficking*   *128*

Chapter 12. *Gang Profiles: Crips and Bloods*   *141*

Chapter 13. *Terrorism Conspiracy Case Study*   *147*

Preface

Terrorists, drug traffickers, and street gangs increase their likelihood of success when they organize. Someone acting alone is more likely to change his mind about committing a crime than someone who is involved with others in a criminal conspiracy. Because of their far-reaching effects, conspiracy investigations have been proven to be some of the most effective means to dismantle entire criminal organizations.

Arresting individual low-level terrorists, drug dealers, and street gang members does little to stop their supervisors, managers, organizers, and facilitators from continuing their criminal enterprises. However, these criminal organizations are especially vulnerable to comprehensive conspiracy investigations. Thanks to Judicial Interpertation of existing conspiracy laws, these groups can be dismantled by making *all* members of a criminal conspiracy subject to indictment, arrest, and conviction for the crimes each member of the organization commits in furtherance of the conspiracy.

Conspiracy Investigations: Terrorism, Drugs, and Gangs explains in detail what a conspiracy is, what the elements of the crime are, how the law allows prosecutors to attach criminal liability to all members of a conspiracy, and the many other advantages of charging defendants with these statutes. The book guides the reader through a series of realistic examples to reinforce important teaching points that focus on how to investigate and successfully prosecute these cases. It also discusses the techniques used by federal agencies to perform extrajudicial renditions to bring international conspirators to the United States to face justice, regardless of whether an extradition treaty exists.

While an instructor at the Office of Training for the U.S. Drug Enforcement Administration (DEA), I taught new special agents, intelligence analysts, diversion investigators, state and local police officers, and members of the intelligence community how to conduct comprehensive conspiracy investigations. As a member of a DEA international training team, I also taught many foreign law enforcement officials how to apply their newly ratified conspiracy laws against organized drug criminals.

Conspiracy Investigations: Terrorism, Drugs, and Gangs takes the mystery out of the law and explores the many investigative techniques that can be used to expand criminal investigations to their fullest potential, so criminal organizations can be dismantled. This book also describes how to develop successful investigative and prosecution strategies against organized criminals. Along the way, it introduces the reader to the world of terrorism, drug, and gang organizations and how they operate.

About the Author

Gregory D. Lee retired as a supervisory special agent for the U.S. Department of Justice, Drug Enforcement Administration (DEA) in late 2003. He is now a criminal justice author and consultant.

Throughout his diverse government career, he has conducted and supervised numerous international drug conspiracy investigations, and at one time he was the resident agent-in-charge of the DEA's Karachi, Pakistan, office. While in Pakistan between 1994 and 1998, Mr. Lee became personally involved in several notable terrorism investigations. He participated in the arrest of Ramzi Ahmed Yousef, the mastermind behind the 1993 World Trade Center bombings who was thought by many to be the architect of the attacks of September 11, 2001. He also later testified at Yousef's trial and was cross-examined by Yousef, who elected to represent himself. Through informants, he also assisted the FBI in locating Amil Kanzi, the terrorist responsible for the murder of two CIA employees outside CIA headquarters in 1993. As a result of his terrorism investigation experiences in Pakistan, he has lectured for and consulted with various agencies within the U.S. intelligence community. He also appeared on an episode of the Discovery Channel's *The FBI Files* that included information about his actions during the Kanzi investigation.

Mr. Lee taught conspiracy investigations, drug smuggling, informant management, and many other courses as an instructor at the DEA's Office of Training, located at the FBI Academy in Quantico, Virginia. He developed and taught weeklong conspiracy-investigation seminars for federal, state, and local law enforcement officers and intelligence community analysts around the country. He spent a year as a member of one of the DEA's international training teams, visiting many countries to provide conspiracy and drug enforcement training to foreign law enforcement officials.

He is the author of the textbook, *Global Drug Law Enforcement: Practical Investigative Techniques,* published by CRC Press, and he has written several articles on drug enforcement topics for professional publications, including the *FBI Law Enforcement Bulletin* and *The Police Chief* magazine.

Mr. Lee also served as a counselor for the 160th session of the FBI National Academy in 1990.

Prior to working for DEA, he was a police officer for the cities of Salinas and Pasadena in California.

Mr. Lee has a combination of more than 32 years of active duty and U.S. Army Reserve service, and he is a chief warrant officer 5/special agent with the U.S. Army Criminal Investigation Command, better known as CID. As an Army reservist, he is an associate instructor with the U.S. Army Military Police School and is a subject matter expert in counter–drug operations and terrorism.

Shortly after the attacks of September 11, 2001, he was called to active duty and served one year at the U.S. Army Operations Center's Anti-Terrorism Operations and Intelligence Cell at the Pentagon, where he routinely analyzed highly classified intelligence data and briefed the Army's top leadership on terrorism and force-protection issues.

Mr. Lee earned a master of public administration in justice administration degree from Golden Gate University, San Francisco, and a bachelor's of science degree in sociology with dual minors in vocational education and criminology from the University of Maryland. While attending graduate school, he taught a criminal investigation course for Monterey Peninsula College, Monterey, California.

He is a regularly scheduled guest speaker at the Defense Intelligence Agency's Joint Military Intelligence Training Center in Washington, D.C. Mr. Lee has been a guest lecturer for the International Law Enforcement Academy in Bangkok, Thailand, the California Narcotic Officers' Association, and the International Narcotic Interdiction Association. He is a frequent radio talk show guest concerning his DEA assignment in Pakistan.

Acknowledgments

Many thanks are in order to Lieutenant Michael Korpal of the Pasadena, California, Police Department for his invaluable assistance in providing the information necessary to construct the gang conspiracy case found in Chapter 15. His and his fellow detectives' hard work resulted in the dismantlement of one of the most violent street gangs in the city's history.

Thanks are also in order for Chief Deputy Steve Robbins of the Santa Cruz County, California, Sheriff's Department for helping me remember some of the facts of the drug conspiracy case we investigated together. The case is discussed in Chapter 14.

A special thank you to the reviewers: John Boal, University of Akron; John Cencich, California University of Pennsylvania; Dick De Lung, Wayland Baptist University; David Graff, Kent State University Tuscarawas; and Ronald D. Swan, Lincoln College.

CHAPTER 1

Introduction to Conspiracy Law

Criminals increase their likelihood of success when they organize. Law enforcement officials in the United States and elsewhere are faced with the problems of terrorists, drug dealers, and street gangs, as well as traditional and nontraditional organized crime syndicates. These criminal organizations prey on members of their community and surrounding areas, and in many cases their numbers are expanding. Arresting one or two people for individual crimes has no impact on a criminal organization and does little to provide a long-term solution to the dangers the other criminals present.

Many large metropolitan areas experience traditional *and* nontraditional organized crime elements operating within their jurisdiction. Some traditional organized crime groups are defined as part of the Italian Mafia, or *La Cosa Nostra,* which preys on businessmen, entrepreneurs, organized labor groups, and contractors through extortion, loan sharking, and protection rackets.

A nontraditional group may be an outlaw motorcycle gang selling methamphetamine or stolen motorcycle parts, or an Asian street gang, whose members sell drugs and demand money from first-generation migrants of their community in exchange for protection from their criminal activities. Many of these victims will not call the police because their culture dictates they should take care of their own problems without the help of outsiders.

Other nontraditional organized crime groups include the Russian and Israeli Mafias, which frequently join forces with other criminal groups that are involved with drug and weapons trafficking.

A proven way to eliminate all types of criminal organizations is for police investigators to focus primarily on the elements of the crime of conspiracy first and the substantive crimes second. Conspiracy laws are a potent tool in investigators' bags because they enable them to eliminate entire organizations by reaching out and striking devastating blows to all members simultaneously.

The concept of conspiracy originated in England centuries ago and evolved from common law into present-day statutes.

The effectiveness of conspiracy laws was recognized at the United Nations 1988 Geneva Convention Against Illicit Trafficking in Narcotic Drugs and Psychotropic Substances, and many nations adopted both drug-conspiracy and money laundering statutes as a result. These signatory nations also agreed to cooperate in **controlled deliveries**, which is a recognized investigative technique used in conspiracy investigations to determine who is receiving drugs smuggled from one country to another. See Chapter 11 for details.

Terrorist organizations, drug traffickers, street gang members, burglars, robbers, smugglers, fences, truck hijackers, arson-for-hire specialists, and outlaw motorcycle gang members are all equally vulnerable to conspiracy laws.

These laws allow investigators to use the evidence gathered against one conspirator to be used against other conspirators, rather than requiring separate evidence for each. This expands an existing criminal investigation to its fullest.

Many international drug and terrorist organizations have been brought to justice in the United States for violating U.S. conspiracy laws, even though they never have or even intended to visit the country. This is because U.S. federal conspiracy laws are **extraterritorial**, which means they apply to anyone, anywhere, even outside the territorial boundaries of the country if a connection to the United States can be established in some way. Once indicted, they can be tried in the United States when they are located and brought here, regardless of the means. Without extraterritorial conspiracy laws, terrorists and drug lords in foreign nations would be able to operate with impunity.

Because conspiracies are secret in nature and each coconspirator is an agent of each other, prosecutions are often allowed an exception to the hearsay rule of evidence. "Hearsay" is a statement, other than one made by the person testifying at a trial or hearing, offered in evidence to prove the truth of a matter asserted. This means an undercover agent, informant, or cooperating defendant can testify about the words, deeds, and actions of the coconspirators. This is a tremendous advantage over nonconspiracy criminal prosecutions and is reason in itself to charge eligible criminals with conspiracy when applicable.

Conventional drug cases require an inordinate amount of time, personnel, and, above all, money when attempting to secure a conviction for distribution. These and other nondrug cases usually go far beyond what is necessary to convict a suspect for the often-overlooked crime of conspiracy.

Police supervisors and managers concerned with budget restraints should realize that a conspiracy constitutes a separate and distinct offense and does not depend on whether the suspects accomplished the conspiracy's objective.

Undercover drug agents technically do not have to spend money to buy drug evidence during conspiracy cases if they can prove the suspects were engaged in a conspiracy to traffic in drugs. Accordingly, drug investigations that concentrate on the simple elements of proof for conspiracy can achieve many of the same results as more-elaborate investigations with potentially much less cost.

Drug conspiracy investigations are not designed to take the place of aggressive, long-term, multijurisdictional cases that have the promise of large drug and money seizures.

However, they can often achieve the same results of more-traditional drug investigations. People, drugs, and assets can be identified and located using fewer departmental resources. In short, drug conspiracy cases can provide an innovative way to expand existing budgets while potentially eliminating an entire criminal drug organization.

Drug agents know through training and experience that it is virtually impossible to commit a drug crime alone. Conspiracy laws allow drug agents to seek indictments for all of the coconspirators during the course of a single investigation. Without U.S. conspiracy laws such as 21 U.S.C. 846[1] and 963,[2] federal authorities could not indict, arrest, and try suspected international drug criminals who conspire to violate U.S. drug laws outside America's borders.

DEFINITION OF CONSPIRACY

An agreement between two or more people to commit a crime constitutes a conspiracy. It is the *agreement* the investigator seeks to prove. The crime the conspirators agree to commit does not have to be completed in order to commit a conspiracy. Even if the conspirators do not have the means or wherewithal to achieve a criminal goal or if it is factually impossible to do, they can still be found guilty of conspiracy if they had the sincere intent to commit the crime. Impossibility to complete is not a basis for a legal defense.[3]

Every state has conspiracy statutes,[4] and federal criminal codes have a general conspiracy law as well as different conspiracy laws for specific crimes. Some of these conspiracy laws call for the punishment to be the same as for the crime the defendants conspired to commit. This means defendants can potentially receive twice the sentence for the crime they commit if their involvement in a conspiracy can be proved.

Federal and some state laws provide that if a defendant is convicted of a conspiracy to commit any offense involving a controlled substance, the punishment is the same as if the object of the conspiracy had been completed.[5]

An example of a federal conspiracy law that is more general, has a specific sentence, and requires an overt act (see definition that follows) be committed by a conspirator for conviction is 18 U.S.C. §371: "If two or more persons conspire either to commit any offense against the United States or to defraud the United States or any agency thereof in any manner or for any purpose and one or more of such persons do any act to effect the object of the conspiracy, each shall be fined not more than $10,000 or imprisoned not more than five years or both."

The agreement to commit a crime is the crime of conspiracy. Conspiracy does not become a lesser-included offense of the crime the conspirators set out to commit. It is not an attempt to commit a crime. In other words, the charge of conspiracy is not and does not become part of the substantive crime when it is committed, regardless if it is to hijack airplanes, bomb buildings, sell drugs, or have someone killed. Many states, however, require that an *overt act* be committed by at least one member of the conspiracy to consummate the crime.[6] An overt act is simply *anything* done by a conspirator to further the goal of the conspiracy. Some federal statutes do not require this; however, without at least one provable overt act, prosecutors are unlikely to seek an indictment. The more overt acts that are uncovered during an investigation, the better the likelihood a jury will agree with the prosecution theory that the defendants conspired to commit a crime they sincerely intended to commit.

Investigators should always keep in mind that whatever evidence they gather, they must present it to the twelve human beings who comprise a jury. They must keep it simple enough that any juror will conclude that the defendants reached an agreement to commit the crime in question.

U.S. District Court Judge John Martin of the Southern District of New York used the following as a portion of his jury instructions in conspiracy cases:

> Simply defined, a conspiracy is an unlawful agreement by two or more persons to violate the law. Whether or not the persons accomplished what they conspired to do is immaterial to the question of guilt or innocence in regard to a conspiracy. The success or lack of success of the conspiracy doesn't matter, for a conspiracy is a crime entirely separate and distinct from the substantive crime that may be the goal of the conspiracy.
>
> A conspiracy has sometimes been called a partnership in crime in which each partner becomes the agent of every other partner. However, to establish the existence of a conspiracy, the Government is not required to show that two or more persons sat around a table and entered into a formal agreement, orally or in writing, stating that they have formed a conspiracy to violate the law, setting forth the details of the means by which it was to be carried out or the part to be played by each conspirator. Indeed, it would be extraordinary if there were such a formal document or specific agreement.
>
> Thus, it is sufficient if two or more persons, in any manner, through any contrivance, either implied or tacitly, came to a common understanding to violate the law. Express language or specific words are not required to indicate assent or attachment to a conspiracy.*

In investigating conspiracies, investigators should keep in mind that what they are attempting to prove is merely that an ***agreement*** was made between two or more persons to violate the law. Conspirators are not accessories to the crime; they are equal partners under the law.

Drug investigators should also appreciate that an individual purchaser of drugs from a street-level dealer cannot be charged with conspiracy because he *is* the object of the conspiracy.[7]

THE WHARTON RULE

Generally, persons can be charged and convicted of both conspiracy and the completed crime that they agreed to commit. There is, however, an exception to that general rule. The exception, known as the Wharton Rule, provides that a conspiracy cannot be charged if the commission of the substantive offense requires interaction between two people.[8] For example, in order to distribute illegal drugs, there must be both a seller and a buyer. Under

---

*(DEA Office of Training, Quantico, VA)

the Wharton Rule, if two people complete a one-time sale of a small quantity of a controlled substance, the buyer and seller cannot be charged with conspiracy.[9]

However, there is an exception to the Wharton Rule. If an additional defendant who is not necessary for the commission of the crime is involved in the transaction, then the rule will not preclude a conspiracy charge.[10] For example, if a drug trafficker employs someone else to help him in a drug sale to a buyer, the Wharton Rule would not preclude the helper from being convicted for conspiracy.[11]

Another way to defeat a Wharton Rule defense is to establish sufficient evidence that the buyer and seller have a long-standing criminal relationship that involves repeated sales of large quantities of illegal drugs. Such facts would be circumstantial evidence that there is an agreement beyond a simple one-time transaction. Consequently, the buyer and seller could be charged with conspiracy in addition to the substantive drug charge.[12]

Some courts do not apply the Wharton Rule at all to drug cases. Instead, they permit a buyer and seller to be convicted of conspiracy even though there is not a third party present or any other exception to the rule.[13] These courts rely on the U.S. Supreme Court decision of *Jannelli v. United States*,[14] in which the Court stated that the Wharton Rule is merely a judicial presumption that is to be applied in the absence of legislative intent to the contrary. For instance, in *United States v. Bommarito*,[15] the U.S. Court of Appeals for the Second Circuit determined that because the federal drug conspiracy statute, 21 U.S.C. §846, provides that it is a violation to conspire to commit any of the crimes under Title 21, the U.S. Congress did not intend that conspiracy charges under §846 were to be limited by the Wharton Rule.

PUNISHMENT FOR CONSPIRACY

Federal statutes, along with those of many states, provide that when a defendant is convicted of a conspiracy to commit an offense, particularly a drug offense, the punishment is the same as it would have been if the object of the conspiracy had been completed.[16] In other words, the punishment for conspiracy is often, but not always, identical to that given for the crime the conspirators sought to commit.[17]

If a conspiracy ends before its goal is accomplished, this does not absolve the conspirators of being involved in a conspiracy because it is a separate and distinct offense. Conspirators can also be charged with any additional substantive crimes they may have committed during the conspiracy's lifetime.

ELEMENTS OF THE CRIME OF CONSPIRACY

Federal and most state statutes in the United States merely require proof that *two or more* people *made an agreement* to commit a *criminal act* and that at least one *overt act* was committed in furtherance of the conspiracy.

Through training and experience, investigators know that it is practically impossible to commit sophisticated crimes like drug trafficking and launching terrorist attacks without the help of others. A street *gang*, as the name implies, also consists of more than one person.

Most drugs abused in the United States originate from outside its borders. It takes many people to cultivate, harvest, process, package, smuggle, store, protect, and sell drugs. With the possible exception of a domestic, indoor marijuana grow that only involves a cultivator who sells his crop to a select customer base, there has to be a conspiracy. The investigator's job is to identify those persons who agreed to participate in the commission of the crime.

The same concept applies to terrorists and street gangs that have the intent, but not always the means, to commit certain crimes without help from other coconspirators. It's the *agreement* that is the primary focus of any conspiracy investigation.

PLURALITY REQUIREMENT

It is important for investigators to understand that in order to prove a conspiracy, the prosecution must show that *two or more* people were involved in the *agreement* to commit a crime. What is equally important is that undercover government agents and informants are not part of that equation. However, this is increasingly changing. Several states have enacted unilateral conspiracy statutes that allow a suspect to be charged with the crime of conspiracy even if the suspect made the agreement with an informant or undercover agent to commit a crime.[18, 19]

During an investigation it is common for an investigator to meet undercover with a drug trafficker, fence, illegal arms dealer, or other criminal through an informant introduction. For example, during an initial meeting between an undercover agent and a drug trafficker, an agreement is reached on how the sale of a substantial amount of cocaine will take place. The trafficker departs the meeting location to obtain the drugs. He returns shortly afterward and delivers the cocaine to the undercover agent, whose surveillance team arrests him.

In this example, even though three people discussed committing a crime, two of the three are **agents of the government**. In most, but not all cases, the cocaine dealer cannot be charged with the crime of conspiracy because the investigator cannot prove the existence of another member of the conspiracy, despite knowing from his training and experience that others must be involved.

Investigators must show that at least two suspects are involved in a crime in order to arrest a suspect for conspiracy. Investigators *do not* have to fully identify any or all of the other members of the conspiracy; they merely have to prove they exist. The meeting in itself satisfies any requirement that an overt act take place before a conspiracy is consummated.

How can the police prove other suspects are involved in the conspiracy?

The undercover agent should merely ask the drug dealer if he will be returning to the meeting location with anyone else. If the defendant replies that he will be alone when he delivers the drugs, the agent can ask the trafficker to call his drug supplier before he leaves to confirm the drugs are available for immediate delivery. If the defendant replies he already has checked or if he calls someone on his cellular telephone or otherwise admits to the existence of someone else being involved in the crime, the investigator can later articulate in a police report and in court that the defendant called a coconspirator, thus proving the existence of a conspiracy. Even if the person the trafficker called is never identified, the element of proof of *two or more* persons has been satisfied. The defendant's admission to being involved in a crime with others is sufficient to sustain a conviction for conspiracy.[20] The defendant can now be charged with the crime of conspiracy in addition to the possession and distribution of the cocaine.

Why is this important?

The defendant now has *two* substantial charges against him instead of one. He may now be eligible to be sentenced to twice the amount of time in prison. He is also much more likely to cooperate with investigators in order to reduce the charges against him by disclosing the identities of the other members of his criminal organization. Those people can also be charged with conspiracy *and* the distribution of the cocaine to the undercover investigator. (This will be discussed in detail later.) Without the charge of conspiracy, the opportunity to expand this investigation might be forever lost.

A second example: An investigator is told by an informant that he knows someone who is in possession of ten stolen computers that are new in their boxes, and this someone wants to sell them quickly. This investigator knows that a series of commercial burglaries of computer stores recently took place in the city. The investigator is familiar with the sophisticated *method of operation* the burglars used to break in to the stores, and he knows that there probably was more than one burglar involved.

The investigator instructs the informant to arrange a meeting between the investigator and the man with the stolen computers to discuss buying the stolen property. The informant sets up a meeting at a local restaurant.

At the meeting the suspect describes in detail the computers he has for sale. The investigator shows interest and negotiates a price for them. After agreeing to deliver the merchandise at an abandoned building in an hour, the suspect leaves the restaurant. When he arrives at the warehouse with the computers, the police arrest the man for receiving stolen property.

Can the man also be charged with conspiracy?

No. The undercover investigator neglected to further his investigation by proving that other people were involved in the burglaries.

How could he have done so?

Simple. Conspiracy case law only requires that law enforcement prove the existence of other conspirators.

How could the investigator have done this?

The undercover investigator only had to ask the suspect to verify that the merchandise was ready for delivery by calling his partners. If the suspect had said, "I already talked to them, and it's ready to go," or "He told me he can deliver in an hour," or anything similar, than he would have acknowledged that there were other people involved in the crime. This would have been sufficient to charge the original suspect with conspiracy, along with the other suspects when they were identified through further investigation. If during the undercover meeting the suspect denied that others were involved, he might have been telling the truth. Unlike a drug operation, some commercial burglars work alone. His denial might have convinced the investigator, and the jury, that the burglar acted alone.

A third example: An informant introduces a drug dealer to an undercover investigator to discuss the sale of methamphetamine. The investigator knows that he or she and the informant do not add to the equation in the requirement of two or more people to constitute a conspiracy. After discussing the specifics of the delivery, the suspect leaves the public park where the meeting took place. A surveillance team follows him to a residence. Within a few minutes he and another man emerge from the residence. The surveillance team sees the original man carrying a shopping bag that he places in the trunk of a car. The surveillance team follows the pair back to the meeting location, where the car is parked in a public lot. The original suspect exits his car, retrieves the bag from the trunk, and delivers the drugs concealed in the bag to the undercover officer while the other man stays behind in the vehicle. Both men are arrested.

Can they both be charged for the crime of conspiracy to distribute methamphetamine?

Under these circumstances, prosecutors probably will not be enthusiastic about charging the second man with conspiracy. The undercover investigator neglected to ask the original suspect who the other man in the car was or if he was somehow involved. He also failed to ask the original suspect if he would be returning alone to deliver the drugs. The presence of a second person indicates he is there either to supervise the transfer of the drugs or to provide security for the original suspect. Drug dealers rarely, if ever, ask an innocent person to accompany them on a drug deal.

The undercover investigator should have engaged the original suspect in conversation about the existence of other suspect(s). Merely asking the original suspect if his source of supply could deliver the same amount of methamphetamine on a steady basis would have overcome the burden of proving his involvement in a conspiracy. Asking what role the man in the car had might have swayed the prosecutor to file charges on him as well. Because this didn't happen, the investigators must now determine through other means what, if any role, the second person had in the crime. The second person may claim he was getting a ride from the suspect and had no knowledge of the drug delivery. The statement may be true, and the investigators are obliged to determine the second suspect's truthfulness. A search of the vehicle for weapons could indicate the second man was there for protection. Cellular telephones possessed by both men could be indicative of the man acting as a lookout for the presence of the police. Separate, intense interrogations, coupled with a polygraph examination, may be required to prove or disprove the second suspect's involvement in the crime. If the undercover investigator had asked a harmless question about other people coming to deliver the drugs, all of this might have been avoided.

Additional factors that might indicate that the second suspect was involved in the drug conspiracy could be the discovery of the man's fingerprints on the shopping bag or drug package, the location of the gun in relation to where the second suspect sat in the vehicle, or a determination that the second suspect had been convicted in the past for drug distribution. Each additional fact uncovered would help convince a prosecutor to indict the second suspect for conspiracy.

In *United States v. Figueroa* (720 F. 2d 1239 [1983]), the Supreme Court ruled that a defendant's admission to engaging in the drug trade with others is sufficient to sustain a conviction for conspiracy, even if the coconspirators were never identified or indicted.[21]

In these three examples, to prove the existence of a conspiracy, the undercover investigators could have asked harmless questions that would have revealed the existence of other suspects. If the suspects had said that they knew the drugs or merchandise was available because they had called their sources earlier that day, that admission in itself would have been sufficient to prove the existence of a conspiracy.

Conspirators do not have to know each other. There is no requirement that the prosecution prove that each conspirator knew all the other members of the same conspiracy or what their individual roles were in achieving the object of the conspiracy.

A fourth example: A reliable police informant tells an investigator that he has heard there is going to be a robbery of a particular jewelry store tomorrow, but he has no further information. Because the informant has proven to be reliable in the past, investigators decide to place surveillance on the store. They tell the storeowner about the possible robbery plot, and he agrees to allow an undercover investigator to pose as a store employee. The police surveillance team sees a car pull up and double-park on the street in front of the store. The driver remains in the car, but another man, wearing a ski mask and carrying a handgun, emerges. The man enters the store and demands money and expensive jewelry from the undercover investigator he thinks is a store employee. The man receives the loot and runs out of the store to the waiting car, only to be arrested by the surveillance team.

Can either or both men be charged with conspiracy in addition to robbery?

Yes. Clearly these men made an agreement ahead of time to rob the jewelry store. The prosecution does not have to prove when or where the agreement was made. The fact that both men participated in the crime makes them eligible for indictment for the additional charge of conspiracy.

THE AGREEMENT

We know that many conspiracy laws only require that two or more people reach an agreement to commit a crime. However, the purpose of the law is to only punish those persons who have a sincere intent to commit a crime. Investigators must show that a sincere agreement took place among the parties in order to secure a conspiracy conviction.

For example: An off-duty police officer is at a packed sports bar with friends watching a telecast of a professional football game. During one play, the favorite team's quarterback throws an interception that allows the opposing team to score a touchdown, and this eventually results in the favorite team's defeat. The officer hears two men seated next to him angrily discussing the interception and loss. They mention that they lost money in a bet because of the poor skills of the quarterback. One of the men remarks to the other, "Someone ought to kill that guy. Not only did he lose the game, he caused us to lose our bet!" The other man agrees by saying, "Yeah, we ought to kill that guy!" The men finish their drinks and depart their separate ways. The police officer obtains their license plate numbers, identifying the men.

Can the police officer later arrest the men for conspiracy to murder the quarterback?

No! There is absolutely no evidence to suggest the men are sincere in their agreement. Loose talk in a bar could never be construed as either a sincere agreement or a conspiracy.

An agreement does not have to be formal. The prosecution does not have to produce a written contract or video and audiotapes showing the conspirators reaching an agreement. Further, a police informant or undercover investigator does not need to be present at the time the agreement is made. Indeed, it would be highly unlikely to have an informant present at the time a conspiracy is hatched. However, it is not that unusual for investigators to discover detailed plans or instructions either in writing or on computer hard drives and floppy disks. There have been many cases in which investigators have recovered written instructions by organizers and managers of a conspiracy for subordinate members to follow. Figure 1–1 is a handwritten document seized from a briefcase of a conspirator, incidental to his arrest, instructing members of a cocaine distribution conspiracy not to use drugs while conducting business. A questioned document examiner later identified the person arrested as the writer of the instructions.

As another example, the al-Qaeda terrorist organization produced a document more than 100 pages long, (commonly referred to as the *al-Qaeda Training Manual*), that was uncovered by British police. It details how to avoid police surveillance, how to commit acts of sabotage, conduct assassinations, make discrete contact with other members, and the like. This training manual is powerful physical evidence that can be used against those who possess it because it tends to demonstrate that they agreed with others to commit terrorist acts.

A different training manual on how to conduct suicide bombings was found in 2002 in the possession of one of six men in Lackawanna, New York, who were believed to be members of an al-Qaeda "sleeper cell" operating in the United States. The document was written in Arabic, and it was described as "chilling" and "scary" by federal prosecutors. The document, titled *Definition of Martyrdom Operations and Their Effects on the Enemy,* was used as evidence that the men agreed to participate in a conspiracy. It also was used to convince a judge not to grant them bail pending the outcome of the trial. The document noted that the common practice in suicide bombings is to "wire up one's body, or a vehicle or suitcase with explosives, and then to enter amongst a conglomeration of the enemy . . . and to detonate in an appropriate place there in order to cause the maximum losses in enemy ranks."

"As for the effects of these operations on the enemy," the document continues, "we have found, through the course of our experience, that there is no other technique which strikes as much terror into their hearts, and which shatters their spirit as much."[22]

Finding such documents can be powerful evidence to prove a prosecution theory that not only did a conspiracy exist, but that the people who possessed the documents agreed to be involved.

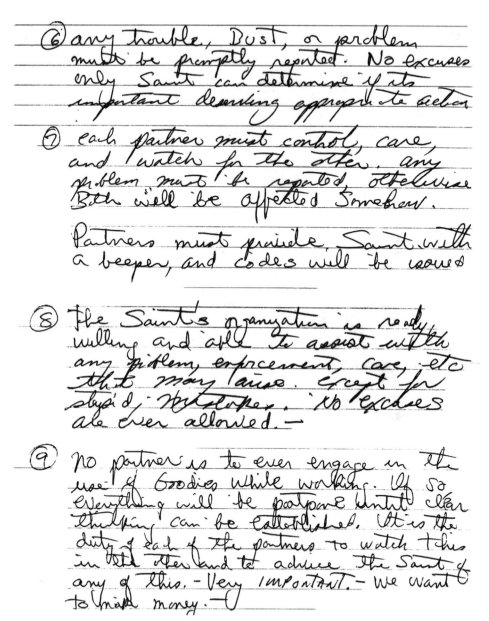

Figure 1–1   Written page of instructions to conspirators. Other pages were never located.

Merely associating with conspirators or having knowledge of the existence of a conspiracy does not constitute agreeing to join the conspiracy. Only those people who made a specific or an implied agreement to carry out the object of the agreement, as evidenced by overt acts, can be charged.

It is also not necessary that a person actually say anything at the time of an agreement to be charged with the crime of conspiracy if other circumstantial evidence indicates that the person tacitly agreed to become a member of the conspiracy. As an example, in *U.S. v. Baptista-Rodriguez,*[23] the defendant attended several meetings to plan a cocaine-importation scheme. The defendant was later identified by others at one of the meetings as one of the "boat people." The court affirmed the defendant's conspiracy conviction by applying common sense. The court said "[i]t is highly unlikely that conspirators attempting a 500 kilogram smuggling operation would have tolerated the recurrent presence of a mere bystander, especially during the operational stage of the scheme."[24] The court reasoned that even though the defendant never said anything during the meetings, it was reasonable to infer that he was a willing participant in the conspiracy and not a bystander.

In another case, the simple nodding of the suspect's head satisfied the court in *U.S. v. Alvarez*[25] that he was guilty of conspiracy in a ***reverse-sting operation***. A reverse-sting operation occurs when law enforcement officers pose as drug traffickers in order to arrest drug buyers and seize the money they would have spent on the drugs they intended to purchase. Alvarez met with undercover agents from the U.S. Drug Enforcement Administration (DEA), one of whom asked him if he would be present at a remote landing strip to help unload a plane that would be returning from Colombia. The DEA agent never made any mention that the plane was supposed to be full of marijuana when he asked the question. Alvarez merely nodded his head to indicate that he would be there. The agents arrested Alvarez. The U.S. Supreme Court upheld his conviction after concluding that, by nodding his head in agreement to help offload the plane, Alvarez had knowledge of the conspiracy and was a willing participant.

A girlfriend, wife, child, or parent of a conspirator may know about the existence of the conspiracy, but that knowledge doesn't make them members of it. However, the fact that they knew about the conspiracy and failed to report it to police authorities may make them liable for another crime, such as misprison of a felony.

If someone furnishes equipment or other items to the conspirators so they can achieve the object of the conspiracy, can that person be charged in the same conspiracy?

It depends on whether the equipment or other items can be commonly found and do not have restrictions on their possession.

In the 1940 case *U.S. v. Falcon,*[26] suppliers sold yeast and sugar to a member of an illegal distilling conspiracy. The U.S. Supreme Court found that although the evidence showed the suppliers knew the recipient of the yeast and sugar was making illegal moonshine, that alone did not make them members of the conspiracy. Such knowledge by itself is insufficient to establish that a person is guilty of being a part of a conspiracy. Investigators must produce evidence of an agreement.

However, when someone supplies and encourages known criminals to purchase supplies that are ordinarily difficult to obtain and that are used in illegal activity, it can be inferred that he is promoting the illegal enterprise. As an example, in *U.S. v. Grunsfield*[27] the U.S. Supreme Court ruled that a chemist was in a conspiracy with illegal drug manufacturers because he supplied large amounts of chemicals and equipment on three or four occasions to individuals who the chemist knew were illegal PCP manufacturers. The supplier did more than merely supply commodities to the conspiracy; he promoted the illegal enterprise and made large profits on the sales of the chemicals. Unlike the defendant in the *Falcon* case, the chemist in *Grunsfield* supplied materials that were difficult to obtain and were often used in the production of illegal drugs.

The reasoning behind these and other cases can easily be applied to someone who supplies automatic weapons to gang members, a silencer to a contract killer, or Pseudoephedrine, the essential ingredient for methamphetamine, to known clandestine-laboratory operators.

OVERT ACTS

Reaching an agreement, in itself, is usually insufficient to commit the crime of conspiracy. In most cases the prosecution must also prove a member of the conspiracy committed an overt act in furtherance of the conspiracy.

Investigators can prove a person's sincerity in agreeing to be a member of a conspiracy by proving he committed **overt acts**. Also, even though some statutes may not require it, as a practical matter, prosecutors will seldom charge suspects with conspiracy unless investigators can prove the conspirators committed at least one overt act in furtherance of the conspiracy.

An overt act is *anything* done to carry out the object of the conspiracy. Overt acts do not have to be criminal in nature. Purchasing or stealing a boat to transport drugs from South America to the United States is an overt act made in furtherance of a smuggling conspiracy.

When prosecutors prepare a conspiracy indictment to present to a grand jury, they will list major overt acts uncovered during the course of the investigation to support the theory that these particular defendants were engaged in a conspiracy. Meetings to discuss details of the plan, travel to a meeting place, and renting a car or stealing an airplane to deliver drugs are all examples of overt acts.

Members of a conspiracy do not need to know what overt acts other members committed. Further, investigators do not have to uncover all of the overt acts committed by each member of the conspiracy. One is sufficient. However, it stands to reason that the more overt acts uncovered, the more convincing it is for a jury to conclude that a conspiracy was formed and that the defendants made a sincere agreement to carry out its goal.

In another example, eight men meet in a hotel room in Florida to discuss the smuggling of five tons of marijuana from Colombia. Each man is assigned a specific role during this meeting. They agree that four of the conspiracy members will sail a boat to a designated location, where they will meet the other four members, who will transfer the drugs to them. These men will then sail the boat to a deserted island among the Florida keys, where an off-loading party will meet them. The day after the meeting, one of the men visits a boat dealership and purchases a 60-foot sailing vessel to use in the venture.

Has the crime of conspiracy now been consummated?

Yes. The purchase of the boat is a clear indication that these men are sincere in their agreement to smuggle drugs into the country. The conspiracy is not completed until at least one overt act occurs. The investigation is not completed until as many overt acts as possible are uncovered.

Examples of overt acts are telephone calls; the act of traveling to meetings to discuss the details of the crime; the meetings themselves; drug sales; the theft of supplies used in the crime; and the renting of cars, storage facilities, equipment, boats, or airplanes used to carry out the object of the conspiracy. The establishment of cellular telephone service used to communicate with coconspirators is a common overt act committed by organized criminals.

PINKERTON THEORY OF VICARIOUS LIABILITY

In a 1946 U.S. Supreme Court case,[28] the justices ruled that conspirators can be charged with substantive offenses committed by coconspirators throughout the life of the conspiracy, provided that: (1) They were in the conspiracy at the time the offense was committed; (2) the offense was committed in furtherance of the conspiracy; and (3) the offense was a foreseeable consequence of the conspiracy. This principle is called the Pinkerton theory of Vicarious Liability.

As an example, street gang members A, B, C, and D agree to commit a drive-by shooting to kill a rival gang member. To avoid detection by the police, defendant A orders defendant D to borrow a car to be used in the shooting from someone living in another area. Unknown to A, B, or C, D instead steals a car because he couldn't find anyone willing to lend him a vehicle. He subsequently is caught in the stolen car just before he is to pick up A, B, and C to conduct the drive-by shooting. He admits to the police he stole the car so he and the others could commit the murder. The police locate and arrest A, B, and C and find them in possession of four loaded firearms. After being interrogated by police investigators, they all admit they were going to shoot rival gang members using the vehicle "borrowed" by D. The police charge them with conspiracy to commit murder.

Can A, B, and C, be charged with auto theft along with D?

Yes. A, B, C, and D can all be charged with auto theft by virtue of their involvement in a conspiracy at the time the car was stolen. The auto theft was a foreseeable consequence of the crime they conspired to commit. The fact that A specifically instructed D to borrow a car is no legal defense to the crime. Although A, B, and C did not know about the vehicle theft, this fact has no bearing on the charges, even if D corroborates the others' denial.

Each member of a conspiracy acts as an agent for other members and is liable for any crime committed in furtherance of the original conspiracy. It's irrelevant whether other members knew the crimes were going to be committed or even if they discouraged other members from committing those crimes.

New members of a conspiracy can only be charged with crimes committed by other members *after* they entered the conspiracy. They cannot be held responsible for crimes previously committed by other members.

In order to charge all eligible conspiracy members with all pertinent crimes, the prosecution must show the crimes were committed to further the goal of the conspiracy. Prosecutors do not have to prove that as a member of a conspiracy, a defendant either participated in, or even knew of the existence of these crimes. They only must prove that he was a member of the conspiracy at the time the crimes were committed. This is an effective tool police and prosecutors can use in bringing criminal charges against all members of a criminal organization, which facilitates its dismantlement. It is one of the major benefits of conducting conspiracy investigations.

In this example, if D had kidnapped a woman and raped her in the stolen car before getting arrested, could A, B, and C, also be charged with rape?

No. D's kidnapping and rape of a woman clearly had nothing to do with the object of the conspiracy, which was to commit a drive-by shooting.

WITHDRAWAL FROM THE CONSPIRACY

The most common legal defense used in a conspiracy case is that the defendant withdrew from the conspiracy before any substantive crimes occurred. In other words, he may be guilty of conspiracy, but he is not guilty of the often many substantive crimes other members of the conspiracy may have committed during the life of the conspiracy.

In order to withdraw, a conspirator must either inform the police about the conspiracy or inform all the other known coconspirators of his intention to withdraw.

The conspirator who wishes to withdraw from a conspiracy must do something affirmative to show his intent to withdraw. Merely staying away from or avoiding the other conspirators does not constitute withdrawal.

For fear of being arrested, there is little chance that a member of a conspiracy will voluntarily inform the police about his involvement in a conspiracy. These admissions generally come only after a person has been arrested and is caught up in a legal dilemma that prompts him to cooperate with the authorities. However, if during the course of a conspiracy investigation investigators learn through undercover meetings, wiretaps, or formal interviews that someone did tell other members he no longer wanted to be involved in the conspiracy, this exculpatory information must be made available to his defense attorney.

The burden of proof that the defendant withdrew from the conspiracy without going to the police ultimately lies with the defendant. This means other members of the conspiracy must be willing to testify that the defendant informed them he no longer wished to be a member. The likelihood of this is extremely remote; therefore, the only practical way to withdraw from a conspiracy is to reveal it to the police.

As an example: On July 24, a department store detective arrests a man for shoplifting. A search of the man reveals several checkbooks in different names, none of which is his own. During an interview, the suspect admits to the security officer that he is involved with others in passing these stolen checks at local businesses. The police are called. They know that bad checks from these checkbooks have been passed throughout the city, but they did not realize the connection. The police arrive at the store and take custody of the suspect. He admits to them that he and several of his friends have been entering office buildings and going through unsecured purses looking for checkbooks, credit cards, and cash. These stolen checkbooks are the ones they have been using to write bad checks. He says that he and his friends pool their stolen property and checkbooks together and that they practice forging the victims' signatures before the checks are passed.

The police conduct their investigation and arrest the persons identified by the shoplifter on August 2. They continue to receive reports of stolen checks being passed in the community until August 1.

Can the original defendant be charged with the bad checks that were passed after his arrest on July 24?

No. The man has effectively withdrawn from the conspiracy by admitting his involvement. However, he can be charged for bad checks passed up to July 24, and in most jurisdictions, with the burglary and theft of the purses and their contents before he withdrew. He can also be charged with conspiracy, because withdrawing from the conspiracy does not absolve him of that crime; it only shields him from being charged with future substantive crimes committed by other members of the conspiracy.

Unless an individual member of a conspiracy formally withdraws from the conspiracy, he is liable for all substantive crimes committed to further the object of the conspiracy until the object of the conspiracy ends in failure or success. As additional crimes are discovered that were committed by conspiracy members, it's important to know which members were active at the time in order to charge them with the offenses. It is equally important to know which members legally withdrew from the conspiracy so they are not charged with crimes for which they are not criminally liable.

It is also important to note that many conspiracies continuously add and remove members throughout their lifetimes. Sometimes a member may be so incompetent the other members agree he should leave. His rejection by the others would probably constitute withdrawal.

TERMINATION OF THE CONSPIRACY

The lifetime of a conspiracy ends in one of two ways: either the object of the conspiracy is completed, or the object is not completed.

Knowing when a conspiracy ends is important because, as just mentioned, all members of the conspiracy can be charged with the substantive crimes that are discovered during its lifetime provided they were members of the conspiracy at the time the crimes were committed.

Some criminal organizations have been involved in the same conspiracy for decades; others engage in new conspiracies one after another.

When the organizers, managers, and supervisors of a criminal organization are arrested, this does not mean the conspiracy has terminated. The head of the organization may continue to direct the activities of others from within prison, or another trusted member might take over the vacated leadership role.

An example of a conspiracy ending in failure is when a vessel used by a marijuana-smuggling organization sinks in international waters before reaching its destination to pick up the drugs. If the conspirators obtain a second boat and attempt the same thing again, a defense attorney might argue that the original conspiracy ended and an entirely different conspiracy was formed. (See chapter 8, "Defense Attorney Tactics.") An example of a conspiracy ending in success would be if the marijuana-laden vessel makes its way back to the United States and is off-loaded by the other conspirators, who later distribute the drug undetected.

In 2003, the U.S. Supreme Court ruled that members of a conspiracy can be convicted of the crime of conspiracy even when the police discover the plot and make it impossible for the conspirators to achieve their goal.[29] The case stemmed from a controlled drug delivery investigation in which a truck driver transporting cocaine and marijuana was arrested in Nevada. He decided to cooperate with the police. Under the supervision of drug agents, he delivered his cargo in Idaho to the intended recipients, who were arrested immediately after taking possession of the truck. The Supreme Court's unanimous decision validated controlled deliveries as a legal investigative technique, not only in drug enforcement, but in terrorism and gang investigations as well.

Justice Stephen G. Breyer wrote in the opinion for the Court: "Where police have frustrated a conspiracy's specific objective but conspirators have neither abandoned the conspiracy nor withdrawn . . . special conspiracy-related dangers remain. So too remains the essence of the conspiracy—the agreement to commit the crime. In our view, conspiracy law does not contain any such 'automatic termination' rule," saying it was "inconsistent with our own understanding of basic conspiracy law."

VENUE

Under federal law, venue lies in any jurisdiction in which an overt act occurs, where the conspiracy agreement was made, or in Washington, D.C., if the agreement or overt acts took place outside the territorial boundaries of the United States. In most states, venue lies in whatever county or government jurisdiction in which the agreement was made or where an overt act occurs.

Venue is an important consideration for investigators because this determines what specific U.S. or state attorney's office has the responsibility of prosecuting the matter.

Investigators may find that members of a complex terrorism, drug, or gang conspiracy operate throughout several states or federal judicial districts committing criminal and other overt acts. Every time a criminal or overt act is identified in a particular venue, the prosecuting authority has the ability, but not the obligation, to adopt the entire case and prosecute each member of the conspiracy in his or her particular jurisdiction.

The prosecutor can also reach an agreement with the other affected jurisdictions about what part of the conspiracy they will prosecute, essentially sharing the responsibility. One prosecutor may determine his office does not have the time, enthusiasm, or resources necessary to prosecute all or part of a complex conspiracy investigation, whereas another prosecutor, in another jurisdiction where venue also exists, may be more aggressive and view the same conspiracy as a routine matter.

Investigators can use venue to their advantage. As an example, an undercover drug agent may have the opportunity to pick the location where he or she will take delivery of a substantial amount of drugs. The agent knows from personal experience that one particular county's district attorney's office doesn't have the manpower to prosecute a complex conspiracy case or that the judges there do not view drug crimes as being very serious. On the other hand, an adjacent county has a stellar team of highly competent prosecutors who aggressively prosecute such cases, and the judges have a well-deserved reputation of handing out severe penalties to drug dealers.

Even if an undercover drug agent orchestrates in which county a drug delivery takes place, venue applies. The drug agent may legally arrange for an overt act, such as the delivery of drugs or the conducting of a meeting, to occur in any venue during an ongoing conspiracy investigation for the sole reason of establishing court jurisdiction there.

A downside to multiple venues is that many problems may occur in the coordination and logistics of prosecuting a matter in more than one jurisdiction. This coordination with prosecutors is necessary to eliminate duplication of effort and double jeopardy issues, especially when these jurisdictions are far apart. Another downside is that a jury may believe that in order for the defendants to receive more punishment than they may have otherwise received, the drug agent purposely created venue in a particular jurisdiction. This can create jury apathy toward the defendant and harm the prosecution.

Jury nullification can also occur when drug agents purposely orchestrate the delivery of drugs on or near school grounds in order for a defendant to receive enhanced punishment as provided by law.

DURATION OF THE CONSPIRACY

Conspiracies run from the time an agreement is made until the object of the conspiracy ends in either success or failure. It is usually impossible to determine when the original agreement was made; however, it is often possible to determine when it ended.

Investigators should be cognizant that just because the police have arrested some members of a conspiracy, this does not mean the conspiracy has ended. It only ends when the object of the conspiracy has been completed or the attempts of the conspirators to reach the goal of the conspiracy have failed. Many times members of a conspiracy are tried for their roles in ongoing conspiracies because other members of the conspiracy are continuing their criminal activities.

As an example, five American Islamic men agree among themselves to do whatever they can to conduct *jihad,* or holy war, against the United States, and they want to assist Osama bin Laden's al-Qaeda terrorist organization. None of them have ever met a member of the al-Qaeda organization; however, they intend to travel to a foreign country to try to meet with al-Qaeda representatives and offer their assistance.

The men decide that they should try to train themselves in the United States in the use of weapons prior to traveling overseas. One of the men rents a secluded mountain cabin to practice shooting rifles that the other two men have purchased. One of the men also conducts extensive research on the Internet to learn how to construct homemade bombs.

After several months of target practice and successfully fashioning and testing several improvised explosive devices, the men are observed by a forest ranger, who notifies an FBI Joint Terrorism Task Force (JTTF), which initiates an investigation.

The JTTF investigation reveals that the five men conspired to essentially wage war against the United States and to provide material support to a terrorist organization. They obtain arrest warrants and go to the mountain cabin, where they arrest four of the five suspects. They learn through interrogation that the fifth man has traveled to Afghanistan, hoping to meet members of al-Qaeda and assist them in carrying out operations.

Has the conspiracy ended with the arrest of the four men in the United States?

No. It continues on because a member still intends to follow through with the object of the conspiracy. Any crimes the one outstanding suspect commits could be attached to the others unless they effectively withdraw from the conspiracy by cooperating with law enforcement.

STATUTE OF LIMITATIONS

Under federal law, and in many states, the statue of limitations runs five years from the last overt act, or when the conspiracy ends, whichever is later. The statute of limitations is especially important to know when investigators are conducting **historical conspiracy** investigations, which will be discussed in detail in Chapter 2.

If an investigator discovers a conspiracy that has ended, he or she may still open a case, but time may run out before the investigation is completed and an indictment is returned by a grand jury. Any informants involved in such a case must be carefully interviewed to determine if the conspiracy has ended or when the last overt act occurred and if it is possible to corroborate the information through witnesses, documents, or other means.

If an informant tells investigators about a previously unreported crime, such as a drug deal, occurring at a particular hotel room, it might be possible to obtain the registration card to establish when the offense took place. The date will be important in determining when the statute of limitations will expire.

SUMMARY

Criminals increase their likelihood of success when they organize. People acting alone are more likely to change their minds about committing crimes than people who are involved with others in a criminal conspiracy. Because of the far-reaching effects of conspiracy laws, including the ability to attach criminal liability to all members of a conspiracy equally, they have been used for years by the federal government to successfully dismantle entire criminal organizations. Conspiracy laws are one of the most potent legal tools an investigator can use against terrorists, drug traffickers, and gang members.

A conspiracy is an *agreement* reached between *two or more people* to commit a crime. The entering into an agreement *is* the crime and is a separate offense from any other crimes the conspirators may commit or attempt to commit during the lifetime of the conspiracy. Undercover agents or informants are not counted in the number of persons within the conspiracy because they are agents of the government. Two or more genuine members of a conspiracy must be known to exist.

Conspirators can be charged with substantive offenses committed by coconspirators throughout the life of the conspiracy, provided that: (1) They were in the conspiracy at the time the offense was committed; (2) the offense was committed in furtherance of the conspiracy; and (3) the offense was a foreseeable consequence of the conspiracy. Mere association or knowledge of the existence of the conspiracy does not constitute joining.

Conspirators are agents of each other. They do not have to know each other or what each member's role in the conspiracy is. Killing someone during a drug deal is a foreseeable consequence of a drug conspiracy. Shoplifting a six-pack of beer on the way to a drug deal is not.

Most conspiracy statutes require that the prosecutor demonstrate that at least one conspirator committed an *overt act* in an effort to reach the goal of the conspiracy. An overt act is *anything* done to carry out the object of the conspiracy, and it does not have to be criminal in nature. Overt acts demonstrate the conspirators' intent to carry out the object of the conspiracy. The prosecutor does not have to prove that any of the participants in the conspiracy knew that coconspirators committed overt acts.

In most conspiracy trials, the prosecution has the added advantage of having an exception to the hearsay rule of evidence that allows for testimony of an informant, undercover agent, or cooperating defendant about the words, deeds, and actions of the conspirators.

The most common legal defense in a conspiracy case is that the defendant withdrew from the conspiracy before any substantive crimes occurred. In order to legally withdraw, a conspirator must inform the police about the conspiracy or inform the other known coconspirators of his or her intention to withdraw. Withdrawing from a conspiracy before a substantive crime occurs does not absolve the defendant from the original crime of conspiracy.

The conspiracy terminates when either the object of the conspiracy has been completed or the object of the conspiracy has not been completed.

Venue for conspiracy trials lies in any jurisdiction in which an overt act occurred, where the agreement was made, or in Washington, D.C., if the conspiracy was initiated outside the territorial boundaries of the United States. The extraterritorial aspects of conspiracy laws allow the government to indict and prosecute foreign drug traffickers and terrorists who have never visited the United States.

The duration of a conspiracy runs from the time an agreement is reached until it ends in either success *or* failure. Arresting one or more of the conspirators does not necessarily mean the conspiracy has failed or ended.

The statute of limitations for the federal crime of conspiracy runs five years from the last overt act or when the conspiracy ends, whichever is later. Most state conspiracy statutes are the same.

NOTES

1. Conspiracy to distribute controlled substances.
2. Conspiracy to import controlled substances into the United States.
3. *U.S. v. Jannotti,* 673 F. 2d 578, 591 (3d Cir. 1982), cert. Denied, 457 U.S. 1106, overruled in part on other grounds by *Mathews v. U.S.,* 485 U.S. 58 (1988).
4. Investigators should check their individual state conspiracy statutes for the elements of proof and prescribed punishments.
5. U.S. Sentencing Commission, *Guidelines Manual,* sec. 2D1.4(a) Nov 1991.
6. State and local criminal investigators should check their individual state statutes for details concerning the requirement of an overt act.
7. The Wharton Rule may preclude a conspiracy charge when there is only one buyer and one seller agreeing to violate the law. See *Iannelli v. United States,* 420 U.S. 770 (1975).
8. *United States v. Varelli,* 407 F. 2d 735, 748 (7th Cir. 1969) (Conviction for conspiracy reversed because the single crime of purchasing stolen goods required an agreement between buyer and seller).
9. E.g., *United States v. DeLutis,* 722 F. 2d 902, 905 (1st Cir. 1983); *State v. Utterback,* 485 N.W. 2d 760 (Neb. 1999), overturned in part on other grounds by *State v. Johnson,* 256 Neb. 133, N.W. 2d (Neb. 1999). Also see *Johnson v. State,* 587 A. 2d 444, 452 (Del. 1991) (The Wharton Rule does not prohibit the charging of conspiracy in addition to a charge of possession with intent to distribute drugs because possession with intent to distribute does not require concert of action between two people in order to commit it).
10. *Curtis v. United States,* 546 F. 2d 1188, 1190 (5th Cir. 1977).
11. *United States v. Jones,* 801 F. 2d 304, 311 (8th Cir. 1986).
12. *United States v. Moran,* 984 F. 2d 1299, 1302–04 (1st Cir. 1992); *Commonwealth v. Cantres,* 540 N.E. 2d 149, 152 (Mass. 1989).
13. E.g., *United States v. Philips,* 959 F. 2d 1187, 1190 (3d Cir. 1992); *Commonwealth v. Cantres,* 540 N.E. 2d 149, 152 (Mass. 1989).
14. 420 U.S. 770 (1975).
15. 524 F. 2d 140, 144 (2d Cir. 1975).
16. U.S. Sentencing Commission, *Guidelines Manual,* sec. 2D1.4(a) Nov 1991.
17. Investigators should check their individual state conspiracy statutes for details.
18. *New York v. Schwimmer,* 394 N.E. 2d 288 (New York 1979) (Defendant conspired with an undercover agent and an informant to steal diamonds); *Ohio v. Marian,* 405 N.E. 2d 267, 270 (Ohio 1980) (Defendant conspired with an informant to murder his wife); *State v. Null,* 526 N.W. 2d 220, 229 (Nebraska 1995) (Defendant was in a conspiracy with a party who feigned agreement).
19. State and local investigators should always check with their prosecutors for case law affecting their state.
20. *United States v. Figueroa,* 720 F. 2d 1239 (1983).
21. *United States v. Goodwin,* 492 F. 2d 1141 (1974).
22. Josh Getlin, "New Evidence Delays Bail Ruling for 6 N.Y. Terror Suspects," *Los Angeles Times,* October 3, 2002.
23. 17 F. 3d 1354 (11th Cir. 1994).
24. Id. at 1374.
25. 625 F. 2d 1196 (5th Cir. 1980) (en banc).
26. 311 U.S. 205, 211 (1940).
27. 558 F. 2d 1231, 1236 (1977).
28. *Pinkerton v. United States,* 328 U.S. 640, 66 S. Ct. 1180, 90 L.Ed. 1489 (1946).
29. *U.S. v. Jimenez Recio, et al,* No. 01-1184 (2003).

CHAPTER 2

Types of Criminal Conspiracies

There are seven types of criminal conspiracies that investigators will frequently encounter: ongoing, no dope, historical, chain, cell, wheel, or any combination of conspiracies that occur when two or more separate criminal organizations have combined their efforts and resources.

ONGOING CONSPIRACIES

Ongoing conspiracies are those currently under way, in which the object of the conspiracy has either not yet been achieved or the conspirators have met their goal and are currently engaging in criminal activities.

Investigating ongoing criminal conspiracies, especially in drug cases, frequently involves an undercover agent or a confidential informant to gather physical evidence and identify all members of the criminal organization.

Police do not have to wait until the object of the conspiracy is achieved before taking action. Because a conspiracy is a separate and distinct offense in itself, arrests can be made to thwart a drug transaction or terrorist act before the conspirators have an opportunity to commit it.

An example of an ongoing conspiracy: Police investigators are told by an informant that members of a terrorist cell are preparing to set a bomb off in a crowded theater in their city, and they have asked the informant to assist them. Based on additional information obtained from the informant, the investigators establish surveillance of the suspects. The informant decides to help the investigation and agrees to wear a recording device during future contacts with the alleged terrorists. The police electronically monitor the informant while he attends meetings with the terrorists at various hotels and restaurants. The police record the men discussing engaging in jihad, "death to the infidels," and "death to America," but no mention is made of blowing up a threater. The informant reports that he has seen one of the men making sketches of the floor plans of a theater.

The next day the surveillance team follows the men to a truck rental agency, where they obtain a seventeen-foot truck and drive it to a fuel depot, where they purchase eight empty 55-gallon drums and load them into the truck. The men then drive the truck to a local shopping center that has a multiscreen theater and legally park. A short time later, a passenger car arrives driven by a man the informant identifies as another cell member, and the men from the truck get into the car and drive away.

Is there an ongoing conspiracy?

Yes, a conspiracy has definitely occurred. Without the intelligence provided by the informant, these acts would appear to be innocent, but coupled with the informant's information and the tape recordings, the men's actions take on an entirely different meaning.

Should the police arrest the men now?

From a practical standpoint, it would probably be premature to arrest the suspects without further investigation. Because the overt acts they have committed are not criminal in nature and there is no evidence they have the means to explode a bomb, the investigators should continue surveillance with the goal of identifying other members of the conspiracy. The meetings in a restaurant and a hotel, the drawing of the sketch, and the rental of the truck are all examples of overt acts in furtherance of the conspiracy, but a defense attorney is likely to point out to the jury that none of these acts is illegal. A prosecutor would be reluctant to seek indictments or file charges until more evidence is gathered. The members of the jury have to ultimately decide if a conspiracy was ongoing, but they are often reluctant to convict if the goal of the conspiracy is not realized (e.g., the theater blowing up), unless there is overwhelming and compelling evidence.

Further, the informant could get scared and run away, making himself unavailable for future court proceedings and severely weakening the case. Also, the sketch of the theater has not yet been found. Without the informant's testimony and more physical evidence, indictments would be unlikely at this point.

Overnight, a team of investigators interviews a hotel clerk where one of the meetings was held. They retrieve the registration card that was filled out at the time the room was rented. They discover that the room was paid for in cash, and the name on the registration card is later determined to be fictitious. A check of the hotel records for telephone calls made from the room reveals that some were made to foreign countries that are known to harbor terrorists.

The employees at the rental-truck agency explain to another team of investigators that the men paid cash for the truck. The information on a photocopy of the renter's driver license is later determined to be fictitious.

Should the police now make their arrests?

With this added information, the burden of the defense would be to explain why someone would use a false name to rent a room and produce a fraudulent driver's license to rent a truck. The circumstances would tend to show that the men were involved in some nefarious activity. However, assuming adequate manpower existed to continue the surveillance of the suspects, further investigation is still warranted.

The next day, investigators staking out the parked rental truck observe the men being dropped off at the shopping center by the same car and driver that picked them up the previous day. The men in the truck and the driver of the car are followed to a lawn and garden shop, where they pay cash for numerous large bags of ammonium nitrate fertilizer. The surveillance team sees the men load the truck with the fertilizer and observes one of the men opening a bag and pouring the contents into one of the 55-gallon drums before closing the truck's rear sliding door. The men then drive to a truck stop, where they are seen filling each of the 55-gallon drums with diesel fuel. The investigators know that this combination of diesel fuel and ammonium nitrate fertilizer can produce a powerful bomb similar to those used in the 1993 World Trade Center and Oklahoma City bombings.

Should arrests now be made?

Investigators would be wise to contact their prosecutor from the onset of their investigation and give him or her continuous updates on their progress in order to seek guidance about when he or she believes enough evidence has been gathered to arrest and successfully prosecute the suspects. To delay any further at this point runs the risk of jeopardizing public safety. There is the additional risk that the surveillance team could lose the suspects before they have the opportunity to arrest them. They should arrest the suspects before they have the opportunity to fully develop a bomb to destroy the theater. No matter if the suspects are later convicted, the public's safety comes before the prosecution merits of the case.

NO DOPE CONSPIRACIES

Ongoing and historical drug conspiracy cases that do not result in the seizure of drug evidence are called **no dope**, or **dry conspiracies**. These cases are usually initiated when an informant, whether motivated by revenge, greed, or fear of prosecution, admits to police that he has participated in past drug transactions.

Drug evidence is not necessary in prosecuting people who were involved in either a historical or an ongoing drug conspiracy, but investigators should make every effort to obtain it. A prosecutor's enthusiasm in seeking indictments in such a case usually increases, or diminishes, with the amount of drugs and money seized by investigators during the course of the investigation.

Corroborating as much of the informant's information as possible will enhance dry drug conspiracy investigations. If he says he met with other conspirators at a restaurant to discuss a drug transaction, investigators should attempt to verify this by obtaining credit card information and conducting photo lineups of the suspects to employees. Documentation of hotel room stays, rental car agreements, airline ticket purchases, purchases of chemicals and weapons, the rental of storage facilities, coupled with the testimony of a credible informant who is a former member of the conspiracy, can lead to indictments and convictions. These documents may prove the overt acts that members of the conspiracy engaged in to reach their goal.

An example of a no dope ongoing conspiracy: A man is arrested for possession of several ounces of cocaine that were found in his car when police officers investigated a traffic accident in which he was involved. Narcotic detectives turn the man over to Drug Enforcement Administration special agents, who interview him. The defendant admits the cocaine found in his vehicle was the last of a multikilogram shipment he received from a drug smuggler who routinely flies his private plane to Colombia and brings back an average of 60 kilograms of cocaine to sell at a time. The now defendant–informant agrees to cooperate with DEA and the detectives. After arranging a meeting with the smuggler, the informant introduces an undercover detective to him. The detective tells the smuggler he is looking for a new source of cocaine and he wants to buy a portion of the next load the smuggler brings in from Colombia. To appear convincing, the detective displays a DEA-provided *flash roll*, or the money that supposedly will be used to purchase a portion of the smuggler's cocaine. The greedy smuggler tells the detective he has flown to Colombia five times in the past year and has a good working relationship with his cocaine source, so obtaining the drugs should not be a problem. The smuggler agrees to sell the detective a portion of the cocaine when he returns from his next trip to Colombia.

The smuggler later flies to Colombia to obtain cocaine, only to learn that the authorities have arrested his source of supply and have seized all of his drugs. The smuggler telephones the informant from Colombia with the news, which is tape-recorded by DEA special agents. The smuggler returns to the United States empty handed.

Can the smuggler be arrested and prosecuted for conspiracy to import controlled substances into the United States, even if there was no dope seized?

Yes. The suspect's behavior meets all the elements to prove his involvement in a conspiracy, despite the fact that he was unable to obtain any cocaine through no fault of his own. He obviously had reached an agreement with his source of supply to smuggle cocaine to the United States, and his intent was to provide the drugs to the undercover detective for distribution in the United States. He admitted to being involved in the crime with his source of supply, and he committed several overt acts by meeting with the undercover investigator. The smuggler then traveled to Colombia to take possession of the cocaine. Seeking an indictment for the smuggler would be appropriate because he would most likely make future attempts to smuggle drugs into the United States once he establishes a new drug connection in Colombia. DEA agents would also attempt to identify the source of the smuggler's supply through Colombian police contacts and telephone records of the smuggler.

The smuggler's attorney most likely would argue that the police seized no drugs during the investigation because the smuggler never intended to deliver the drugs to the agent. Despite the testimony of an undercover detective and the defendant–informant, investigators should always attempt to electronically record all conversations with a suspect(s). They also could have verified that the smuggler possessed a pilot's license, had access to an airplane, and had filed real or fraudulent flight plans. A search warrant to retrieve his passport with entry and exit stamps and visas for Colombia would prove he had traveled there in the past. The totality of the evidence would help a jury decide if the smuggler actually intended to deliver the drugs.

HISTORICAL CONSPIRACIES

Historical conspiracies are those in which the object of the conspiracy has usually been achieved and the conspiracy has terminated. There is no requirement to prove the crime that was the object was accomplished, because the conspiracy in itself is the crime being investigated.

Historical conspiracy investigations are usually initiated when a former member of a conspiracy has been arrested and offers to provide law enforcement with information about a conspiracy he was involved in, along with the identities of the other members, in return for consideration in his legal situation. In these cases the informant will be providing the bulk of the investigative leads and usually will be required to testify against his former conspirators.

Historical conspiracies are investigated in the same manner as any other reported crime—that is, by locating and interviewing witnesses, conducting search warrants, gathering physical evidence including documents, and by interrogating suspects. The main difference is that the investigator's focus is on proving that the members of the conspiracy reached an agreement to commit the specified unlawful act and then committed a series of overt acts in an effort to achieve their goal.

Investigators should be cognizant that informant information is almost always presumed to be unreliable until it is corroborated. It is the investigator's job to corroborate all of the informant's information to lend credibility and competency to his claims. The credibility of the informant will weigh heavily in the prosecutor's judgment in seeking an indictment against members of a historical conspiracy. If the informant appears to be untruthful or is proven to be so, the likelihood of prosecution is remote.

If the prosecutor chooses not to seek an indictment against the conspirators, investigators may opt instead to initiate a fresh investigation and use the informant's information for intelligence purposes and as the basis for conducting surveillance of the suspects. Because historical conspiracy cases are investigated in the same manner as other reported crimes, the investigator's goal is to prove that an agreement to violate the law existed between two or more persons.

In historical conspiracy cases, the probable cause required to obtain search warrants to seize drugs, weapons, or other physical evidence probably will not exist, but search warrants for documents can, in most cases, be justified. Drug traffickers maintain paper and computerized *pay and owe sheets*, and terrorists have been known to maintain computer files that chronicle the details of future terrorism events. Both can help identify other members of conspiracies. Drugs, weapons, explosives, or other contraband found during the execution of a document search warrant are admissible as evidence and may lead to substantive charges. Historical drug conspiracy cases frequently locate money and other proceeds of drug transactions that are subject to seizure.

For example, police investigators arrest an eighteen-year-old man while he is driving a stolen automobile. When auto theft detectives interview him, the young man volunteers that ten days ago, he met with several members of a local street gang at an apartment in the city to discuss transporting methamphetamine from the city to other parts of the country. The defendant, now turned informant, professes to the detectives that of the six gang members attending the meeting, he only knows the true identity of the man who invited him into the conspiracy and at whose apartment the meeting took place. Further, the informant claims that the person who recruited him had road maps and made copious notes during this first meeting that detailed to what cities the drugs were going to be delivered and who specifically was going to make the deliveries. The notes also included descriptions of the vehicles that would be used to transport the drugs and the drivers' specific travel routes.

The defendant–informant maintains that at a subsequent meeting five days later, in the same apartment, he was told the methamphetamine they were supposed to distribute had been given instead to another group of established drug couriers and the deal was now off. He claims he is admitting this to the police for consideration in his pending legal matter concerning the stolen automobile. The man is willing to testify against the other members of the conspiracy.

The police drive the informant past the apartment complex where the meetings allegedly took place, and he points out the exact apartment where the main suspect lives. He also provides the police with the full name and physical description of the man. He describes this man as one of the leaders of the street gang.

The main suspect named by the informant is known to narcotics detectives to be a suspected methamphetamine dealer who has been arrested several times but never convicted. A copy of the suspect's last booking photo is obtained. When it is shown to the informant, mixed with five other booking photos of similar-looking men as part of a photo lineup (sometimes called a *six-pack*), he readily picks out the suspect.

Investigators see from past booking sheets that the main suspect listed his home address as the apartment identified by the informant.

The police investigators subpoena the local telephone company for records of toll calls made from the main suspect's apartment. The records show numerous telephone calls made to Los Angeles within the past several months. A further check of the telephone numbers with the DEA reveal that these same numbers are known to be associated with major methamphetamine manufacturers in Mexico. Many of the subscribers to these telephone numbers have in the past been subjects of investigations conducted by the DEA.

The police coordinate with their local assistant district attorney, and together they apply for a search warrant for the main suspect's apartment, specifically to look for notes and other documentation related to the drug distribution scheme.

During the search of the apartment, not only do they find the road maps and notebook used by the suspect during the meetings, but they also discover eighteen pounds of methamphetamine hidden in the suspect's bedroom closet.

Police drug investigators later learn from an unrelated informant that the main suspect had negotiated a deal with a different methamphetamine trafficking organization to transport drugs for them throughout the United States.

Have the investigators proven that a historical conspiracy to distribute methamphetamine took place?

Yes. The defendant–informant's testimony, coupled with the physical evidence of the notebook and road maps, would be sufficient to justify a document search warrant. The facts that the telephone in the apartment had called known methamphetamine traffickers in Los Angeles and that they had called others in Mexico adds to the prosecution's theory that a conspiracy had taken place. The fact that eighteen pounds of methamphetamine were located in the apartment further corroborates the informant's information, and it may make the gang member liable for involvement in a different ongoing conspiracy.

Thoroughness is key to convincing the prosecutor, the judge, and ultimately the jury, that an agreement to violate drug laws must have taken place because the informant information about the meeting was corroborated by the notes and road map.

If the suspect denies writing the notes or knowing anything about the road maps, a handwriting expert may be able to testify that the suspect's handwriting matches that found in the notebook. A fingerprint examination should also be conducted of the notebook and road map, and it could further corroborate the informant's information.

Investigators might have further proven the main suspect's involvement by instructing the informant to make a recorded telephone call to the man to see if there was any news about what happened to the methamphetamine they were supposed to distribute.[1] The recorded telephone call could have resulted in the suspect corroborating the informant's information by admitting to, or at least having knowledge of, the scheme.

They could also have asked the informant to wear a recording device and meet with the suspect to capture conversations between them concerning the transportation of the methamphetamine.[2] This recording might be critical in convincing a prosecutor and the jury that a conspiracy actually did take place. However, if the suspect denied any knowledge of the drugs, it could work against the police investigation and possibly diminish the credibility of the informant.

In any such investigation, a thorough background investigation of the informant must be made for any past criminal activity or bad acts that could destroy his credibility. The defense attorney surely will conduct such an investigation in an effort to erode the effectiveness of an otherwise-credible witness. Past crimes committed by an informant involving moral turpitude, perjury, income tax evasion, and the like may quickly nullify a jury.

The jury will decide for themselves why the suspect had notes and road maps and was making telephone calls to known methamphetamine traffickers. Any suspect statements that can be refuted will enhance the credibility of the informant and the prosecution's theory that the suspect is lying to conceal his involvement in the historical drug conspiracy.

To further bolster the case, once other members of the conspiracy are identified, prosecutors might consider granting selected individuals **use immunity**[3] to provide additional eyewitnesses other than the informant to testify about the overt acts, both criminal and non-criminal, that occurred during the short life of the conspiracy.

Investigators are cautioned that before initiating any historical drug conspiracy case, they should coordinate with their supervisor and local prosecutor to get their feelings and guidance. They should also strive to obtain drug evidence through controlled purchases of drugs from the suspect by the informant or undercover investigator. When probable cause exists, search warrants should be executed to find supporting documentation and drug evidence against suspects.

Historical conspiracies are often used as the basis for launching fresh investigations into the criminal activity of the person(s) identified by informants.

CHAIN CONSPIRACIES

Like the name implies, all members of **chain conspiracies** are connected despite being directly linked to only one or two other defendants (see Figure 2–1).

Each link of the chain represents a member of the conspiracy. An example of a chain conspiracy is when defendants A and B make an original agreement to break into a freight train car to steal merchandise and fence it. A and B obtain the necessary tools to break into the car. They break the locks of a freight train car and steal fifty DVD players. B contacts C and provides him with twenty of the DVD players, and he distributes ten of them throughout the city. C in turn, solicits D to help in the sale of the ten stolen DVD players. D drives to another city, where he sells the remaining stolen players with the help of E, who knows they are stolen.

Link A only knows about the existence of link B. B obviously knows about A and C because he solicited C's help in distributing the stolen DVD players. C knows about the existence of B and D, but has no knowledge of A or E. D knows C, who solicited him to distribute the remaining ten DVD players, and E, who helped him sell the players. D has no idea who A and B are. E only knows D.

In a chain conspiracy, not all members know each other, and no single member knows everyone involved. Despite this, because of the Pinkerton theory of vicarious liability, all the members of this chain conspiracy can be charged with the actual burglary of the freight train and the other criminal acts committed in furtherance of the conspiracy.

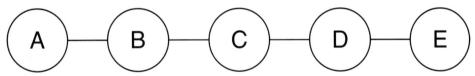

Figure 2–1 Chain conspiracy.

It is not unusual that only the police investigators will ultimately know the exact number of conspirators and the role each member of the conspiracy played, depending on the size and sophistication of the criminal organization.

CELL CONSPIRACIES

A *cell conspiracy* has a hub, which represents the leader. As the leader, suspect F knows the identities of all the cell members: G, H, I, J, K, and L (see Figure 2–2). Each member knows suspect F, but they do not know each other. This is a classic example of a *cell operation* used by drug and terrorist organizations. These conspiracy cells are designed this way so if any one member of the cell is arrested, he is able to disclose to the police the identity of only one other member. This technique of **compartmentalization** has been effective in thwarting law enforcement efforts to expand investigations and identify other members of a criminal or terrorist organization. Some terrorist organizations are believed to have *sleeper cells* located throughout the world that are waiting for instructions from their leadership to perform terrorist acts.

Despite their only knowing F, the cell head, suspects G through L can be held responsible for the criminal actions of each member of the conspiracy.

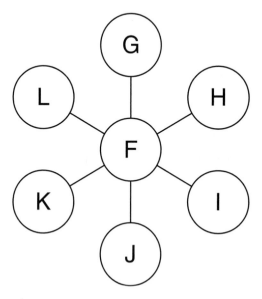

Figure 2–2   Cell conspiracy.

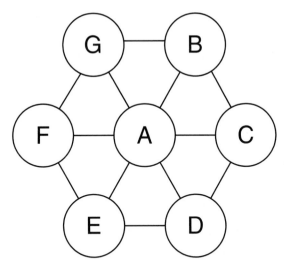

Figure 2–3   Wheel conspiracy.

WHEEL CONSPIRACIES

Wheel conspiracies differ from cell conspiracies in that each member knows some of the other members, but not all of them (see Figure 2–3). These types of conspiracies are also found in terrorist and drug trafficking organizations when the leadership finds it necessary to disclose the identities of some of the other members for operational purposes. They are still effective in concealing all the members of the conspiracy through compartmentalization. Each member is criminally liable for the actions of all members of the group.

COMBINATION CONSPIRACIES

A *combination conspiracy* is when one or more of the members of two different conspiracies interact, and they become a part of the same conspiracy (see Figure 2–4).

This combining of conspiracy groups is not unusual and can be found in a variety of conspiracy cases that have been investigated.

In 1957, New York State Police Sergeant Edgar Croswell noticed an unusual group gathering at the rural estate of a businessman soft drink bottler in the small town of Appalachin. Mr. Joseph Barbara supposedly was hosting a "soft drink convention" there.

Sergeant Croswell had observed suspected criminals at the estate before and was naturally suspicious. Along with his partner, Trooper Vincent Vasisko, Croswell started writing down license plate numbers of the many luxury cars in the driveway.

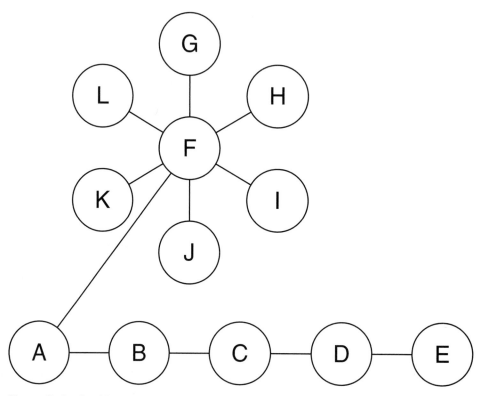

Figure 2–4   Combination cell and chain conspiracy.

When Barbara's guests noticed the troopers, they panicked. Some fled to the woods; others dashed to their cars. Sergeant Croswell ordered roadblocks and eventually detained 62 "guests" in order to check their identification. Among them were Joseph Bonanano, Russell Bufalino, Carlo Gambino, Vito Genovese, Antonio Magaddino, Joseph Proface, John Scalish, and Santos Traficante—a veritable Who's Who of what we now call the Mob, the Mafia, or *La Cosa Nostra*.

Sergeant Croswell's important detective work exploded nationally. Concerns had been expressed that a secret network of connected criminal enterprises existed. But many, including FBI Director J. Edgar Hoover, had disagreed. They said crime was a serious problem, but there was no evidence that a conspiratorial web linked racketeers across the country. Now there was evidence. Hoover got to work, ordering his field executives to develop maximum information on crime bosses in their areas of jurisdiction. This "Top Hoodlum Program" produced a wealth of information about organized crime activities. In a 1960 Letter to All Law Enforcement Officials, Hoover wryly commented: "If we must, let us learn a lesson from the barons of the underworld who have shown that cooperative crime is profitable—cooperative law enforcement can be twice as effective."[4] This spirit of cooperation between law enforcement agencies still exists today.

Once again, each member of these conspiracies can be held criminally responsible for the actions of each member of both conspiracies. The investigation must show that each separate conspiracy relied on the actions of the other to conduct its criminal enterprise.

Examples of this are when a drug trafficking organization relies on a group of other conspirators to launder their drug proceeds and when a terrorist group reaches out to others to obtain financing through fraudulent charities.

SUMMARY

There are seven types of criminal conspiracies that investigators will frequently encounter: ongoing, no dope, historical, chain, cell, wheel, and a combination of any of the two, when two or more separate criminal organizations have combined their efforts and resources.

Ongoing conspiracies are, as the name implies, in the process of conducting their criminal enterprise.

No dope or *dry* conspiracy cases frequently fail to seize any drug money or assets, but law enforcement can prove that the members of the conspiracy conspired to import or distribute drugs. The focus of these investigations is on the agreement rather than on the substantive crimes the conspirators committed. These investigations are usually initiated when a former member of a conspiracy has been arrested and now wants to cooperate with the police in return for consideration in an unrelated legal matter.

Historical conspiracies have ended in success or failure, but they are still investigated in the same manner as any other reported crime if the statute of limitations has not expired. In the case of a historical conspiracy, each member can be charged with not only the crime of conspiracy, but also with the criminal acts they may have committed during the lifetime of the conspiracy.

Conspiracies can take on many shapes and sizes. It is not uncommon for investigators to discover conspiracies that can be described as a chain, cell, wheel, or any combination thereof. Regardless of what shape a conspiracy takes, each of the members is criminally liable for the actions of the other members, despite not knowing the existence or the identities of the other conspirators.

NOTES

1. Investigators need to check their local laws and policy to determine if such a technique can be used in their jurisdiction.
2. Check with local prosecutors before using this investigative technique.
3. Use immunity protects the defendant from this crime only, not others that are not connected to this conspiracy.
4. "*A BYTE OUT OF HISTORY*: Organized Crime and 'Joes's Barbecue,' " fbi.gov, 11/13/2003.

Advantages of Conspiracy Investigations

One of the biggest advantages of conducting conspiracy investigations is that they can result in the elimination of the entire criminal organization. Targeting one or two individual members of an organization does little to stop it from functioning.

Conducting a traditional drug investigation by making several small controlled purchases from the same defendant can eventually reach the point of diminishing returns. Drug enforcement budgets deplete rapidly when prosecutors, seeking to establish the most compelling case possible to secure a conviction, demand that several buys be made in order to thwart a possible entrapment claim by a defendant. Thus, a smaller police department's entire "buy money" budget could be exhausted on just one or two investigations. Further, the jury might interpret additional buys as an agency's attempt to set up a defendant for more prison time than might be warranted. In contrast, investigators can satisfy the elements of proof for drug conspiracy early on in their investigations and reap benefits not normally associated with more-traditional investigations, such as the exception to the hearsay rule of evidence.

SIMPLICITY

Prosecutors risk losing cases when they are too complicated for a jury to understand. Charging defendants with crimes under "Continuing Criminal Enterprise" (CCE) and "Racketeer Influenced and Corrupt Organization" (RICO) statutes may be professionally appealing, but proving the essential elements of these crimes can sometimes be overwhelming to a jury.

The CCE statute requires the government to prove that a defendant was an organizer, supervisor, or manager of five or more others in order to secure a conviction. This may not always be possible. Another element of proof in a CCE case is that the defendants derived "substantial" income or resources from the criminal conduct. What may be substantial to one juror could be insignificant to another.

In RICO cases, the government must prove the participants were engaged in a "rack-eteering activity," meaning any act involving murder, kidnapping, gambling, arson, robbery, bribery, extortion, dealing in obscene matter, or dealing in controlled substances, which is a felony. The statute is so specific and complex that it can be easily challenged by defense attorneys.

The sheer magnitude of a multidefendant trial can cause a jury to lose sight of even the simplest elements of the crime. During the course of a long and complicated drug trial, the defense has ample opportunity to portray the defendants as the victims of an intrusive, overzealous police agency.

CCE and RICO statutes were designed to give defendants substantial prison terms if convicted. Since their enactments, the federal sentencing guidelines have substantially increased the amount of time a defendant is likely to serve for conspiracy, without having to prove specific criminal conduct.

Conspiracy cases avoid these problems because the prosecution needs only to prove that two or more defendants made an agreement to commit a crime. Prosecutors and investigators only must prove to the jury's satisfaction that an agreement took place and that one member of the conspiracy committed at least one overt act to reach their goal. Individuals involved in RICO and CCE cases should always be charged with conspiracy as well.

CRIME PREVENTION

Historical and no dope conspiracy cases are a form of crime prevention. To identify and arrest defendants who agreed to sell drugs in the community before they had a chance to do so, or who are prepared to do it again, is a noble goal, one that appeals to any jury.

Additionally, in many jurisdictions the penalty for conspiracy is the same as the penalty for the substantive crime the defendants conspired to commit. Since 1987, in federal drug cases, the law mandates that the punishment for conspiracy to commit a drug crime be the same as what the defendants would have received if they had carried out their plan.[1] Drug conspiracy laws, coupled with mandatory minimum sentences, are powerful crime prevention tools for drug enforcement because they discourage people from becoming involved in drug trafficking. Many states have comparable laws.

When investigators learn of a conspiracy to rob a convenience store, often they will stake out the store and await the arrival of the robbers. Obviously, public safety issues are raised when the police knowingly allow such a crime to take place for the purpose of arresting the suspects in the act. As an alternative, through surveillance and close coordination with the prosecutor, a search warrant may be justified, possibly leading to the recovery of weapons, masks, and other evidence substantiating that a robbery has been planned. Arrest warrants can then be requested and the suspects possibly taken into custody before the robbery actually takes place.

The media often question police tactics that allow a crime to actually take place when the opportunity to prevent that crime was ignored for the sake of having a more "sexy" case to prosecute. The same logic can apply to drug and terrorism cases. Arresting persons who have sold drugs in the community in the past prevents them from dealing drugs in the future. Police managers have to weigh the safety of their officers and the community against arresting the culprits in the act.

LEVERAGE

Thanks to *Pinkerton,* conspiracy cases also give prosecutors added leverage during plea-bargaining sessions because all members of a conspiracy can be charged with crimes committed by any of the members. However, the crime must have been a foreseeable consequence and in furtherance of the conspiracy.

For example, if one suspect steals a boat to transport a drug shipment into the country, everyone in the group can be charged with that crime, if they were members at the time of the theft. However, if the suspect stops at a liquor store and steals a six-pack of beer on the way home from stealing the boat, the others cannot be charged with that theft because it was clearly not committed in furtherance of the conspiracy to transport drugs.

Murders sometimes occur in the course of drug sales and organized crime activities. The courts consider these crimes to be foreseeable consequences of these types of conspiracies, and prosecutors can charge each member of the group with murder.

Prosecutors often will drop some or all of the substantive charges against some or all of the conspirators if they agree to plea guilty to straight conspiracy. Without the charge of conspiracy, this option is lost.

EVIDENCE CAN BE USED IN MULTIPLE TRIALS

Evidence against one defendant is evidence against all of the defendants in a conspiracy case. The evidence investigators gather against a single member of the conspiracy to prove he committed a substantive crime can be used in the trials of other defendants in the same conspiracy. If ten defendants in a conspiracy case are tried in two separate trials, the identical evidence can be used in both trials. There is no requirement to gather additional evidence, and in many cases it may not exist. The ability to use evidence in multiple trials against all the defendants saves valuable investigative time.

Many conspiracies contain numerous members, far too many to be tried simultaneously. The prosecutor can opt to try a more manageable number of the conspirators at a time, and in each subsequent trial, the same evidence used in the original case can be used against the additional defendants. Independent evidence against each defendant during each trial is not necessary.

As an example: Twenty members of a street gang have been arrested and charged with conspiracy and many substantive crimes they committed, such as robbery, burglary, discharging of firearms, and drug dealing. In the first trial the leadership of the gang is tried and convicted of conspiracy and several other substantive crimes. Later, other gang members are tried for conspiracy and the substantive crimes, even though they may not have actually participated in their commission. This is because of the criminal liability that attaches to all members of the conspiracy when a crime is committed. The prosecution may use the identical evidence in the first trial against the second group of defendants. Once the first set of conspirators is convicted, they can be compelled to testify against the other members of the conspiracy.

EXCEPTION TO THE HEARSAY RULE OF EVIDENCE

An added benefit to conspiracy prosecutions is the exception to the hearsay rule of evidence. Because conspiracies are secretive by nature and coconspirators are agents of each other, the rules of evidence usually allow a cooperating defendant, investigator, or informant to testify about the words, deeds, and actions of others, even if they did not actually witness the events. In other words, an informant could testify about overhearing the defendants talking about selling drugs, committing robbery, or murdering someone. Without the charge of conspiracy, the prosecution may be burdened with producing witnesses who can testify directly about particular things they saw or heard. These witnesses are almost always going to be coconspirators, who cannot be compelled to testify against themselves unless they are offered immunity. Other witnesses could be convicted criminals with questionable backgrounds and credibility. Law-abiding solid citizens may not have to testify because a police officer can testify on their behalf about what they saw or heard.

In contrast, when defendants are indicted for aiding or abetting or being an accomplice, the hearsay rule usually applies, and additional witnesses will be necessary. Therefore, prosecutors can help their cases and probably increase the punishment the defendants are likely to receive by indicting them for conspiracy.

Conspiracy cases that net large numbers of defendants are often handled in trials of increments of five or fewer. Prosecutors will usually indict a handful of defendants at a time in order to make the case more manageable and to streamline the process. In a twenty-defendant conspiracy, four trials of five defendants may be in order. The evidence used in the first trial can be used in all subsequent trials.

ASSET FORFEITURE

In drug conspiracies, the government can seize anything of value derived as a result of drug trafficking, including real property and other items used to facilitate the crime. Often these assets are returned to the police departments involved in the conspiracy investigation to supplement their drug enforcement budgets.

Asset-forfeiture laws apply to drug conspiracy cases, just as they do for any other drug law violation. Many federal and state civil seizure laws do not require that defendants be convicted of substantive drug crimes in order to make their property subject to seizure.

Although asset-forfeiture funds can supplement lean budgets, supervisors in law enforcement agencies must resist the temptation of targeting drug traffickers based solely on their assets. The suspect who poses the biggest threat to the community may own little property in the United States. The focus of any drug investigation should be people, drugs, and assets, in that priority. When police investigate an organization with conspiracy as the primary focus of the investigation, drugs and assets will inevitably follow.

SUMMARY

Because of the many advantages police and prosecutors enjoy when defendants are indicted for the crime of conspiracy, this charge should be the *primary* focus of their criminal investigation when multiple defendants are involved.

The burden of the government is merely to prove that an *agreement* took place between two or more of the defendants and that at least one overt act was committed to reach conspiracy's goal. This element of proof provides simplicity in enforcing the statute, unlike complex statutes such as CCE and RICO statutes. Juries are much more likely to understand that the defendants agreed to commit a crime, rather than they managed a corrupt organization, as required in the RICO statute.

Arresting suspects for conspiracy before they have the opportunity to sell drugs, commit robbery, or break into businesses is a noble goal juries will appreciate. It is a form of crime prevention in which the defendants, in many cases, can receive the same punishment as if they had committed the crime they conspired to commit.

Charging the defendants with conspiracy provides prosecutors with the leverage they need to negotiate plea bargains. Because most conspiracy statutes carry substantial punishments, it gives defendants an added incentive to admit their guilt and cooperate with investigators in expanding an investigation.

Conspiracy case law usually reflects an exception to the hearsay rule of evidence. Charging defendants with conspiracy may be the only way to allow informants to testify about the words, deeds, and actions of all the defendants.

In federal and many state drug investigations, financial assets held by the defendants that were derived from drug dealing are subject to seizure by the government. Conspiracy investigations often reveal the means of laundering money that was used by these drug traffickers through direct evidence or from the cooperation of other defendants. Money and assets seized by law enforcement are often returned to police department budgets.

NOTE

1. U.S. Sentencing Commission, *Guidelines Manual*, sec. 2D1.4(a) Nov. 1991.

Disadvantages of Conspiracy Investigations

Despite the many advantages to conspiracy cases, certain disadvantages must be considered before a large-scale, complex conspiracy investigation is undertaken. Many of these disadvantages, however, can be overcome with planning and close coordination with prosecutors.

PROTRACTED IN NATURE

Many months can be spent gathering evidence against what could turn out to be numerous members of a conspiracy. However, these months of investigation can net many defendants who might otherwise escape detection and punishment.

As mentioned, multiple venues often pose logistical and sometimes political problems for investigators and prosecutors alike. Prosecutors may not view drug prosecutions as a priority for their office, or they may not be willing to devote the time necessary for a complex drug case. On the other hand, the prosecutors in every area in which venue has been established may all want to take the lead on a particular high-profile significant prosecution. Prosecutors early on must resolve their conflicts over venue in any large-scale conspiracy investigation.

In any event, investigators should make every effort to get a firm commitment from the prosecutor's office to devote the necessary amount of manpower before any long-term, significant conspiracy investigation gets under way.

MANPOWER INTENSITY

Some large-scale multijurisdiction conspiracy investigations will require extensive manpower expenditures. Supervisors may balk at committing the required manpower an investigator requests. Manpower requirements could sometimes dampen the enthusiasm of supervisors, who may have other enforcement priorities. Often supervisory investigators may direct their staff to wrap up a particular case so they can move on to something else without taking into account the time necessary to complete the case and its prosecution.

Many police agencies have more work than they can handle and their budgets are tight. The demand for quick resolution of cases has always existed. The demand for police services when inadequate manpower and money exist places pressure on police managers to streamline their procedures. When an investigator proposes initiating a conspiracy investigation that may take months or years to complete, it may not be well received by police management.

To help overcome this, investigators should point out that by targeting an entire criminal organization, as opposed to opening cases on each individual within it, in the long run will expend fewer investigative resources. Further, the evidence against one defendant can be used at trial against all the other defendants, requiring less time in its gathering.

VERIFICATION AND CORROBORATION

In major conspiracy investigations, witnesses must be found and documentary evidence must be located, seized, and analyzed. The most damning evidence will come from testimony from coconspirators; however, the prosecutor, judge, and jury will always view these witnesses as being inherently unreliable.

Investigators may spend a significant amount of time and money locating evidence that corroborates the testimony of informants and coconspirators. This evidence can include many different car rental contracts, vehicle registration documents, bank loans, or business licenses. It all must be identified, located, and seized, often in different parts of the country or the world, adding to the already mentioned manpower expenditures.

If an informant says he was told by drug smugglers they stayed at a resort hotel in Hawaii while the sailing vessel they used during the smuggle was being repaired, it may be necessary for investigators to travel there to seize registration records to corroborate the information. If terrorists met in a hotel room in Vienna, Austria, to discuss future targets, the same applies. Seizing documentary evidence, no matter where it may be, is crucial in the successful prosecution of conspiracies.

NO DOPE CONSPIRACIES

A prosecutor's enthusiasm for filing conspiracy charges against drug traffickers will be diminished if drugs or money are not seized during the course of the investigation. Prosecutors need physical evidence and compelling testimony for jury appeal during trials. The lack of seized drugs, guns, or money sometimes plays into the hands of defense attorneys, who ask where the drugs are if this organization is as prolific as the police investigators claim.

Investigators must strive to recover physical evidence during any conspiracy investigation they conduct, and they need to assure their supervisors and prosecutors that this is one of the main objectives of the investigation. Some cases that start off with the promise of huge drug or money seizures end up with none only because of the incompetence or misfortunes of the conspirators. The drug business is like any other business; sometimes sources of supply cannot deliver as they promised. When that happens, these cases need to be pursued as no dope conspiracies because these drug traffickers sincerely intended to sell drugs and they will not otherwise be deterred from continuing in their illegal enterprise. The same logic applies to terrorism and gang investigations.

Investigators should receive a firm commitment from a prosecutor before initiating any drug case in which there is a chance the suspects may not be able to deliver the drugs as promised.

For example, an informant introduces an undercover investigator to several large-scale drug traffickers who are looking for customers to buy portions of a substantial load of drugs they intend to import into the country soon. The investigator displays a large sum of money to them to prove he or she has the means to purchase the drugs. All of the investigator's conversations with the traffickers are recorded, and from these recordings there is no question the suspects intend to deliver the drugs as agreed. Surveillance fails to detect when the suspects departed the country to retrieve the drugs. On the day of the promised delivery, the suspects call the informant and say they have suspicions that his "friend" may be a drug agent, and they are refusing to deal with him or her. Or, they may demand payment in advance of any drugs being delivered, something the drug agent is unwilling or able to do.

Will the prosecutor now seek the indictments of these conspirators?

If the prosecutor did not commit to prosecuting the members of the conspiracy prior to the initiation of the investigation, he or she may not seek indictments. Before starting any formal conspiracy investigation, the investigators should demonstrate to the prosecutor that the suspects are worthy targets of prosecution.

The investigation may be salvaged if the drug agent can convince the traffickers he or she is not involved with law enforcement. Additional surveillance of the traffickers may lead to other customers or stash locations that generate probable cause to obtain search warrants. The results of these search warrants may produce drug evidence after all.

Even if the conspirators do not have the wherewithal, are inept, or are inexperienced in committing the crime they conspired to commit, this is *not* a legal defense for the crime of conspiracy.

SUMMARY

The advantages of focusing on conspiracy as the primary objective of a criminal investigation far outweigh the disadvantages. Many conspiracy investigations have large numbers of defendants involved, which requires extensive manpower commitments. Because of the time and attention to detail each defendant requires, these investigations can be protracted and sometimes arduous. Supervisory investigators who are not familiar with the length of time required to conduct a thorough conspiracy investigation may want their staff to prematurely terminate a case in order to go on to other pressing matters. This demand for time, coupled with the expense of gathering evidence that is sometimes in multiple jurisdictions, can make these cases unattractive for some police managers.

Sometimes verifying and corroborating information provided by an informant in a conspiracy investigation is easier said than done. Without corroboration, prosecutors will be reluctant to indict members of the conspiracy or to authorize arrest warrants. Because many conspiracies stretch into many other jurisdictions, the expense involved in gathering evidence or corroborating what an informant claims can be costly.

In drug cases, supervisors and prosecutors may not be enthusiastic about supporting a no dope conspiracy case, in which the defendants can only be charged with conspiracy because they have not yet delivered drugs to an undercover investigator or informant. Investigators engaged in drug enforcement should always strive to recover drugs and assets during the course of a given conspiracy investigation. They should also receive a commitment from a prosecutor that indictments will be sought against the defendants even if they cannot be found in possession of drugs. Without a firm commitment from a prosecutor, conducting an investigation may be a waste of valuable manpower and limited department resources.

CHAPTER 5

Conspiracy Case Development

Every investigative technique used in modern criminal investigations is utilized in conspiracy case development. Conspiracy cases involving terrorism, drugs, and gangs often require a larger variety of investigative techniques than traditional after-the-fact cases.

CONFIDENTIAL INFORMANTS

Because many conspiracy cases are ongoing, they frequently are initiated through information provided by confidential informants. Many of these informants are defendants who are cooperating with the police in return for judicial consideration in unrelated legal matters. Informants also are motivated to provide information by revenge, egotism, self-preservation, the desire to play an important role in something, or money.

Nearly all drug conspiracy cases begin with an informant. Almost every drug case conducted by the Drug Enforcement Administration (DEA) or state or local police is self-initiated, stemming from information supplied by either an informant or a former coconspirator. Other drug conspiracy cases are usually historical conspiracies in which drugs are found abandoned on a commercial airliner or a secluded beach, or a suspect is caught in the act of smuggling contraband without benefit of an informant's information.

The investigator's job in proving any criminal conspiracy is to produce witnesses and evidence to support the prosecutor's theory that an agreement was reached between the suspects to commit a crime. Evidence may consist simply of documents such as car rental agreements, hotel receipts, and phone bills. These seemingly innocent transactions take on a different appearance when a confidential informant testifies that the suspects used a hotel room to privately discuss the details of an upcoming drug deal or terrorist event. The investigation into the informant's information may also show that phone calls from the hotel room were made to known drug dealers or terrorists; that one of the suspects, using a fictitious name, paid for the room with cash to avoid creating a paper trail through a credit card receipt; and that scientific examination positively identified the handwriting and fingerprints on the registration card as that belonging to the same suspect.

Because conspiracy cases usually allow for the exception to the hearsay rule of evidence, informants can testify about the words, deeds, and actions of the defendants. However, because the courts and the public view informants as inherently unreliable, their information must be corroborated whenever possible. For example, if an informant claims to have attended a meeting at a hotel on a certain date, investigators can verify this information through hotel registration records. Hotel employees may further corroborate the informant's information by identifying suspects who occupied the room from a *photo lineup*.

All of these factors tend to corroborate the informant's information. The jurors can then decide for themselves why a person would pay cash to rent a hotel room using a fictitious name and then meet with, and telephone, known criminals from that room. Although much of the evidence by itself has no meaning, the totality of the evidence gathered through an investigation will help secure a conviction.

Most states require that an overt act (anything that furthers the goal of a conspiracy) take place before the crime of conspiracy is consummated. Simply stated, overt acts show sincerity and intent by the members of the conspiracy to reach their criminal goal. The greater the number of overt acts uncovered, the easier it is for a jury to conclude that the defendants actually intended to commit the crime.

Informants are usually in a position to help identify many of the overt acts conspirators committed during the lifetime of a conspiracy. However, they may not recognize the significance of these seemingly innocent acts or their importance in proving that the conspiracy existed. Investigators must educate their informants, as well as codefendants who are now cooperating, about the definition of overt acts. Informants and cooperating defendants must be thoroughly debriefed in order to identify all the overt acts they have witnessed or heard about taking place.

As mentioned, informants have a variety of motives for supplying information to the police. These may include providing information for money, working off criminal cases they are facing, revenge, altruism, or in drug cases, eliminating the competition.

Investigators are cautioned to determine the true motivation of the informant. Often a true motive is hidden by an informant to make himself appear to be noble when he is not. Investigators will experience problems controlling informants and their actions in conspiracy investigations when the motivations that drive them are not identified.

Investigators should never completely trust an informant or his information. Some individuals are unsuited as informants because their backgrounds may cause such credibility issues that they cannot be effective in court. An example may be a convicted child molester or a murderer who offers information about an ongoing burglary ring. One crime may have nothing to do with the other, but the prosecutor may be unable to overcome the issue of the informant's credibility in court.

The credibility of an informant also can easily become an issue at trial if the defense can prove the informant lied or exaggerated to investigators or engaged in criminal activity while providing information to the police. Investigators must do a complete criminal background on any informants used during conspiracy investigations to evaluate their trustworthiness. Prosecutors need to bring out previous bad acts committed by informants early on in any trial so they do not give the impression they are hiding their pasts, or the defense attorney's will have opportunities to destroy what little credibility they may have.

When an informant with an extensive criminal background is used to initiate a conspiracy investigation, investigators may want to only use him to introduce an undercover agent to the conspirators, effectively cutting him out of future interaction with them. If they keep such an informant involved in the ongoing case, he becomes a witness who may be called to testify. His testimony is useless if he is not credible. However, by limiting his role to introducing undercover agents to the suspects, his credibility should not be an issue.

UNDERCOVER OPERATIONS

One of the most effective ways of determining the intentions and targets of conspirators is through undercover operations. A police investigator working undercover can locate evidence and provide effective testimony no informant can match. Undercover investigators can usually become expert witnesses who can testify about the events they see or hear. Their work provides highly effective ways to gather firsthand information about conspirators and to move the progress of cases forward rapidly.

Informants are often used to introduce undercover police investigators to significant suspects within a conspiracy. These investigators may be in a position to purchase drugs or stolen property or to provide needed services to help the conspirators reach their goal. Investigators can legally smooth the path of criminals for the purposes of gathering evidence and arresting them later.

Thorough debriefings of informants are important in analyzing where a criminal organization is most vulnerable to the introduction of an undercover operative. For example, a drug trafficking organization's need for a truck driver to transport drugs from one location to another is an opportunity to interject an undercover agent. Terrorist and drug organizations work the same way as many legitimate outfits, and they always need dependable, trustworthy employees. Terrorist organizations may need weapons, explosives, or training. A street gang may require special equipment or a place to store their drugs or stolen goods.

ASSET SEIZURES

Members of large-scale drug trafficking organizations amass large amounts of money and property through their dealings. They have to launder their money to give it the appearance of being derived through legitimate means. This laundering process may take the form of purchasing rental property, businesses, and other real estate. Alternatively, some organizations simply transport their money to a foreign country in an attempt to keep it out of reach of U.S. law enforcement.

Once members of any conspiracy are identified, they should be routinely checked through indices for any real property they may either own or occupy. How they acquired that property may lead to the discovery of other crimes, such as bank fraud, mail fraud, or tax evasion.

As an example, in 1988, in Santa Cruz County, California, nine tons of marijuana and numerous vehicles were left abandoned on a secluded beach. Sheriff's deputies responded there to investigate a tip from a passerby that a possible off-loading of drugs was taking place. On arrival, they estimated as many as fifty people had fled the area, mostly on foot. The Coast Guard later that day captured a fishing vessel in Monterey Bay with several additional tons of marijuana onboard.

Investigators discovered that the registered owner of one of the abandoned pickup trucks had earlier acquired a California driver's license after presenting a deceased person's birth certificate to the Department of Motor Vehicles as proof of his identity.

Further investigation revealed that the abandoned pickup truck had been purchased at a local new-car dealership and was financed through a federally insured bank. The bank loan was obtained through the submittal of a false application that used the name on the fictitious driver's license, which constituted bank fraud.

Because driver's licenses in California only can be obtained through the mail, the suspect also committed a mail fraud. Because of the Pinkerton rule, all members of the conspiracy who were members of the conspiracy when the bank and mail frauds occurred were charged with these offenses (see chapter 14 for details).

Federal agents seized the vehicle as a proceed of drug trafficking that was also used to facilitate the drug crime.

In the same case, a conspirator admitted to investigators that the off-loaders who removed the marijuana from the boat met at a coconspirator's home before going to the beach. The defendant–informant told agents that while they were on the coconspirator's property, the off-loaders formed several teams and were given instructions and equipment to quickly remove the marijuana from the boat. The owner of the home received a fee for the use of his secluded property to conduct the meeting and facilitate the crime.

An affidavit was filed in support of seizing the property because it was used to facilitate a drug smuggle by concealing the preparation for the off-loading event. DEA agents and U.S. marshals seized the property after a magistrate issued a federal seizure warrant.

Investigators should always identify property, vehicles, money, and bank accounts that may be subject to seizure during conspiracy investigations. Seizure warrants can be obtained at any time during an investigation after such property and vehicles have been identified.

Examination of vehicle and real-property records may reveal **straw purchasers**. A straw purchaser is someone who, for a fee, poses as the buyer of a property in order to conceal the identity of the real owner. These people are subject to indictment in the same conspiracy cases as the owners.

FIXED AND MOBILE SURVEILLANCE

As in any proactive investigation, physical and electronic surveillance of known suspects will frequently identify other members of a conspiracy.

Because of the paranoia that committing a crime creates, many criminals assume they are under constant surveillance. To relieve their paranoia, they often drive their vehicles in a manner to disguise their ultimate destination. They will frequently drive down cul-de-sacs to see who follows them and go around city blocks several times before parking, even though plenty of parking spaces are available. Some conspirators, especially drug and terrorist suspects, will practice these and other driving techniques even when they are merely going to a grocery store or conducting legitimate business.

Investigators' patience will pay off when conspirators are followed to their ultimate destinations. When a meeting between two conspirators takes place and there is an insufficient amount of manpower to follow both suspects, the lead investigator must decide which of the two suspects is more important to follow. If the suspects are involved in a drug deal, they will ultimately lead the agents to the upper management of the organization, because they are the ones who usually control the drugs and money. In all cases, if investigators observe the transfer of money from one suspect to another, *follow the money*.

Suspects have unwittingly led surveillance teams to **stash houses**, where drugs and money are stored; homes of other conspirators; travel agencies they use; and other businesses that provide services to their organization. Surveillances also have shown investigators places where stolen property is stored and where vehicles used in crimes and weapons used in violent crimes are hidden.

Investigators can use fixed surveillance equipment that can be mounted on telephone and power poles disguised as transformers or other apparatuses. The development of these types of surveillance devices is only limited by the imagination of the person designing them for use by law enforcement.

PEN REGISTERS

Also known as dial digit recorders, **pen registers** can be installed in a police facility, with the knowledge and assistance of a telephone company, to capture the telephone numbers dialed from target telephones. Each device is activated when the telephone instrument's receiver is picked up or the telephone is turned on, and it records the time this occurred. The device then makes a written record of the outgoing telephone number dialed by anyone from that particular phone number and documents the time the hand receiver was returned to the cradle of the phone or the telephone was turned off. It does not record incoming telephone numbers or voices, only outgoing telephone numbers.

Most of this information can be captured later from telephone company long-distance toll information; however, pen registers record *all* telephone numbers that are dialed, including local calls, instantaneously. The machines also record any numbers dialed while the telephone line is in use. The devices frequently record credit card numbers, prepaid-telephone-card account numbers, personal identification numbers, and bank account numbers when suspects call their banks to use automated banking services.

The use and installation of these devices requires a court order.

TECHNICAL LISTENING EQUIPMENT

Wiretaps

Telephone wiretaps and technical listening devices have been used for many years to identify coconspirators, how they operate, and what crimes they may be planning.

Both federal and state judges have the authority to order wiretaps after investigators establish there is probable cause to believe that not only are suspects involved in certain criminal activity, but they also are using telephone(s) to facilitate the crimes. Not all states allow their law enforcement agencies to engage in wiretap investigations,[1] and some states limit the use of wiretaps to only certain violations of the law. The federal government also has such restrictions.

Many criminals, especially drug traffickers and terrorists, assume that the government is constantly monitoring their telephones and other communication devices. They spend large amounts of money on electronic equipment that supposedly will detect the presence of listening devices in their homes, on their telephone lines, and on persons with whom they are meeting. Many of these devices, thankfully, do not work; however, some of them are effective. If the suspects in a conspiracy investigation are known to discipline themselves about what they discuss on the telephone, the use of wiretaps may be rendered moot. Investigators must debrief their informants for this type of information before launching any wiretaps due to the time, expense, and manpower commitment involved in these types of cases. It's true that some criminals, regardless of how much telephone discipline they display, may occasionally drop their guard and talk about criminal activity on the telephone as the police are monitoring it. However, oftentimes this same information may be available through other investigative means, such as recorded undercover conversations and informant debriefings.

Suspects often talk in code about criminal activity while they are on the telephone, thinking they are clever enough to fool law enforcement officers who may be listening. They often substitute the name of a drug with some harmless commodity, such as "white shirts," "green shirts," "tires," or something similar. They sometimes get confused while using codes and are forced to discuss selling one half-shirt, or one half-tire, as if such a sale were possible. When presented to a jury, this type of recorded evidence goes far in proving that suspects obviously are talking about something illegal.

Because communications are so important for any criminal organization to survive and flourish, organizers, managers, and supervisors must use some sort of telecommunications device. Many of these conspirators buy prepaid cellular telephones, using phony names, and then dispose of these telephones rather than pay for additional service. By constantly changing telephones, they believe they will keep law enforcement officers off balance and prevent them from successfully conducting wiretaps to learn about their criminal activities. If investigators know a particular suspect frequently disposes of prepaid cellular telephones, they may want to abandon the idea of conducting a wiretap on that suspect. Investigators still may be able to capture this suspect's conversations by tapping the telephones of coconspirators he frequently calls. They also may be able to have an informant provide the suspect with a disposable telephone provided by the police.

Conducting a conspiracy investigation involving wiretaps is a long and arduous process that requires many man-hours. There are constant court-mandated reporting, expensive equipment, and other requirements, and they don't always lead to large drug or money seizures, or to the identities of other conspirators.

If the main target of an investigation is known to dispose of cellular telephones regularly, or is known to seldom discuss business on any telephone, investigators must weigh the benefits of pursuing a wiretap against its extensive manpower and cost requirements.

Through a court order, investigators can obtain permission for a ***clone pager***, which gives law enforcement the same messages as a suspect whenever someone pages the suspect. The requirements for a clone pager are almost identical to the requirements for a wiretap, and investigators must coordinate with prosecutors before attempting such an investigative technique.

Despite having a court order, not all phone conversations conducted on a targeted telephone can be monitored. If when monitoring a captured telephone conversation an investigator determines that it is not related to criminal activity, he or she is obligated to perform ***minimization***, to turn off the recording equipment until this innocent conversation has ended. An example of an innocent conversation may be a discussion between a suspect's wife and an employee at a dentist's office when the wife makes an appointment to get her teeth cleaned.

Once the authorization for a wiretap has expired, copies of the tapes used to record the telephone conversations are provided to each defendant's attorneys before trial. All persons who had their telephone conversations recorded and who can be identified must be notified that their conversations were captured during the course of the investigation.

Defense attorneys usually will attack the probable cause outlined in the affidavit for a wiretap. They also will look for technical violations or omissions in the wiretap affidavit, or abuses that may have been committed during the investigative phase of the case, hoping the court will rule that the tape recordings of the telephone conversations are inadmissible. If the defense does not achieve this, many defendants will then seek a plea bargain or plead guilty because wiretap evidence is very damning to a defense.

The number of wiretaps conducted by the DEA and the FBI rose significantly in the 1990s. Both agencies rely on them now more than ever. Wiretaps however, are no substitute for old-fashioned police work. Surveillance teams must be positioned to act when significant conversations are captured on a wiretap. For example, if the main suspect in a methamphetamine drug case tells someone on the telephone he is going to "go to the lab," surveillance officers must be poised to follow the suspect. Investigators cannot rely solely on a wiretap to expand their investigation. It must always be coupled with surveillance teams ready to respond to any given situation overheard during a suspect's telephone conversation.

Electronic Transmitters

Unlike wiretaps, ***electronic transmitters*** may be installed in homes, businesses, hotel rooms, automobiles, and other places to overhear conversations between suspects. However, many states do not have laws allowing state and local law enforcement officials to install them. Even if they are legal, the mechanics of installing them can be challenging because they must be concealed in areas frequented by conspirators. Investigators installing such devices may be seen by the suspects or their friends, who could report to the suspects. Investigators have become innovative in avoiding detection, including posing as telephone repairmen or as gas- or electrical-company employees.

The DEA, FBI, and other federal agencies have technical agents who are trained to enter a building or vehicle, plant a device(s), and leave without a trace.

The questions that an officer or informant asks a defendant during undercover recorded conversations can reveal the truth about a defendant's intent to commit the crime that is the objective of the conspiracy.[2] A skillful undercover agent can elicit responses to the same questions jurors may have during a trial.

Recording conversations during undercover meetings can be done in several ways. A hotel room can be equipped with a secret microphone that transmits the sound by microwaves to another room where it is monitored and recorded. Or an undercover investigator or informant can be equipped with a hidden transmitter that is monitored and recorded nearby. In the latter method, the investigator or informant should also have a small tape recorder concealed on his person in the event the transmitter suddenly fails. Small microcassette or digital recorders are manufactured for this purpose and available to law enforcement. Some have an added feature that prevents the informant from intentionally or accidentally switching the recorder off.

Some informants are afraid to wear a recording or transmitting device, fearing it may be found during a personal meeting with the suspects. Their fears are well-founded. Informants, as well as investigators who are suspected of being informants, have been hurt or killed by suspects in retaliation for their attempts to secure recorded evidence about criminal activities. Criminals are far less likely to knowingly kill or injure law enforcement officials under these circumstances.

More-sophisticated suspects will actually search undercover investigators or informants before talking about their criminal intentions. Conducting a meeting in a room already equipped with a concealed microphone eliminates the need to place a transmitter on an informant or investigator. However, sometimes the meeting place suddenly changes and there is insufficient time to place a concealed microphone or transmitter at the new location. Informants should always be asked ahead of time if the suspects are known to search anyone new to them before talking about their criminal business.

Another situation can arise in which a suspect refuses to go to a designated hotel room to conduct a meeting for fear of the room containing listening devices. For example, an undercover agent might have a particular hotel room wired for audio and video in anticipation of conducting a meeting with a suspect. The suspect arrives at the hotel and meets with the undercover agent in the lobby. When the undercover agent tells the suspect he has already rented a room to discuss business privately, the suspect balks. He insists on renting a room himself so he'll feel more comfortable. He goes to the registration clerk and rents a room, and the meeting instead takes place there, defeating the agent's efforts to record their conversations.

The undercover agent should have given the appearance of renting a room at the spur of the moment to discuss business with the suspect. By coordinating with a trusted hotel staff member ahead of time, the undercover agent who "instinctively" rents a room to conduct a meeting will receive the key to a room that has already been equipped with recording devices. This way the paranoid suspect will feel more comfortable with his surroundings, and the undercover agent does not have to come up with excuses about why a different room should be used.

Transmitters available to law enforcement can be concealed in items commonly found in any home or hotel room, including alarm clocks, smoke detectors, and thermostats.

Larger items such as table lamps and televisions may also hide a small camera that captures images that are recorded on a videocassette recorder in a nearby location.

Investigators should caution informants that in some states, if an informant leaves a room for any reason, the continued recording of the remaining suspects' conversation cannot proceed until the informant returns because the person who has consented to have his conversation be recorded has left the room. Authority to record conversations when no party of the conversation has given permission is only authorized by a court order.[3]

If investigators feel there may be even the slightest chance of a suspect searching them or their informant for any concealed transmitting devices, they should not be worn. The investigator can always later explain to the prosecutor or the jury during trial that if the suspect had discovered such a device on them during their undercover role, it could have seriously jeopardized their safety. Alternatively, an investigator might be able to wear a recording device at a second or subsequent meeting in which the suspects recap what was discussed at the meeting when a transmitter or recorder was not worn.

Recording conversations with members of a criminal conspiracy is important. During undercover meetings a suspect may admit to the undercover agent having sold drugs "hundreds" of times or may boast of an ability to obtain "any drug" in "any amount." When the agent expresses doubt, a suspect may brag about having never been arrested for past drug sales and other crimes he has committed.

Such a tape provides evidence that is hard to dispute. Even if the defendant makes no admissions under formal questioning after being arrested, the recording alone satisfies an element of proof for conspiracy because the defendant committed an overt act simply by meeting with the undercover agent. In addition, a defendant's admission to being engaged in crime with others is sufficient to sustain a conviction for conspiracy,[4] even if the other coconspirators are never identified or indicted.[5]

Investigators are cautioned that if they decide to use a concealed recording device for an initial conversation with a suspect, they should then strive to record all subsequent conversations. The reason is simple. When an undercover investigator or informant does not record one of the conversations, even the most innocent one, it leaves them vulnerable to a defense attorney later at trial. The attorney may imply or outright state that it was during that particular unrecorded conversation that his client wanted to "withdraw" from the conspiracy but was threatened by the undercover agent or informant if he did so. Withdrawing from a criminal conspiracy is a legal defense in which the defendant cannot be charged with subsequent criminal offenses committed by other members of the conspiracy. Despite repeated denials from the investigator or the informant, this ploy may create a doubt in a juror who is looking for a reason to acquit the defendant.

It is good policy and practice for police managers to require that all undercover and telephone conversations be recorded to guard against this defense. Recording all conversations makes the investigation more thorough and provides evidence of overt acts. Recording telephone conversations between an informant and a suspect is especially important because informants are viewed as inherently unreliable in the eyes of the jury, and recording such conversations poses no safety risk.

Investigators should equip all informants involved in a case with a simple tape recorder and telephone microphone so there can be no reason why their conversations with the suspects are not recorded. Informants have been known to make direct or implied threats to suspects to follow through on their agreements to commit a crime. Informants will sometimes do this because they want to justify the largest reward they can receive from the law enforcement agency. They may believe that if the targeted suspect honestly withdraws from the conspiracy, the informant's credibility will diminish, and it could jeopardize his future role in other criminal investigations. This is especially true if the informant is providing assistance to law enforcement for the first time or is providing assistance in exchange for a reduced sentence stemming from his own recent arrest.

Informants simply cannot be trusted. They have been known to have hidden agendas and to work against the interests of law enforcement. Requiring them to record *all* telephone conversations with each member of the criminal conspiracy they talk to will help eliminate this.

SURVEILLANCE CASES

Police intelligence may lead investigators to initiate surveillance on known or suspected criminals in the hopes of observing them commit a crime in their presence. An example of this may be when an informant reveals that a gang member has told him he is planning a daring bank robbery and he will require help from several others. The informant may not want to get any further involved, but his information can be used as the basis for a surveillance of the suspect to monitor his activities and see with whom he meets. The surveillance could result in learning the identity of other robbery conspirators and could prevent the crime from occurring.

Police investigators may place surveillance on parolees who have recently been released from prisons to see if they are associating with other known or suspected criminals in violation of their conditions of parole.

Investigators may also receive information from other law enforcement agencies about suspected criminal activity occurring in their jurisdiction. This intelligence, coupled with physical surveillance of the suspects, may lead to the initiation of a formal criminal investigation.

Tenacious investigators who monitor the activities of known or suspected criminals in their particular jurisdictions often make prosecutable cases. Based on what they observe, investigators may gather enough probable cause to obtain a search warrant for the home or business of their suspect(s). The search may result in evidence leading them to believe a conspiracy exists between the suspect and others to commit a crime.

Experienced surveillance teams can detect criminal activity when it is not obvious to the general public. Their observations and experience may lead them to identify crimes that may otherwise go undetected and can lead to the recovery of stolen property, drugs, and money.

For example, a DEA office in North Carolina is conducting an investigation of an outlaw motorcycle gang that is selling large amounts of marijuana. The DEA has discovered that the main suspect in North Carolina frequently calls another suspect who lives in California and is believed to be somehow involved in related drug trafficking activity. However, because the focus of the federal case is in North Carolina and there are manpower restraints, no action against the suspect in California is anticipated soon.

The DEA notifies police investigators in California and provides them with the full name of the suspect, along with his telephone number. The police initiate physical surveillance of the suspect after determining where he lives through information provided by the Department of Motor Vehicles. They also receive a copy of the suspect's driver's license photograph.

Late at night, the police investigators follow the suspect to a location fifty miles from where he lives, and he is observed meeting another man in a secluded parking lot. From seclusion, the investigators see the original suspect open the trunk of his car and remove a large duffle bag and place it in the backseat of the other man's car. While this activity is going on, the investigators check the vehicle registration of the second man's car and determine that he also lives a substantial distance from the meeting place, but in the opposite direction from the first suspect's home. Investigators watch the transfer of the duffle bag and follow the second suspect when he leaves.

The suspect with the duffle bag appears to be heading in the direction of his home. The investigators call for a marked police unit to rendezvous with them, and they ask the police officer to stop the suspect's vehicle if the driver commits a traffic violation. They want the officer to ask the man for permission to search his vehicle and to determine where he is going and where he just left. They do this to prevent the suspect from knowing that he is the subject of a police surveillance.

The suspect fails to make a complete stop at a stop sign and is pulled over by the officer. He obtains the man's driver's license and writes him a citation. The officer also asks him what is inside the duffle bag in the rear seat. The suspect becomes nervous and denies knowing what is inside the bag. He says it belongs to someone else and he is merely doing the man a favor by transporting it for him. The driver gives the officer permission to open the bag, and inside fifty pounds of high-grade marijuana are found.

The man is arrested and the police continue their investigation into the first suspect, who furnished the man the marijuana. Through interrogation and further surveillance, there is an excellent chance the investigators can obtain search warrants for both men's residences. They should be able to prove that a conspiracy took place between the two and that they are most probably tied into the criminal conspiracy involving the outlaw motorcycle gang members in North Carolina. Further, both of the vehicles used by the men can be seized for facilitation of the crime.

THE GRAND JURY

After coordinating with the U.S. attorney's office or district attorney, investigators will routinely testify about the findings of their investigations to a grand jury and seek the ***indictment*** of targeted suspects. An indictment formally accuses a suspect of committing a crime. ***Accusatory grand juries*** indict suspects, making them ***defendants*** in criminal matters. Once someone is indicted, a judge immediately issues an arrest warrant, and the defendant is promptly entered into the FBI's National Crime Information Center and state indices as being a wanted person. A direct indictment eliminates the need for a preliminary hearing after the defendant's arrest. The next step is to go straight to trial after any motions by the defense are heard.

A grand jury hears testimony of investigators and other witnesses brought to it by the prosecutor. Defense attorneys are not allowed to accompany witnesses or potential defendants into the grand jury room during questioning. The testimony of the witnesses is considered secret and cannot be disclosed outside the grand jury room, even to other investigators, unless sanctioned by the supervising judge.

Grand juries have the power of subpoena. They hear requests from investigators to issue subpoenas for records of individuals and businesses. On a federal level, grand jury subpoenas are required before banks and other institutions, including brokerage houses, have to surrender financial records. Once the records are obtained, the investigators must return to the grand jury with their findings.

Federal grand juries consist of twenty-four individuals who reside in the judicial district. They usually serve an eighteen-month term. Investigators should communicate early in their investigation, and often, with a grand jury. Depending on the length of the investigation and when the grand jury's term expires, it my be strategic to wait for a new grand jury to be sworn in before approaching it with complicated matters that may lead to indictments.

In complex criminal investigations, the grand jury needs ample opportunity to understand what the investigation has revealed and who is involved. By explaining the investigation in increments rather than in one long session, the grand jury members become interested and look forward to periodic updates. Also, in many large jurisdictions, police agencies compete for limited grand jury time, and asking for a long session may not be feasible. After learning a complex investigation in increments, the grand jury usually has to spend little time in making a decision when an indictment is sought because it is already thoroughly familiar with the case.

Federal and state grand juries make it possible to subpoena suspects involved in criminal conspiracies to appear before them and give testimony.

Unindicted coconspirators and other *material witnesses* can sometimes be compelled to testify before a grand jury, locking in their testimony before trial begins. This also gives the prosecutor an opportunity to learn how good a witness is. (e.g., Is he believable? Is he not credible?)

Grand juries also serve as a means to convince reluctant "witnesses" that they should cooperate with the government instead of running the risk of being indicted and possibly going to prison.

COORDINATION WITH OTHER LAW ENFORCEMENT AGENCIES

Most conspiracy cases will lead investigators into multiple jurisdictions and venues. They must include law enforcement agencies at all levels in their investigations in order to glean criminal intelligence, to obtain manpower assistance, and to foster good working relationships between different agencies.

Because conspiracies often involve many persons who live in different areas of the state or country, the cooperation of all agencies affected must be solicited unless there is a compelling reason not to seek that assistance. Many federal agencies routinely solicit the co-operation of local law enforcement in areas where they may be affected. Combating criminal organizations is a mission bigger than any one investigator or law enforcement agency. It requires the cooperation and coordination of all affected jurisdictions.

Law enforcement investigators who frequently share criminal intelligence with other law enforcement agencies usually receive similar information in kind, making them more-effective criminal investigators.

Uniformed police officers assigned to patrol duties can advise investigators whom to talk to, when to talk to them, and what information they may be able to provide. Good patrol officers know their beat like no one else in the community. Patrol officers can provide information and insights that investigators may never otherwise be able to gain about a particular suspect, neighborhood, or area of a city or county.

ANALYTICAL INVESTIGATIVE SUPPORT/TOLL ANALYSIS

Intelligence analysts provide valuable services and enhancements to any conspiracy investigation. They can perform the groundwork that uncovers background information and raw criminal intelligence about suspects and their organizations, allowing investigators more time to perform enforcement activities.

By conducting telephone toll analysis, analysts can show evidence of knowledge and association between different suspects when they show, through long-distance toll records and cellular-telephone records, that one suspect is telephoning another.

Analysts can provide link diagrams and flow charts to enhance an investigation and make a complex investigation more understandable by clarifying which suspects do and don't know each other. These charts display circles and squares that represent suspects and businesses, with lines connecting them to one another, making it easy for agents and juries alike to understand the relationships between suspects and what their roles are in the criminal conspiracy.

Intelligence analysts begin toll analysis by having subpoenas sent to various telephone companies that compel them to provide long-distance or cellular service and billing information pertaining to the suspect. A subpoena will most likely ask for the records of at least the past six months of toll calls that were made from the suspect's home or business telephone number and the records of all calls made from cellular telephones. Once these are in hand, the analyst can then ask the telephone companies for the names of the subscribers of each of these telephone numbers, as well as records of the toll or cellular calls made from those phones. With subscriber information, analysts can begin criminal-history and intelligence records checks on each subscriber and can look for telephone calls made between the subscribers and the suspects. A link diagram can be drawn that illustrates which suspects interacted with each other, making it much easier to discern what overt acts each member of the conspiracy may have committed. As more information is received through surveillance or other investigative means, analysts can add to the link diagram.

USE OF PUBLIC, PRIVATE, AND GOVERNMENT RECORDS

Investigators use many public and private records during the course of their investigations.

When a suspect is followed to an address that has never been identified in an investigation, a check with the local utility company can provide information about who is paying the utility bills at the address. This name can be given to intelligence analysts or other investigators to start the tedious, but necessary, process of checking through different indices to search for criminal information on the suspect. The subscriber to the utility service is often connected to the conspiracy. In fact, everyone connected to the suspects should also be considered potential suspects until proven otherwise.

Public and government records are necessary in determining if a suspect owns a home, other real property, a business, or an automobile, or if he holds any licenses. They reveal if he has ever paid taxes, what his mailing addresses are, when he was born, and what he looks like. Other records show if he is a native or naturalized citizen, where he migrated from, if he holds a passport, if he has ever been granted a U.S. visa and when it expired or expires, where he went to school, who his parents are, and if he is registered to vote.

Private records will reveal his credit rating, where he banks, and if he holds stock and mutual funds. These records also show his loans, how much money he's borrowed and from whom, and who his doctor is. Private records also divulge where he took a commercial airline, what rental car company he used, what hotel he stayed in, what phone calls he made from the room, and the names of the subscribers to the numbers he called.

Investigators will routinely review public and private records during the course of their investigations, and they will rely heavily on them for quick, accurate information.

POLYGRAPH EXAMINATIONS

A useful tool in criminal investigations is the **polygraph**, which is sometimes called a **lie detector**. The findings of the device cannot be used in court; however, it is an effective investigative tool that is highly accurate and is used to enhance interrogations. It is often used to clear a suspect's involvement in a crime.

A polygraph simply measures bodily functions that cannot be voluntarily modified. The machine measures a person's breathing, galvanic skin responses, heartbeat, and blood pressure. It operates on the theory that when a person is confronted with danger, certain involuntary physiological reactions occur within the body to help it overcome the danger. To name just a few, the autonomic nervous system automatically transfers blood where it is needed most, and it regulates heartbeat and breathing.

As an example, when someone is walking on a desert path and suddenly encounters a rattlesnake, that person's autonomic nervous system will automatically transfer additional blood to his legs and regulate his breathing to ensure a quick getaway.

A person taking a polygraph examination who is asked a question he intends to lie about also goes through involuntary physiological changes as a defense mechanism to lying. The machine measures these "fight or flight" responses, and it, coupled with the skill of the examiner, can tell with much accuracy if the person is being truthful when he answers questions using a simple yes or no format.

At the beginning of a polygraph session, the examiner fully explains the functions of the polygraph to the suspect before the exam begins so he will have an appreciation of how it operates. The questions the suspect is asked are directly related to the matter at hand and will not deviate to other unrelated topics. The suspect also will know exactly what questions will be asked, although they may not be in the same order during each examination.

Polygraph examinations help investigators further their conspiracy investigation by uncovering hidden assets and unknown suspects, and by determining if a cooperating defendant is being completely truthful about his and others' involvement in the crime. This is accomplished by asking a suspect if he knows for sure if other people are involved and if there is anything he is not revealing to the examiner.

Any plea bargain between a prosecutor and a criminal defense attorney on behalf of his client should always be based on the defendant revealing everything he knows about the other members of the conspiracy and the assets they have accumulated during its lifetime. These agreements should always state, in writing, that the defendant is subject to a polygraph examination that will be administered by a police or government agent, at the government's discretion, to determine if the defendant is being truthful with the investigators. It is important that prosecutors not agree to allow a private examiner working for a defense attorney to administer a polygraph examination to the defendant to avoid any possible conflict of interest.

The polygraph should never be used as a bluff but should be given to the defendant to determine his truthfulness and sincerity in wanting to cooperate with the police in return for consideration in his legal dilemma. After an initial in-depth debriefing of the defendant, a polygraph should be administered before investigators act on leads provided by him. This is important because most defendants will attempt to minimize their roles in a conspiracy, and they may attempt to conceal the involvement of others. The condition of continued consideration in the defendant's legal situation should always be contingent on taking a polygraph examination. If a defendant is determined to be deceptive, the police and prosecutor will not be obligated to honor any promises made to him about receiving consideration. Further, the defendant should be clearly informed that if he lies or refuses to take any police-administered polygraph examination, the government will use any information it already has obtained from him in any future court proceedings against him.

If a small police department does not have a qualified polygrapher, they should seek the support of a state or federal agency to have the test administered. Without the presence of a qualified polygraph examiner for the test, the defendant will almost always underexaggerate or outright lie about his involvement and the involvement of others in the conspiracy.

For example, police investigators arrest someone who is a significant player in a criminal conspiracy. He reluctantly agrees to cooperate with investigators as part of his proffer in return for legal consideration. The investigators interview the suspect in the presence of his attorney about his involvement in the crime. He tells his version of the story to the investigators, who become skeptical about the defendant's truthfulness. The investigators offer him a polygraph examination to prove his veracity.

Whether the defendant agrees or refuses to take a polygraph examination, the investigators have just given him the **instant polygraph examination**. Merely offering someone a polygraph examination can be synonymous with giving him a formal examination. Guilty people will almost always decline a polygraph examination because they know they will be discovered as liars. In contrast, truthful people will usually agree to an examination because they know they are telling the truth, but not everyone trusts the accuracy of the polygraph instrument.

Investigators should rely on the polygraph examination to keep a defendant honest. They should tell the defendant they will administer a polygraph examination to him whenever they feel it is appropriate. The defendant should be told that if he does not agree, he will seriously jeopardize any further consideration in his legal matter. Investigators are truth seekers; there is no room for half-truths in the proffer process.

MAIL COVERS

A **mail cover** occurs when the U.S. Postal Service provides law enforcement with the names of senders of first-class mail to a suspect's address within a thirty-day period. A mail cover does not authorize agents to look at the contents of mail, only to determine who is sending it.

Mail covers can potentially accelerate and bolster any conspiracy investigation by quickly providing numerous investigative leads. The average suspect receives many pieces of mail from various persons, businesses, and organizations during any single month. This mail will most likely include bills from the suspect's long-distance telephone carrier, correspondence from brokerage firms and mutual fund companies, advertisements or statements from his travel agencies, credit card billing statements, letters from automobile and mortgage companies, and property tax bills. Each piece of mail gives investigators insights into the personal, financial, and recreational dealings of the suspect.

Once the long-distance carrier is identified through the mail, it can be subpoenaed or otherwise compelled to provide toll and subscriber information for the suspect's telephone. Brokerage houses and mutual fund companies can be served with grand jury subpoenas for financial information of the suspect that may eventually lead to assets and proceeds from criminal activity. Travel agencies sending the suspect literature may have arranged for his travel in the past or may be arranging future travel, and their records can be queried. Credit card companies can provide information on where and when purchases were made. They also are helpful in determining where the suspect has recently traveled or frequented, what specific hotel he stayed in, and later, what telephone calls were made from his room.

The postal inspector in charge of the area where the suspect's mailbox is located should be consulted on how to begin a mail cover. Mail covers do not require a court order. They can be accomplished by providing a letter from the agency head to the postal inspector in charge that outlines the basic facts of the investigation and the reason for the request.

Information gleaned from a mail cover can be found through other formal methods; however, it serves as a quick and simple way to determine the lifestyle and spending habits of a suspect. It may also provide enormous investigative leads that may reveal other members of a conspiracy.

TRASH RUNS

Trash runs, physically sorting through suspects' discarded trash, provide another easy way to determine long-distance toll carriers, bank affiliations, telephone tolls, and travel itineraries. Trash runs will probably provide investigators with the contents of the mail a suspect has recently received.

Physical evidence may surface when clothing worn by a suspect at the time of a robbery or burglary, such as a mask, shirt, shoes, or gloves, is discarded in his trash.

In drug investigations, investigators may find pay-and-owe sheets, packaging material, empty Pseudoephedrine bottles, plastic bags, empty rolls of duct tape, and other items indicative of involvement in drug trafficking or manufacturing.

Usually investigators must wait for the trash to be placed on the street of the residence or to be discarded in a common-area waste receptacle before it can be collected.[6]

As an example of the potential rewards of conducting a trash run, investigators go to the residence of an elderly woman to look for her son, who is a wanted fugitive in a conspiracy investigation. They have no direct knowledge he has been at the residence, but they decide to solicit the woman's cooperation in finding her son. She denies seeing or hearing from her son lately, and she claims to not know his whereabouts. The mother seems convincing, but one of the investigators, without her knowledge, decides to collect trash that was at the curb in front of her house. They take the trash bag to their office and examine its contents. Inside they find, among other things, eight empty spark plug boxes, eight used spark plugs, a used automobile oil filter, an empty box for a new filter, and five empty quart-size oil cans. There is also a paper bag from a local auto supply store that contains a credit card receipt in the suspect's name for a recent purchase for spark plugs, engine oil, and an oil filter. The investigators remember seeing a small foreign-made vehicle in the woman's driveway that probably has a four-cylinder engine. Because of the trash run, the investigators correctly deduce that the mother lied when she said her son had not visited her, because he most likely performed a tune-up and oil change of his eight-cylinder vehicle at her residence. They conduct a surveillance of the residence and, in a short time, arrest the suspect when he returns to his mother's home.

PHOTO SPREADS

In order to develop witnesses other than paid informants, investigators should seek out any opportunity to display photographs to solid, law-abiding citizens to verify that suspects were present at a particular location.

As an example, an informant tells auto-theft investigators about a private meeting that took place between him and several others at an auto repair shop on a particular day to discuss stealing luxury automobiles for shipment overseas. The informant identifies the main suspect by name. The investigators obtain a previous booking photo of the man and show it to the informant, who identifies him as the man he and the others met with to discuss future car thefts. The investigators drive past the auto body shop and notice a gasoline station next door. In an attempt to corroborate the informant's information, the investigators contact the owner of the gas station. They show the business owner a series of photographs of similar-looking men, known as a *six-pack*, and he identifies the man named by the informant as being at the auto body shop on the day in question. He says he remembers the man because he was driving an expensive car he has always wanted to own and it did not have any body damage.

This further verification and corroboration by a good citizen, as opposed to another informant, can go a long way in convincing a jury that the informant is being truthful. It brings credibility in the eyes of the jury when they realize the government is not relying solely on the testimony of an informant who probably has something to gain by the defendant's conviction.

Any opportunity an investigator has to inject a good citizen into an investigation should be taken. Even though the citizen in the example did not know what was discussed at the meeting at the auto body shop, the information given might be enough corroboration to launch a formal investigation.

EXECUTION OF SEARCH WARRANTS FOR DOCUMENTS

Although in some cases probable cause to obtain search warrants to seize drug evidence may not exist, sufficient probable cause may be present to look for documentary evidence.

In ongoing and historical conspiracy investigations, warrants for documents, the contents of computers, and e-mails usually can be justified, especially in drug and terrorism cases. Investigators know through training and experience that traffickers maintain meticulous records chronicling past drug transactions and the amounts of money paid and owed for drugs. These documents often identify other members of the conspiracy. These records also reveal how extensive an individual's or drug organization's trafficking has been. If controlled substances are found during the execution of a documentary search warrant, these items, along with other contraband, are admissible in court so long as the basis for the search was done in good faith. In fact, historical drug conspiracy cases frequently locate bank accounts and proceeds from drug transactions that are subject to seizure.

SUMMARY

Every investigative technique used in modern criminal investigations is utilized in conspiracy case development. Conspiracy cases involving terrorism, drugs, and gangs often require a larger variety of investigative techniques than traditional after-the-fact cases.

Confidential informants, undercover agents, and surveillance operations against known criminals often result in the initiation of conspiracy cases, especially in the drug-enforcement and terrorism arenas. When coupled with wiretaps, mail covers, trash runs, pen registers, intelligence analysis, polygraph examinations, and photo lineups, these cases are frequently expanded to identify other coconspirators. The use of public, private, and government records, along with the subpoena power of a grand jury, can significantly expand a conspiracy investigation even further, often leading to the seizure of contraband and the fruits of the crime earned from illegal activities. Search warrants justifying looking for computers, e-mail, and documents associated with a crime can often result in the seizure of drugs, money, and other contraband.

NOTES

1. Investigators must check with their prosecutors before initiating any investigations using wiretaps.
2. Conversations recorded with the consent of at least one involved party do not require a warrant. However, because consensual eavesdropping rules vary, officers should always consult with their state attorney's office before using this technique.
3. State and local investigators should check with their local prosecutor concerning consensual recordings before this technique is used.
4. *United States v. Figueroa,* 720 F. 2d 1239 (1983).
5. *United States v. Goodwin,* 492 F. 2d 1141 (1874).
6. Under federal law, individuals have no expectation of privacy in trash set on the street for pickup. See *California v. Greenwood,* 108 S.Ct. 1625 (1988). However, officers should check with their local prosecutors to determine the law in their jurisdictions.

CHAPTER 6

Drug Interdiction Conspiracy Cases

INTRODUCTION

Every day in the United States, teams of drug agents and investigators from the federal, state, and local levels arrest drug couriers and seize money from them at airports, train stations, and bus terminals. Almost all of these arrests and seizures are self-initiated without the benefit of any criminal intelligence or information provided by a confidential informant. Through keen powers of observation and skillful questioning of these people, who frequently exhibit certain characteristics, law enforcement officers have seized millions of dollars of drug proceeds and tons of controlled substances.

Many of these drug couriers travel alone. Drug agents know through training and experience that it is nearly impossible to commit a drug crime alone. Many people are required to produce, package, sell, distribute, and transport drugs to customers. Every drug interdiction case in which a lone courier is arrested has the probability of being expanded into an international drug conspiracy investigation.

The International Narcotics Interdiction Association (INIA) each year trains hundreds of investigators to identify and conduct consensual encounters with suspected drug or money couriers at airports or other transportation nodes. The INIA offers outstanding training around the world that has expanded to include the identification of suspected terrorists, who often exhibit characteristics similar to drug couriers. The INIA has long recognized that each single arrest has the potential of being expanded into a large-scale conspiracy investigation, and it offers training in that regard. The INIA has always stressed that when a drug or money courier has been arrested at a transportation hub, it is the beginning of a conspiracy investigation. Drug agents already know that at least two other people are involved: the person who furnished the drug-laden luggage and the intended recipient. Merely booking the suspect and going on to another case does nothing to expand the investigation and identify other suspects involved.

Despite increased passenger and luggage screening in the wake of the events of September 11, 2001, drug smuggling on airlines continues. Couriers have adjusted their methods of operation to compensate for increased security. Drugs can easily be secreted in common items found in luggage and in the luggage itself, and they can be fashioned in other ways to disguise them from x-ray machines. Traffickers have also recently increased the use of express-package-delivery services to move drugs to avoid detection at passenger terminals. Drug couriers and smugglers are risk takers who are willing to chance going to prison to receive their often-lucrative fees.

COURIER PROFILING

Drug couriers come in all races, shapes, and sizes; however, they usually exhibit certain traits that will alert an experienced drug agent that they may be couriers. One way to detect couriers is by using proven courier profiling techniques. None of these profiles is based on race.

Some couriers are more experienced than others, and others are better at concealing their emotions and nervousness. However, drug agents have seen a pattern of activity that remains consistent with people engaged in transporting drugs in airplanes, trains, and buses. When investigators detect one or more of these traits in a passenger, they must decide whether or not to approach the person and make an initial inquiry. The drug agent's objective is to voluntarily obtain certain information from the suspect that will give him or her the necessary probable cause to conduct a search and possibly arrest the person for possession of drugs or other contraband.

Approaching a suspected drug courier cold at an airport, train station, or bus terminal is not unlike the experience of a patrol officer who stops a suspicious motorist or pedestrian on the street to inquire about his presence. Several U.S. Supreme Court decisions have had a direct impact on what drug agents can do during an interdiction operation or consensual encounter.

The U.S. Supreme Court in the famous 1968 decision *Terry v. Ohio* (392 U.S. 1, 30), distinguished between an investigative stop and an arrest and between a frisk and a full-blown search requiring a warrant.

A decision in 1989, *U.S. v. Sokolow* (490 U.S. 1), affirmed the method that DEA special agents use when conducting investigative stops of potential drug couriers. These same methods are widely taught and used by drug interdiction investigators assigned to transportation nodes throughout the world. INIA President Dick Kempshall was the DEA special agent who arrested Sokolow and legally validated the use of the following investigative techniques in consensual encounters with suspected drug couriers.

In 2002, the U.S. Supreme Court ruled in *U.S. v. Drayton* (231 F. 3d 787) that police conducting interdiction operations are not required to inform passengers they wish to question or search that they have the right to refuse to cooperate. This ruling gives considerable latitude to drug agents as long as they can show that the answering of questions and any subsequent search was clearly voluntary.

Some of the traits drug agents look for when profiling passengers include:

- Passenger appears exceedingly nervous, furtive, or evasive.

- Passenger's ticket was purchased with cash, not credit card.

- Ticket is good for one way only.

- Ticket was purchased the day of travel or the previous night.

- Ticket was purchased through a travel agent in a city not near where the passenger resides or at a location that is inconvenient to his residence or work address.

- Passenger has little or no luggage.

- Passenger has excessive amounts of luggage.

- Passenger makes excessive amounts of phone calls from a cellular phone or a public phone booth at the terminal before leaving and or upon arriving at his destination while still at the airport.

- Airline records reflect an erratic pattern of travel between passenger's departure point and destination. Length of stay varies with each trip.

- Passenger has a return ticket the following day from a city where the length of stay would normally be longer due to distance traveled (e.g., Los Angeles to New York or Miami to Seattle).

- Passenger lives out of the normal service area of the airport where the flight originates.

- Passenger does not remember how he got to the airport.

- Passenger cannot remember the name, address, or telephone number of the person he is visiting.

- Passenger does not know if this person will be picking him up at his final destination.

- Passenger does not know the combination to the locks on his suitcases.

- Passenger cannot recall the name of the travel agency where he supposedly purchased his ticket(s).

- Narcotics detection K-9 (dog) reacts to the presence of controlled substances in the passenger's checked or carry-on luggage.

- Passenger is the first one on the airplane to be seated.

- He is the last passenger of the airplane to depart upon arriving at his destination.

- Baggage has nametags of someone other than the ticketed passenger.

- Passenger claims to live in one state, but has a driver's license from another.

- Passenger is extremely uncooperative.

- Passenger is extremely cooperative.

- Passenger's heart rate and breathing increase significantly; he begins to perspire and or begins to shake when confronted by law enforcement authorities.

- Passenger has a criminal history.

These characteristics are not all-inclusive and may change from time to time based on experience gained by a courier and his handlers. Drug agents need to recognize that a drug trafficker's methods of operation are often modified or entirely changed when they no longer work.

Drug agents should cultivate airline and bus ticketing agents to solicit their assistance in identifying travelers who exhibit these characteristics.

APPROACHING THE PASSENGER

Drug agents must keep in mind that they have no legal authority to open a traveler's bag or search his person for tickets, passports, or other travel documents without a search warrant or incidental to an arrest. The drug agent's objective is to solicit the traveler's cooperation and permission to search his luggage.

How a drug agent initially approaches a traveler suspected of being a drug courier may well determine if he or she will be successful in obtaining permission to search the traveler and his luggage. Tact is extremely important. A chess game of sorts takes place once drug agents make their initial contact, and they must be prepared to handle what could easily turn into a fluid situation. Drug agents should avoid approaching a suspect alone, and they should always have a partner to act as a witness and to offer protection. If another drug agent is unavailable, a uniformed police officer is acceptable.

When approaching a suspected courier, the drug agents should always be courteous and professional. They need to communicate early on to the traveler that they are soliciting his voluntary cooperation.

After asking to see the suspect's airline ticket, agents probably will ask many questions after they examine it. Transportation-node drug agents usually know the meanings of certain characters and codes that appear on tickets. These codes normally are indicative of special restrictions and conditions on the sale of the ticket that may not be obvious to the traveler.

Many of the drug agents' questions will elicit the responses previously outlined. Many suspected couriers will either not know or will lie about how they received their ticket, why it was purchased a certain way, or whom they are visiting.

The totality of the circumstances will dictate what actions the drug agents will take. If a narcotics detection K-9 is available, the dog should be allowed to examine the suspect's bag without opening it. In the event the dog alerts to the presence of controlled substances inside, the passenger and his luggage can be held at the airport office while a search warrant is sought before opening the luggage.

If a K-9 is not available and the traveler does not allow the drug agents to search the bags and insists on boarding his plane or bus, the agents have the option of calling the airport or bus terminal where the passenger will be arriving to have other drug agents further observe the suspect's actions, where he goes, and with whom he meets. If the traveler is met by another person who drives him in a private automobile, the name of the registered owner of the vehicle can be obtained and a criminal history check can be conducted. The person picking up the traveler may have a reputation or history of being involved in drug trafficking.

If the traveler is observed checking into a hotel, he can be placed under surveillance and further observed.

While the passenger travels to his ultimate destination, the drug agents have the opportunity to run the name of the traveler through a series of indices for any drug intelligence that may exist about the person, as well as any criminal record he may have. This information can then be provided to law enforcement at the traveler's destination.

HOTEL PROFILING

After many years of experience, airport interdiction investigators have recognized characteristics of people staying in hotels who may be drug couriers or who may be otherwise involved in the drug trade. Often these people are identified by a police source of information working as a hotel clerk, who in turn notifies drug agents.

Investigators will ask their sources of information to look for hotel guests who check in either without a reservation or with one made very recently. Drug couriers have a tendency to pay cash for their stay, order room service instead of going out or only eat in the hotel restaurant, refuse daily maid service, and receive few visitors. These suspects usually remain in their room inordinate periods of time, and they may stay at a hotel for a week or more with no apparent reason for being there. Drug agents know that hotel guests who exhibit this behavior may be waiting to have either drugs or money picked up from them, or they may be awaiting the delivery of drugs or money to take with them on their return trip.

When alerted by a source of information, drug investigators will conduct a preliminary investigation into who a person is, how he got to his destination, and what telephone calls he has been making while a guest at the hotel. An analysis of the telephone calls made can determine if the name of the traveler and the telephone numbers he is calling are known to have a history of involvement in drug trafficking. The results of the drug agents' inquiries will determine whether or not the hotel guest will be placed under surveillance to see what develops.

Hotel profiling has been highly successful in identifying courier routes and members of drug smuggling organizations, and it has been responsible for the recovery of large amounts of drugs and drug proceeds.

After a suspected courier is arrested at a transportation node or hotel, his personal belongings should be thoroughly examined for clues concerning where the drugs were to be delivered, where they came from, and who else may be involved. Any address book found should be seized or photocopied for later analysis. Every courier case is an instant conspiracy investigation waiting to be launched through the investigative skills of the drug agents.

EXPANDING THE INITIAL INVESTIGATION

A typical drug interdiction case begins when a drug agent combs through the passenger manifest of a flight arriving at his or her airport that originated in a city known for distributing drugs or for receiving money from drug sales. As an example, large U.S. cities close to the Mexican border are considered major distribution centers for methamphetamine, marijuana, and cocaine after they have been smuggled into the United States. Outbound flights from Los Angeles have a tendency to carry drug couriers, and incoming flights have a tendency to have couriers returning with large amounts of money generated from the sales of these drugs.

Drug investigators will sometimes target individuals on these flights after reviewing a flight's manifest for passengers who purchased tickets in unusual ways, possibly in an attempt to conceal their original points of departure or destination. A good example is a passenger who has paid cash for a one-way ticket at a travel agency that is an unusually long distance from the point of departure or the passenger's home and then has exchanged the ticket for a different flight to the same destination twenty-four hours before departure. Or the same person purchased a ticket to fly across the country, only to return the next day.

Some transportation-terminal drug investigators have K-9s specially trained to detect the presence of drugs. Upon arrival of the suspect flight, a dog handler will walk the dog past the unloaded baggage from the flight before it reaches the terminal to see if the dog alerts to the presence of drugs within the suitcases. Cash frequently has trace amounts of drug residue on it, which alerts these K-9s.

When a K-9 alerts on a traveler's luggage without his knowledge, drug agents may decide to conduct a controlled-delivery investigation in lieu of confronting him at the terminal, in order to determine who the receiver of the drugs or money is. However, if a surveillance team is unavailable or due to other circumstances, the drug agents may have no option but to confront the passenger after he retrieves his baggage. The passenger usually will be arrested at this point.

This is when the drug agent's interview and interrogation skills will come into play. Assuming the passenger waives his right to counsel and agrees to answer questions, he most likely will deny he had any knowledge that any money or drugs was in his baggage, despite the fact that he carried the bag with him onto the plane instead of checking it in (see **blind mule** defense tactic, chapter 8). Drug agents should always check the **pocket litter** of the suspect. This includes every piece of scrap paper on his person or in his baggage. Photo-copies of the paper and his ticket should be obtained for further analysis. Telephone address books are especially helpful, as well as the address books contained within the memory of cellular telephones the suspect may possess. Numbers recently dialed and telephone numbers of those who called the suspect also may be obtained from the cellular telephone.[1]

Agents also should make an effort to locate any vehicles owned or operated by the suspect that may be parked in an airport or transportation node's short- or long-term parking lot. The vehicle may be occupied by an accomplice, or it may contain valuable evidence linking the suspect to other members of the conspiracy.

Drug agents should always ask for the suspect's cooperation after he has been arrested. If he agrees, agents should direct the suspect to call the person he is working for to report to him that all went well and that he is about to leave the airport with the drugs or money. This phone call, which should be recorded if possible, may verify that the person called acknowledges he is aware of the courier's activities. His acknowledgement could lead to conspiracy and other substantive charges against him. The acknowledgement of a second person involved in the drug transportation scheme also makes the courier liable for conspiracy.

In the event the drug agents learn the telephone number of the contact person but the courier refuses to cooperate, the agents may consider calling the number themselves as a ploy to draw the suspect into the open. Using this approach depends entirely on the circumstances. It is not appropriate in all situations.

An agent may pose as a representative of the airlines or as a relative of the courier who was asked to call the number and leave a message. The agent can tell the person on the telephone that the suspect is in the hospital and has asked that he be called to pick up his bag, or any other reasonable explanation of why the original suspect is unable to make the telephone call himself. Just the mere acknowledgement that the person called was to meet the suspect at the airport, hotel, or other location may lead to future conspiracy charges. A phone call like this will not always get the desired results, but it is an investigative technique that should at least be attempted.

Agents should also be mindful that the receiver of the drugs or one of his representatives may already be at the airport or bus terminal and may have witnessed the arrest of the courier.

The telephone number subscriber's name and address should be determined as soon as possible. Checking with the Department of Motor Vehicles for driver's license information about the subscriber might reveal an additional address where a surveillance can be initiated. A copy of the subscriber's driver's license photograph can be obtained and shown to the cooperating defendant in a photo lineup to further corroborate his incriminating statements.

Drug agents should further attempt to solicit the suspect's cooperation in conducting a controlled delivery of the money or drugs to its intended recipient. If the suspect does cooperate, drug agents will have the opportunity to arrest the person who arrives at the predetermined location to retrieve the drugs or money. Often this person is not a significant member of the conspiracy but is himself another courier hired to merely transport the items to someone else. However, he may be a significant player in the conspiracy. The same offer to cooperate should be given to this person whether or not he is the ultimate recipient of the drugs or money. He is in a position to reveal the identities of other members of the drug conspiracy.

After the arrest of the recipient of the drugs or money, a search warrant can be sought for his residence because it could contain records or other drugs and money belonging to his criminal organization.

Once these people are fully identified, telephone toll information should be obtained from the local telephone companies that service their residences and cellular telephones. The toll numbers should be run through indices to determine if these numbers have appeared in other drug investigations or if their subscribers have a history of involvement in drug trafficking.

Surveillance can be initiated at the houses or businesses where these telephones are located to determine who frequents them. License plates from their vehicles often will identify them and where they live. Those locations can also be placed under surveillance for additional intelligence on persons who visit them.

If the drug or money courier claims to have no knowledge of the presence of contraband in his luggage and refuses to cooperate, additional steps can be taken to disprove his claim. These include fingerprint comparison on the packaging of the contraband with the suspect's fingerprints. They may also include a polygraph examination to prove or disprove his claim of not being involved. A criminal records check that shows the suspect has prior arrests for drug trafficking is powerful circumstantial evidence that may be later introduced in court. Again, pocket litter can identify other persons involved, and their subsequent surveillances and interviews may lead to their admission of their and the courier's involvement in drug trafficking. No single piece of evidence will ever be sufficient to indict or to result in a conviction; the totality of evidence will often lead to indictments and convictions. The more circumstantial evidence the drug agents can obtain, the better are the chances for conviction.

OTHER CONSIDERATIONS

Drug couriers have been arrested from every racial and ethnic group. However, from experience drug investigators know that statistically certain groups are more involved in drug trafficking than others. Organizers of drug courier and smuggling rings believe that conservatively dressed Caucasians, especially older women, are the least likely to be approached or noticed by drug agents at transportation nodes. Drug agents need to be cognizant that smuggling rings often specifically employ Caucasians for this very reason; however, no matter how innocent looking these people may appear, they will still exhibit other profile traits such as nervousness, cash purchase of tickets, and the like. Drug agents should not be lulled into believing that only non-Whites are involved in the drug smuggling trade. Couriers come from all walks of life and socioeconomic backgrounds.

SUMMARY

Drug and money couriers heavily rely on airlines, buses, and trains for transportation. Recognizing this, law enforcement has established teams of drug investigators to identify couriers and seize their money and contraband. Each year in the United States, thousands of pounds of controlled substances and millions of dollars in cash are seized by drug agents.

Couriers make efforts to blend into the multitudes of other passengers conducting legitimate business; however, they often reveal the true nature of their travel by exhibiting certain characteristics. These characteristics include the way they purchase tickets for transportation as well as their length of stay, physical appearance, and inability to answer simple questions about their travels. These characteristics often can be applied to terrorists moving about the country.

When an investigator conducts a consensual encounter with a suspected drug courier, it is not much different from when a uniformed police officer stops a motorist or pedestrian to inquire about his activity.

The success of airport and transportation-node profiling has been expanded to hotels, where many drug and money couriers wait aimlessly to be contacted by the recipient of the contraband. They also may be waiting in a hotel room to receive another suitcase that contains drugs or money to take to another destination.

In each case in which an arrest is made, a conspiracy investigation is waiting to be born. Drug agents know that at least two other people are involved: the person who furnished the drug-laden luggage and the intended recipient. It is now the job of the drug agents to identify the other members of the drug trafficking organization.

Searching the courier's possessions and pocket litter will often reveal contact telephone numbers, addresses, and other information leading to the identities of the others involved. Drug agents should exploit each bit of information for analysis of who else is involved. To merely book the courier and go on to another case throws away a golden opportunity to arrest others involved in the same offense.

Drug agents involved in transportation interdiction should recognize that drug traffickers will often hire Caucasians, especially older women, as drug couriers in order to defeat any profile they think may exist. Agents are advised not to be complacent, and they should realize that couriers come in all shapes, sizes, socioeconomic backgrounds, and races.

NOTE

1. Check with the prosecutor who will handle the matter before attempting to either retrieve stored telephone numbers or answer any incoming calls received by the suspect's telephone.

SUGGESTED READING

Lee, Gregory D. *Global Drug Enforcement: Practical Investigative Techniques,* Boca Raton, FL: CRC Press, 2004.

CHAPTER 7

Coordination with the Prosecutor

Many problems and misunderstandings can be avoided when the investigator and the prosecutor come to a mutual understanding before any conspiracy case is initiated.

Prosecutors know the legal community and sitting judges best. They have experience with people who make up the jury pool in their particular jurisdiction. They know which judge will be more receptive than others to multidefendant conspiracy trials in which there may be only circumstantial evidence presented to a jury.

Investigators should always approach their prosecutor before initiating a complex conspiracy investigation. Prosecutors may need to have advance notice for scheduling and personnel management for many of these types of cases. They need to know what the goal and scope of the conspiracy investigation will be, how many defendants may ultimately be identified, and of that number, based on the evidence, which ones are most likely to be convicted.

Investigators and prosecutors should conduct strategy meetings early and often to determine what direction an investigation is going and what specific evidence the investigation is likely to produce. Opinions should be shared about which suspects are likely to cooperate by testifying against other conspirators. Prosecutors need to know the availability of potential witnesses and how the evidence is likely to be collected. They need to share with investigators their honest assessment of the case and what anticipated legal defenses they will most likely encounter during trial. Together, investigators and prosecutors can formulate a viable strategy or investigative plan as members of the same team.

A technique in "pitching" the case to the local prosecutor is to give him or her a realistic view of the scope and potential of the investigation. Are there too many defendants or not enough to warrant prosecution? These numbers will vary greatly depending on the policies and resources of the prosecutor's office. Before embarking on any long-term conspiracy investigation that may require substantial prosecutorial assets, the investigator is well advised to consult with his or her local prosecutor. Nobody likes surprises.

Prosecutors know the jury pool in their district, and they are in the best position to gauge the probable outcome of any trial. Many deputy district attorneys and assistant U.S. attorneys have wide discretion on whom to indict and prosecute. However, some elected or appointed officials may be more restrictive, and they may have to be personally convinced to begin a potentially massive undertaking by virtue of the numbers of defendants and complexities that may arise during the case. If an investigator finds an aggressive career prosecutor willing to try a case on less-than-substantial physical and circumstantial evidence, he or she should consider himself or herself fortunate. Many prosecutors will reject conspiracy cases because they lack substantial physical evidence. This is why investigators must strive to submit the best quality case they can with as much documentary, physical, and testimonial evidence as possible.

If a prosecutor in one district balks at prosecuting a particular conspiracy investigation, the investigator should explore the possibility of contacting another prosecution office where an overt act has been or is anticipated being committed. As mentioned earlier, venue rests in any place where an overt act has taken place or the agreement has been reached.

CHARGING ALL CRIMES COMMITTED BY CONSPIRATORS

Investigators who have thorough knowledge of state and federal criminal statutes will prepare the most accurate criminal indictments possible.

Members of criminal conspiracies frequently have committed other violations of law in addition to the original crime that they agreed to commit. A complete listing of all violations uncovered during the course of a conspiracy investigation should be discussed with the prosecutor when they are discovered. The defendants should be indicted for all of their crimes, not just the ones that are the easiest to prove. These added criminal charges can be used to facilitate plea-bargaining agreements because they may substantially add to the punishment the defendants will receive. Remember, because of the Pinkerton rule, all members of a conspiracy can be charged with the crimes that were committed by others in the conspiracy that are connected with achieving the object of the conspiracy if the members were in the conspiracy at the time the crimes were committed. The following list of federal criminal statutes is usually duplicated in state penal codes. Many of these types of crimes will be uncovered during conspiracy investigations:

- *18 USC 4—Misprision of felony.* This requires persons knowledgeable of crimes that have been or are about to be committed to inform law enforcement authorities. An example may be a person who is not directly involved in a conspiracy but who has intimate knowledge of it being prosecuted for not reporting the offenses to the police. This may apply to a girlfriend or wife of one of the conspirators who had some active participation in concealing the crime. Their indictment may compel them to testify against the defendants in return for use immunity.

- *18 USC 111—Assaulting, resisting, or impeding federal officers.* If a witness or suspect purposely sends investigators in a direction leading nowhere in an attempt to protect himself or his friends, he has impeded the investigation and may be charged with this or a similar offense.

- *18 USC 924 (C)—Use or possession of a firearm during and in relation to a federal drug trafficking crime (five-year mandatory minimum).* Even if a firearm is not found on a person who delivers drugs, he may still be charged, and this offense applies to all other members of the drug conspiracy under the Pinkerton theory of vicarious liability.

- *18 USC 1001—False statements.* Lying to federal agents is a crime during the course of a federal criminal investigation and is a felony.

- *18 USC 1071—Concealing person from arrest (harboring a fugitive).* Someone who knowingly conceals a fugitive or assists them in hiding from authorities is subject to being charged with this offense.

- *18 USC 1073—Flight to avoid prosecution or giving testimony.* A member of a conspiracy who temporarily or permanently moves or flees to avoid being prosecuted or giving testimony against members of the conspiracy is guilty of this offense.

- *18 USC 1341—Mail fraud.* Fraudulently obtaining a driver's license or other government identity cards or documents through the mail constitutes this crime. Using the mails to apply for or secure a loan using a fictitious name is an example of mail fraud.

- *18 USC 1503—Influencing or injuring an officer or juror.* This may occur when a conspirator approaches a juror in person and intimidates or bribes him to influence his decision in the conspirator's or someone else's trial.

- *18 USC 1504—Influencing a juror by writing.* Same as above, but in writing.

- *18 USC 1510—Obstruction of criminal investigations.* Destroying potential evidence, shredding documents, or leading investigators on a false trail constitutes obstruction.

- *18 USC 1511—Obstruction of state or local law enforcement.* Same as above, but this applies to obstructing state and local law enforcement investigators during the course of certain gambling cases.

- *18 USC 1512—Tampering with a witness, victim, or informant.* Intimidating witnesses, victims, or informants in order to influence their testimony or prevent them from testifying constitutes this crime.

- *18 USC 1513—Retaliating against a witness, victim, or informant.* Bringing violence or the threat of violence against a witness, victim, or informant involved in a criminal investigation violates this statute.

- *18 USC 1542—False statement in the application and use of a passport.* Terrorists and drug smugglers will often apply for passports by using a false birth certificate or by lying about the circumstance of the loss of their legitimate passport in order to obtain another one. They require a different passport to conceal their foreign travels to countries known to aid terrorists or to produce and export drugs.

- *18 USC 1543—Forgery or false use of a passport.* This most often applies to a "photo switch," in which the photo of a legitimate passport holder is substituted for another in older passports. Alterations of a passport apply to this statute.

- *18 USC 1952—Interstate and foreign travel or transportation in aid of a racketeering enterprise (ITAR).* Whenever a conspirator travels to another state or country in order to aid or facilitate a criminal offense, he has violated this felony statute. Each time the suspect travels to further the goal of the conspiracy he violates the ITAR statute.

- *18 USC 1956—Laundering of monetary instruments.* This includes conducting a financial transaction using money derived from criminal activity or the concealment of the source of the funds.

- *18 USC 1957—Engaging in monetary transactions in property derived from specified unlawful activity.* This involves an attempted or actual transaction in which the value of criminally derived property is over $10,000. An example is when a conspirator purchases an automobile or real estate using money derived through drug trafficking.

- *18 USC 1621—Perjury.* Lying about a material fact after being sworn.

- *18 USC 1622—Subornation of perjury.* Requesting, encouraging, or paying others to perjure themselves while testifying.

- *21 USC 841(a)(2)—Distribution of counterfeit substance.* The defendant sells what he purports to be a controlled substance to an informant or undercover agent when in fact he knows it is not, for the purpose of gaining the buyer's money.

- *21 USC 841(e)(1)—Booby traps on federal property.* Marijuana cultivators are known to place booby traps to discourage, injure, and kill anyone who happens on the field. This statute applies when these devices are found on federal land, usually national forests.

- *21 USC 843 (b)—Use of communication facility to facilitate a drug crime.* Also known as phone counts. Every time a conspirator uses a telephone to facilitate a drug transaction, he commits a felony, even if an undercover drug agent or informant initiated the telephone call.

- *21 USC 849—Distribution within 1,000 feet of a rest or truck stop.* If convicted of this drug-related statute, the defendant can receive double the original sentence.

- *21 USC 859—Distribution to persons under age twenty-one.* Conspirators who sell drugs to juveniles or anyone younger than twenty-one can potentially have their sentences doubled upon conviction.

- *21 USC 860—Distribution or manufacturing in or near schools and colleges.* This applies to the manufacturing and distribution of drugs in any area within 1,000 feet of any school property. This includes adult schools, any time of the day or night, or even when school is not in session. The conviction doubles the original sentence. It does not matter if the undercover agent or informant suggested consummating a drug deal on school property. However, by doing so, the agent runs the risk of nullifying the jury.

- *21 USC 861—Employment of persons under eighteen years of age in drug crime.* Inner city drug dealers often employ children to distribute drugs to customers, because they believe police are less likely to suspect that children are involved in the conspiracy. Convictions will double the sentence of the substantive crime to those who employed children in drug distribution.

- *21 USC 953—Exportation of a controlled substance.* This applies when controlled substances already in the United States are exported to another country. It also applies when the controlled substances are exchanged, out of the country, for money or another drug, (e.g., cocaine smuggled into the United States that is exported to Canada in exchange for marijuana). Also, when any domestically manufactured drug, such as marijuana, LSD, or methamphetamine, is exported.

Each conspirator should be charged with all the related crimes committed by all the other members of the conspiracy after they entered into the agreement. Proper charging gives prosecutors leverage when negotiating plea agreements. It should be clear in each defendant's mind exactly what their potential sentence will be if they are convicted of all the charges. Defendants do not engage in a conspiracy anticipating being arrested. The sentence each defendant could potentially receive is probably substantially more than he ever thought was possible, especially in light of state and federal sentencing guidelines coupled with mandatory minimum sentencing. Bringing proper charges against a defendant is a way of enticing him to cooperate in the government's case by testifying against the other defendants.

Investigators should be cognizant that because of the secretive nature and size of some criminal conspiracies, not all members of the conspiracy will know the existence of every other member or what their role in the conspiracy was. Nor will they know all the overt acts or crimes the other members of the conspiracy committed. However, every defendant knows at least one other coconspirator. Investigators of conspiracy cases may be the only ones who actually know who all the members are and what overt acts and crimes each member committed.

SEALED INDICTMENTS

A prosecutor often asks the court to seal the indictments of the defendants. This prevents the premature disclosure to the defendants of the existence of the investigation and their indictments for the offense(s).

Sealed indictments buy time for investigators to plan strategies for making arrests and locating defendants before they have an opportunity to flee and become fugitives. However, once any member of a conspiracy is arrested, the seal is broken, and the existence of arrest warrants stemming from the investigation and indictments becomes public record.

ARREST WARRANTS

An arrest warrant should be obtained as soon as the prosecutor decides to seek an individual's indictment for participating in a conspiracy. Arrest warrants provide the investigator in charge of the case the needed flexibility in planning case strategy. Fortunately, investigators are not required to arrest someone immediately after an arrest warrant has been issued. In large conspiracy cases, it may be advantageous to arrest all the suspects simultaneously after most or all of the members of the conspiracy have been identified. The immediate arrest of one of the suspects may cause the others to flee. By obtaining arrest warrants during the course of the investigation, valuable time will be saved if circumstances should change.

As an example, during an ongoing investigation of a group involved in the illegal sales of firearms, the supervisory investigator may want to wait until a final shipment of weapons is delivered to the primary undercover agent before arresting the other members of the conspiracy. Arresting them before the object of the investigation is met will not only seriously jeopardize the final delivery of the weapons, it may cause other members of the conspiracy to flee because they fear that they are also about to be arrested. If these fugitives flee to other jurisdictions around the state or to other parts of the country, it can cause unnecessary logistical problems in locating, arresting, and transporting them back to the venue responsible for prosecuting them.

Further, without arrest warrants in hand, other uninvolved law enforcement agencies may hesitate or refuse to arrest someone within their jurisdiction unless an abstract of an arrest warrant can be faxed or e-mailed to them. Arrest warrants offer them a level of comfort because they know that an impartial magistrate has heard the facts of the case and has issued the warrants based on probable cause developed through an investigation. Arrest warrants also shield the arresting officers from civil liability from making a false arrest, because they were acting on good faith based on the existence of an arrest warrant.

This is especially true if a fugitive has fled to another country. Few, if any, foreign police agencies will take action unless they have an arrest warrant in hand that they obtained from Interpol. A phone call from the case investigator to another police agency asking them to make a "probable cause" arrest for someone without an arrest warrant is unprofessional and most likely will not be honored until one is obtained.

In addition to the arrest warrant, investigators should provide the outside agency with a copy of the affidavit used to obtain the arrest warrant. This will give them sufficient background information about the fugitive and the particular role he played in the conspiracy so they can plan how to go about arresting the individual safely.

Prosecutors should request that the court seal the arrest warrants in order to maintain the integrity of the investigation and not alert the suspects they have been discovered and are subject to arrest. However, in doing so investigators should not enter the names of the persons subject to arrest into the FBI's National Crime Information Center (NCIC). NCIC stores information about all wanted persons and vehicles in the United States. If a police officer encounters one of the conspirators and checks his name against the database of wanted persons in the system, he or she will arrest the person, and this may unintentionally jeopardize the continuation of the investigation once it is known that one of the members of the conspiracy has been arrested.

MATERIAL WITNESS WARRANTS

Federal prosecutors will sometimes seek from the court a *material witness warrant* for a person with intimate knowledge of a conspiracy to ensure his presence during future crucial judicial proceedings.[1]

The witness is required to post a bond or may even be incarcerated. This technique is usually reserved for **unindicted coconspirators** who may flee to avoid testifying or fear of later being arrested.

Material witness warrants were issued for many persons early on in the investigation of the events leading to the September 11, 2001, airline hijackings and attacks in Pennsylvania, New York City, and Washington, D.C. Since then, many legal challenges to their use have been made. They are an effective means of placing a legal hold on persons by making them available to give testimony or to be arrested if they are later discovered to be involved in the same conspiracy.

GRAND JURY PROCEEDINGS

A grand jury is a body of citizens who are empanelled at random and who serve for at least a month, sometimes up to a year or more, and who in proceedings outside of the courtroom, decide whether to issue criminal indictments. A "true bill" of indictment is issued when a grand jury decides that evidence in a certain case is strong enough to charge a suspect with a specific crime. Grand juries are usually comprised of twenty-four persons. A quorum is needed before the grand jury can indict.

Grand juries can also issue subpoenas that are required to obtain financial records. Administrative subpoenas, such as those issued by the DEA and other U.S. government agencies, are not honored at banks or other financial institutions. An investigator must appear before a grand jury to request a subpoena. After the service of the subpoena, the agent must return to the grand jury and inform them of the results.

Grand jurors are naturally interested in ongoing criminal investigations, and like most people, they want to be made to feel they are a part of a procedure, which they most certainly are. They may sometimes ask investigators irrelevant questions, but the prosecutor is there to guide them in obtaining the relevant facts before an indictment, or **true bill of indictment**, is requested.

Defense attorneys are prohibited from being inside the grand jury room when a prosecutor questions witnesses, suspects, or investigators as they testify. Investigators are merely asked if they have any evidence to suggest the person in question is not guilty of any crime.

Periodic visits to the grand jury will keep its members apprised of the progress of a complex ongoing investigation. This will often facilitate the expeditious securing of true bills and arrest warrants. The prosecutor may ask that true bills of indictment be returned on suspects as they are identified through the ongoing criminal investigation.

In multidefendant cases, after indictments are returned prosecutors can try one or all of the defendants during a particular trial. However, they may try suspects in increments of five or fewer in order to make the prosecution more manageable. These defendants are usually conspiracy members who had comparable roles, as opposed to mixing a supervisor or manager with defendants who only had minor roles.

IMMUNITY

Prosecutors may grant **use immunity** to selected defendants in order to gain their cooperation in an investigation and subsequent trial(s). Use immunity is granted to shield a defendant from prosecution for a particular offense. **Blanket immunity** shields the defendant from any crime he may have committed during a particular time period. This granting of immunity is done sparingly and only after prosecutors receive guidance from department policy and input from the case investigator. The granting of immunity to one or more selected defendants may provide valuable witnesses otherwise not available.

Before a defendant is offered immunity, he should be thoroughly debriefed by the investigators during what is called a **proffer**. A proffer, or formal offer of information in return for legal consideration, is designed to learn exactly what the defendant knows and what his and others' involvement in the conspiracy is. It also helps the prosecutor and investigators evaluate the defendant's credibility as a witness. If the prosecutor determines that a defendant's testimony is essential in securing guilty pleas or convictions of the other conspirators, immunity should be seriously considered. Conditions should always be attached to the offer of immunity. The defendant must understand and agree that he must fully cooperate throughout the entire investigation and trial phases of the case and that his reneging will nullify the agreement and subject him to prosecution.

The defendant should also be required to submit to a government-administered polygraph examination to prove he is being completely truthful and forthcoming with the investigators. Private polygraph examiners hired by a defense attorney have the potential of being tainted. Many private polygraphers are either unscrupulous or unqualified to administer such important examinations.

The proffer should include the defendant revealing the location of all money and assets accumulated by the conspirators during the lifetime of the conspiracy. Taking the profit out of the crime deters them and others from engaging in future criminal activity. A polygraph examination may prove useful in this regard.

MULTIPLE VENUES

As we learned in chapter 1, in a conspiracy investigation venue lies where the agreement was made or any overt act was committed to further the goal of the conspiracy. Conspirators will often commit crimes, make telephone calls, conduct meetings, and travel to other states or countries to carry out their criminal activity.

Coordination between the different U.S. attorney/district attorney offices where venue lies is required to consolidate cases, eliminate duplication of effort, and avoid double-jeopardy issues.

A decision should be made early on about who will prosecute the conspirators. Even though the same conspiracy can be tried in more than one venue, it is probably better from a logistical and practical standpoint to try all the defendants in a single venue.

Sometimes political considerations are made when deciding where conspirators will be tried. Other times, one venue may be ill equipped or have limited resources to try large conspiracy cases.

ASSET FORFEITURE PROCEDURES

Frequently, real property and other assets of the defendants involved in a conspiracy are located in different venues. Close coordination is required to ensure that all known assets subject to seizure are identified and that civil or criminal forfeiture proceedings are initiated.

It is not uncommon for a prosecutor to exercise his venue over a minor aspect of a large conspiracy case for the sole purpose of justifying his department receiving a portion of the assets seized during the investigation. Investigators are advised to allow their prosecutor and supervisors to resolve any disputes between vying agencies for any assets that are subject to civil or criminal forfeiture.

SUMMARY

Conspiracy investigations should always be conducted in partnership with the prosecutor.

Before any large-scale conspiracy investigation is launched, coordination should be made with the local state or federal prosecutor to receive their valuable input on what evidence they will need to obtain arrest warrants, indictments, and convictions of those involved in the conspiracy. With their help, a viable investigative plan or strategy can be formulated.

It is a good idea to seek the prosecutor's counsel and commitment to go to trial even if the goal of the investigation is not completely realized. Investigators should always strive to identify all members of a conspiracy, to recover all the stolen property or drugs, and to identify any assets subject to forfeiture procedures.

Investigators should document all crimes uncovered during the course of any conspiracy investigation. Conspirators often commit crimes when attempting to achieve the goal of the conspiracy. When they do, the conspirators should be held accountable for those crimes that can be attached to each individual who was a member of the conspiracy at the time the crimes occurred.

Prosecutors can seek sealed indictments and arrest warrants that can be obtained during the course of a conspiracy investigation. Sealing them will guard against unnecessarily or prematurely disclosing the existence of an investigation before it is completed.

Prosecutors may conduct grand jury procedures to seek indictments resulting in arrest warrants and subpoenas for financial records of the conspirators. Financial records can only be obtained through grand jury subpoenas and not through administrative subpoenas.

Through periodic investigator and prosecutor visits to the grand jury to seek indictments and subpoenas, the jurors become apprised of the progress of a conspiracy investigation. In large jurisdictions, this will expedite matters and prevent requiring significant amounts of the grand jury's time later.

The prosecutor is the only person authorized to grant either use or blanket immunity to a particular conspirator in return for his cooperation in an investigation and testimony during trial. The prosecutor will be guided by policy and the recommendations of the investigators involved in the case. Prosecutors will also conduct proffer sessions with defense counsel and their clients to determine if it is appropriate to offer them immunity and how crucial a defendant's cooperation is in securing convictions of other codefendants.

Conspiracy investigations often cross into other venues either within or outside a state and sometimes outside the country. Prosecutors will coordinate with the other affected venues to eliminate duplication of effort and to streamline the prosecution process. Sometimes political considerations are taken into account before a prosecutor will defer his right to prosecute to the venue initiating an investigation.

When conspirators accumulate money, property, and other fruits of their crimes, these should be seized and legally forfeited to take the profit out of the crime. Prosecutors will initiate civil or criminal asset forfeiture proceedings to confiscate the property of the conspirators that was earned or used to facilitate the conspiracy.

Material witness warrants are designed to put a legal hold on reluctant witnesses and unindicted coconspirators to make them available for trial and other court proceedings. Prosecutors can seek a bond, or even incarceration, of these witnesses to ensure they are available later.

NOTE

1. Not all jurisdictions may have the authority to issue material witness warrants.

Defense Attorney Trial Tactics

Through out their careers, investigators and prosecutors will be subjected to a variety of legal defenses launched at them by criminal defense attorneys, especially in high-profile cases. These defense tactics potentially can unravel the prosecutor's case. Some defense attorneys will not represent clients who are willing to agree to cooperate with investigators in return for consideration in their legal matters. They want to maintain their reputations as trial lawyers, not simply negotiators of plea agreements. The extent and cleverness of many of these defense tactics is only limited by the imagination of the attorney involved.

Investigators who are cognizant of the variety of defense-attorney trial tactics that have been used in the past can conduct their investigations in ways that will render them useless. Knowing these tactics also forces investigators to be as thorough as possible while conducting their conspiracy investigations. Thoroughness during an investigation takes away the defense attorney's tools to defend the client. Facts, coupled with evidence, are the defense attorney's worst enemies. The following are some of the most common legal defense tactics that investigators are likely to encounter that are used by criminal defense attorneys and are applicable to any conspiracy trial.

DEFENDANT WITHDREW FROM THE CONSPIRACY

With this tactic, the defendant readily concedes his involvement in the conspiracy at its onset. However, he claims he withdrew from the conspiracy long before its object was met.

By doing this, the defendant shields himself from criminal liability for crimes committed by other members of the conspiracy during its lifetime (see Pinkerton theory of vicarious liability in chapter 1).

Investigators need to focus on exactly when a defendant entered into a conspiracy, and exactly when, if applicable, he took affirmative steps to withdraw from it. Conspirators can only withdraw from a criminal conspiracy by doing something affirmative. One way for a defendant to withdraw from a conspiracy is for him to inform all known members of his intentions to withdraw. This means the other defendants would have to testify on his behalf to corroborate his claim, which is not likely. The other method of withdrawal is when a defendant fully and completely informs the police of his involvement in the conspiracy. This usually only occurs after the defendant has been arrested and admits to his involvement in a conspiracy during his initial interview or interrogation.

While questioning suspects in any conspiracy case, investigators should focus on exactly when a particular conspirator entered into the agreement and, more importantly, if the conspirator legally withdrew from it by informing the other conspirators he no longer wanted to be a part of the scheme. When these points are established early, defendants cannot later falsely claim they were no longer a member of the conspiracy when in reality they made no effort to legally withdraw. Carefully questioning defendants during their initial interviews about their withdrawing or remaining in a conspiracy will help thwart this legal defense.

OUTRAGEOUS GOVERNMENT CONDUCT

Criminal defense attorneys sometimes claim that the conduct of the investigators, and even the prosecutors, during the course of an investigation or trial was so outrageous that a dismissal of the indictment or acquittal of their client is warranted.

The defense attorney wants the judge or jury to believe that the investigators and/or prosecutor conducted themselves in such an outrageous manner that the dismissal or acquittal is justified in order to punish them for their conduct and to deter them from repeating it.

Investigators need to remember that it only takes one juror to agree with this defense theory to create a hung jury that cannot convict. Judges are aware of this defense tactic and are less likely to dismiss a case based on alleged investigator or prosecutor misconduct. Some judges, however, can be as offended as any juror by the techniques used by investigators and prosecutors to bring a defendant to trial. Most of these misconduct issues stem from the use of informants with questionable motives.

Investigators need to discuss with a prosecutor, in detail, any innovative or unusual investigative techniques they intend to use during the conduct of their conspiracy investigations. The use of controversial techniques, although perfectly legal, may be perceived by the judge or jurors as being outrageous, and should be avoided, if possible, to thwart this defense tactic.

A prosecutor can educate a jury by having a disinterested investigator testify as an expert witness to explain how such techniques are deployed. For example, in drug trafficking, terrorism, or gang investigations, the defense attorney is looking for a juror who may be offended at the idea of an undercover investigator or informant disguising his true intentions when associating with the defendants. They may claim that it is dishonest for an undercover investigator or informant to lie to a suspect about whom they really are, where they work, and what they've done in the past. The fact that they were dishonest with the defendants then implies that they are being dishonest with the jury now during their testimony. The disinterested expert witness can explain that lying to suspects during an undercover operation is a routinely deployed investigative technique designed to learn a defendant's true intentions. Even though it should be obvious that a criminal would not be forthcoming with a person he knew was a law enforcement official, the jury may need to hear this.

A skilled defense attorney can make just about any investigative technique appear underhanded and give the false impression that the investigators were relentless in trying to send this particular defendant to prison.

Other examples of possible outrageous conduct may include a female informant who had a sexual relation with one or more defendants or a star witness for the prosecutor, usually the informant, who has a criminal history of multiple arrests and convictions for crimes against women and children. Other jurors may believe that it is outrageous for the police to knowingly use an informant who has never paid federal income taxes. Once an informant is labeled as having done an outrageous act, prosecutors may be leery to use him in any future criminal case.

Another example of possible outrageous conduct is when drug investigators, knowing that defendants can receive substantial punishment enhancements for possessing a firearm during a drug deal or selling drugs on or near a school campus, arrange for these things to occur. Investigators run the risk of nullifying the jury when they arrange for a drug delivery to take place at a school or encourage the defendant to bring a gun for protection. However, if it can be established that the defendant suggested making the drug delivery on or near a campus and told the undercover investigator he was going to be armed, these facts should be made known to the jury.

Prosecutors should bring to the jury's attention early all known past bad acts committed by an informant during his direct examination on the witness stand. If the defense attorney has the opportunity to question the informant about such things during cross-examination before the prosecutor mentions them, the jury gets the indelible impression that the prosecutor intended to hide these facts from them. Because of the exception to the hearsay rule of evidence in most conspiracy trials, the informant can testify about the words, deeds, and actions of the defendants. The informant must admit to his past crimes and indiscretions to the jury, in open court, in order to steal the thunder of the defense attorney, who will make every effort to make the informant–witness appear to be worse then he may actually be.

The prosecutor needs to also inform the jury through the testimony of disinterested witnesses that informants, especially in the drug world, come from within it and good citizens do not normally possess the information needed to infiltrate conspiracies. This leaves the government with little option but to work with members of the drug world.

The objective of the prosecutor is to make the informant appear to be truthful and disinterested in obtaining a conviction, despite his unsavory past and close association with the defendants. Investigators need to provide the prosecutor with all the available information about the informant's past, including matters concerning tax returns, outstanding parking tickets, and relationships with women and former employers. Many defense attorneys will have private investigators conduct full-background investigations on informants who are scheduled to testify in order to find any derogatory information that may exist in an attempt to destroy their credibility.

As an example, through a private investigator, the defense may learn that an informant has recently applied for a bank loan. Part of the loan package includes the informant's past federal income tax returns. The investigator obtains a copy of the returns and discovers that the informant never paid taxes on money he earned in the past as an informant with various police agencies. Under these circumstances, the defense attorney will surely question the informant about not paying his federal taxes, and he will use this information as evidence of his dishonesty and to divert the jury's attention from the facts of the case.

Investigators may not normally ask to see an informant's past tax returns because obtaining them is highly restricted. However, they should quiz informants about them, along with any other matter that a judge or jury might perceive as derogatory. If an informant has seldom or never filed an income tax return, this information should be brought to the attention of the prosecutor immediately, and the informant should be instructed to remedy his tax problems well before trial.

MULTIPLE DEFENDANTS

Most conspiracy trials will include multiple defendants. Sometimes the defendants will turn on each other to save themselves. One group of defendants may coerce another defendant to take the blame for the crimes committed by the other conspirators, thereby exonerating them.

This usually occurs in the middle of a lengthy trial that is going badly for the defendants. Suddenly, one defendant makes it known to the court that he wants to change his plea from not guilty to guilty. His defense attorney announces to the court that the defendant feels guilt and shame for having gotten his "friends" into a legal jam because they had absolutely nothing to do with the crime, despite overwhelming evidence to the contrary. The truth of the matter is that all the defendants are equally guilty. However, this one defendant was either threatened by the others and/or promises were made to him that his family will be well taken care of while he's in prison and they will receive a stipend while he is in prison if he pleads guilty. This defendant is being asked or coerced to essentially take the fall for the others.

Prosecutors need to emphasize to the court that evidence exists contrary to the single defendant's claim, and they should request that investigators be given the opportunity to reinterview the defendant who is asking to change his plea.

ENTRAPMENT

The *entrapment defense* tactic is sometimes presented in conjunction with the *outrageous government conduct* ploy. This is the most common form of defense in drug cases, but it can be equally applied in other conspiracy cases as well. In this situation, the defense attorney alleges that an informant, or undercover investigator, convinced the suspect to commit a crime when he would not normally be predisposed to do so, solely for the purpose of having him arrested.

The defense attorney will attempt to show that the idea of selling drugs, weapons, or stolen property to the undercover agent or informant was planted by the government. The otherwise "innocent" defendant would never have become involved in such a crime if the government agents had not suggested it. The defense will attempt to show that the investigators or informants convinced the defendant he could make a lot of money with very little work and there were few risks involved. The defense will imply that the defendant had no intention of being involved in criminal activity before meeting the informant or undercover agent.

This legal defense usually can be defeated in drug cases when multiple buys of controlled substances are made from a suspect to show that not only was he predisposed to commit the crime, but he also had connections to obtain increasingly larger amounts of drugs to sell to the undercover agent or informant. The defendant's criminal history or police intelligence about him being involved in past drug sales or other criminal activity also can help defeat this defense. Recorded conversations in which the defendant admits to previously engaging in criminal activity is a powerful weapon against this tactic, especially if the defendant has no criminal record or only a minor record.

One caution: Investigators should be sure that their informants are not targeting individuals who truly are not engaged in criminal activity simply for the purpose of making a case to justify being paid.

MISTAKEN IDENTITY

In cases in which someone has been arrested as an out-of-district fugitive, the defendant has the right to what is called an *identity hearing.* At these hearings, the government must prove that the person in custody is the same person named in the indictment that resulted in his arrest. Some defense attorneys have maintained that their client simply is not the person named in the indictment.

This tactic is quickly disproved when witnesses are called during the identity hearing who can testify that the person is indeed the one named in the indictment. Sometimes investigators are forced to spend valuable resources obtaining fingerprint cards, photographs, recorded telephone calls, and the like to prove that the person in custody is the same as the person in the indictment.

Some defendants have been known to continuously deny being the person named in the indictment all the way through trial and their conviction.

FABRICATION OF EXCULPATORY EVIDENCE

A real sign of desperation on the part of a defendant is when his attorney fabricates *exculpatory evidence.* Exculpatory evidence is evidence that tends to prove the defendant is innocent.

Overzealous or unscrupulous defense attorneys may seek out a so-called *expert witness* to testify about certain facts entered into evidence during trial. The testimony the defense attorney seeks is for the expert witness to contradict the findings of the investigative agency in matters concerning scientific evidence or testimony.

These expert witnesses appear in trials most often when there is a question about a scientific fact or police tactics. Their testimony can be concerning fingerprint examinations, blood stains, DNA results, police tactics and training, use of force, and the authentication of audio- and videotapes, to name a few. The defense attorney's objective is to locate an expert witness who will give a contrasting opinion from that already given by a government expert.

Before a witness can testify as an expert, he is subject to **voir dire.** This is an oral examination, under oath, about the witness's education, background, work experience, and other qualifications that would make him an expert in a particular field. The judge determines if the witness is qualified to testify as an expert during a particular trial. Once declared as an expert witness, the witness gives an opinion to the jury, and they have to make their own decision about whether the witness is credible.

A member of the bar, of course, would never knowingly recruit an expert witness to give false testimony about a scientific matter in order to refute the prosecutor's evidence. Many defense attorneys screen numerous expert witnesses until they find one who will testify exactly as they had hoped. Many of these same attorneys unwittingly employ expert witnesses who have convinced them they are credible, when in reality they are not.

When seeking an expert witness, defense attorneys will either intentionally or unwittingly ask these persons questions that make it clear what the attorney is hoping to achieve from the expert's examination. A dishonest expert witness will reach a conclusion that benefits the attorney's client. An attorney who seeks an expert witness to give a dishonest opinion can be disbarred for suborning perjury. The expert can also be charged with perjury if it can be proven he lied about his expert opinion. However, this is extremely rare because the witness is testifying to his opinion, even if it is wrong. There is no crime in being mistaken.

As an example of an actual case, a DEA agent testified in federal court that an audiotape of a recorded telephone conversation between an informant and a defendant was made in his presence and that what was heard on the tape was what was actually said between the informant and the defendant. The defense attorney later asked the assistant U.S. attorney for the actual cassette tape with the recording in order to listen to it himself in the privacy of his office. The assistant U.S. attorney complied with the request.

During the defense portion of the trial, an expert witness testified that his own examination of the audiotape in question revealed that it had been severely tampered with, in that it was a compilation of splices and editing that resulted in the defendant appearing to utter words he did not say. The expert witness displayed the appropriate body language during his testimony (hand on heart, open palms, eyes to heaven, etc.) to signal the jury that he was a disinterested, honest, thoughtful, professional who knew his business well. He testified that he had conducted microscopic examinations of the actual tape, and he was allowed to post photographs of alleged markings on the tape he identified as erasure marks and other probable signs of tape manipulation. He played the recording on an impressive-looking tape machine that was connected to a computer and other instruments that displayed audio waves. He gave the indelible impression that he had proven that the agent had lied under oath in his uncontrollable zeal to convict this particular defendant.

The prosecutor asked for a delay in the trial until a government expert witness could examine the same tape and render his conclusions. For the next four days, a team of FBI forensic audio examiners performed the identical tests conducted by the witness, plus many others that the witness was incapable of conducting because he lacked the expensive equipment to do so.

The FBI expert's credentials and experience in the area of tape authentication were extensive and impressive. He testified that, as a result of his examination, he had concluded that the disputed tape was genuine and tamper-free. He replicated the tests performed by the witness and disputed his methodology, experience, training, and technical expertise to successfully conduct such an examination.

During the FBI's examination of the tape, the expert witness's credibility was further questioned. An investigation into the expert witness was launched, and it was discovered that the academic degree he claimed to possess was never achieved. It is also clear he did not have the formal training or technical experience he claimed to render such opinions. When asked under oath about his college degree, he claimed he "thought" he had earned it. When asked if he could explain the discrepancies between his and the FBI expert's findings, he admitted he "probably made a mistake."

The jury convicted the defendant, and when polled after the trial, said that the expert witness initially appeared extremely credible. A government agent manipulating a piece of physical evidence to make a defendant appear guilty angered them. They wanted to punish the government by acquitting all the defendants on trial. However, once the truth of the matter was known and the expert witness's formal education and training were in question, they wanted to see charges brought against him.

The government elected not to pursue perjury charges against the defense expert witness. This same witness later testified in numerous high-profile trials throughout the United States and Canada, always for defense attorneys, and he helped win acquittals on occasion. He is only one of many so-called expert witnesses who, for a fee, will testify to just about anything a defense attorney would like them to say.

In another actual case, a defense attorney introduced a recently made tape recording of a telephone conversation between his client and the informant that supposedly took place months earlier between them. The tape purportedly showed the informant threatening the man if he did not follow through with the crime. An expert witness authenticated the recording as being genuine, when in reality it was a total fabrication.

A defense attorney might also attempt to introduce a private-sector polygraph examiner as a witness who will testify that a polygraph examination he conducted of a defendant showed him to be completely truthful when he denied any involvement in a conspiracy. Even though this testimony may not be allowed in trial, the attorney may conduct a news conference revealing the results of the examination in an attempt to reach the jurors through television or radio coverage.

Another expert witness may claim to possess a "critical ear" and to hear a defendant's words on a taped confession differently from the police transcripts of the recording. Despite having a tape recording of the defendant saying, "I murdered the man," this expert may testify that, after listening to the tape, he concluded that the defendant actually said, "I did *not* murder the man."

Other expert witnesses may be recently fired or retired investigators who are prepared to testify that the procedures followed by the police are either unsound, unprofessional, or in some way in contrast with the police department's manual or policy.

Many expert witnesses for the defense are legitimate and possess the academic training and experience to render opinions; however, there are an ever-increasing number of people who claim to possess expertise in an area when they clearly do not. These people offer their services to anyone who is willing to pay for them, and after being briefed on a case, in an indirect or roundabout way, they will suggest they can testify to exactly what the defense is hoping for, no matter how unbelievable it may be.

When prosecutors first learn that an expert witness will be called to testify, they should immediately request the witness's curriculum vitae, resume, and case history so their investigators can explore each claim of education, training, employment, and experience in the field. Many of these witnesses assume that no one will check out their qualifications or if they are checked, it will be after the witness damages the government case and it will be too late for the government to recover.

Investigators need to find legitimate expert witnesses in the same field who can replicate any examinations conducted by defense expert witnesses and who are available to testify about why the defense findings may be in error. The federal government, especially the FBI and the military, employ experts with impeccable credentials and world-class expertise who can contradict the findings of any self-educated expert witness who is essentially nothing more than a hired gun for the defense, used to kill the credibility of the government's case.

Some criminal defense attorneys will intentionally seek out unethical expert witnesses to bolster an otherwise-dismal legal defense. Others are genuine victims of consumer fraud or are simply convinced that the investigators, specifically, and the police, in general, routinely fabricate evidence to make innocent persons appear guilty. They firmly believe these expert witnesses validate their prejudices about the police and provide a real service to the legal community by helping ferret out corruption within the ranks of the police.

Investigators should never underestimate the powerful testimony these witnesses provide. Some are extremely convincing, especially when they exhibit the right body language and bring props into the courtroom to conduct demonstrations of how they conducted their examination.

PLACING THE AGENT ON TRIAL

In another attempt to divert a jury's attention from the facts surrounding the prosecutor's case, defense attorneys will attempt to shift the focus of the trial onto the government agent or attorney instead. This usually is done in conjunction with the outrageous government conduct defense, especially when a defense expert witness challenges the findings of the government.

Defense attorneys have employed private investigators to look into the personal lives of investigators and informants to ascertain their financial situations and lifestyles, simply to imply that they are living above their means and may be taking bribes or selling drugs themselves.

Some defense attorneys will attack police investigators directly on the stand, insinuating they are inexperienced, incompetent, immoral, unethical, prejudiced, or ambitious and are only seeking publicity or promotions by generating "big headlines." Investigators need to remain professional and maintain their composure on the witness stand when they are being accused of these things and try not to exhibit body language indicative of being irritated with this line of questioning.

Defense attorneys may exploit an overlooked investigative procedure as the grounds to attack the agent. For example, an investigator collects certain writings by the defendant that tend to show he was involved in the conspiracy. The investigator obtains handwriting exemplars of the defendant for comparison with the handwriting on the original documents. A government expert positively concludes that the defendant authored the documents in question. The defense attorney may ask the investigator on the stand if any fingerprints were found on the document. If the investigator responds that he or she did not request a fingerprint examination because the handwriting analysis showed the defendant wrote the document, the attorney will seize the moment by implying that *if* the document had been examined for fingerprints, the defendant's fingerprints would not be there. This may be contrary to logic, but the defense attorney is attempting to convince at least one juror that the investigator is completely incompetent because a fingerprint examination was not requested or conducted. The attorney also is implying that if a fingerprint examination were conducted and the defendant's fingerprints were not found, then it would have been impossible for him to have authored the document.

Defense attorneys realize that usually the extent of jurors' knowledge of forensic science is what they have seen on television or have read in novels. They may actually believe that if a person's fingerprints are not on a document, then he obviously didn't touch it and, therefore, he couldn't have authored it.

In this type of situation, the prosecutor needs to reestablish that a handwriting expert positively concluded that the defendant wrote the document in question and that fingerprint analysis would have been redundant. However, investigators can avoid these problems by being as thorough as possible and by conducting as many relevant scientific examinations of the evidence as possible to limit the defense attorney's ability to attack the findings and the investigator's professional conduct.

DEFENDANT WAS INVOLVED IN AN ENTIRELY DIFFERENT CONSPIRACY

In another common defense tactic, the defense attorney acknowledges that the defendant is a criminal involved in terrorism, drugs, or gangs; however, he alleges the defendant was involved in an entirely different conspiracy, not the one named in this indictment.

As an example, an undercover investigator has been negotiating with two drug traffickers to deliver narcotics he intends to purchase to his city. The investigator and the drug traffickers continue to negotiate for some time; however, because the traffickers have been arrested in this particular city in the past, they hesitate to deliver the drugs there. The negotiations finally reach an impasse, and they refuse to deliver. They immediately offer to sell an entirely different type of drug they have stored ten miles away in another city that is in the same county. They are eager to deliver that drug to the undercover investigator within a few blocks of where it is stored. The investigator agrees, and the traffickers deliver the second type of drugs and they are arrested. Both are charged in one indictment that includes conspiracy to distribute drugs. Is this an entirely different drug conspiracy case from the first, or is it all one conspiracy?

It may be deemed a different conspiracy if the investigator's reports and testimony are not clear about the negotiations. This legal maneuver is designed to overturn a conviction during an appeal or to have an indictment dismissed outright before trial. Investigators need to amass as much evidence as possible about a defendant's involvement in a particular conspiracy and to be as specific as they can when writing reports and testifying about the role of each defendant in the conspiracy in order to counter such claims.

Investigators need to coordinate closely with their prosecutor to render the proper charges in the indictment in order to avoid a situation that may generate a successful appeal. The traffickers may have to be charged in two different indictments if prosecution is sought for conspiracy to deliver two different types of drugs at different locations. Each investigation is different and must be dealt with individually. Many problems can be resolved by close examination of the facts of a case before an indictment is drawn up and presented to a grand jury.

THE BLIND MULE

This defense is commonly used by defendants who are caught in the act of transporting drugs in privately owned vehicles or rental cars, or on commercial airlines, buses, or trains. The defendant claims he had no knowledge that the drugs found in his suitcase or car were there. He claims to be a victim who was used by drug dealers to unwittingly transport drugs for them. This same type of defense equally applies to terrorists or gang members who have been caught with explosive devices, weapons, or other contraband.

Investigators can counter drug courier defense claims by gathering the facts, being thorough in their investigations, and offering expert testimony. It doesn't make sense for a drug dealer to hide drugs in a car he has no control over. If a rental car had drugs in it before the innocent defendant rented it, how did the owner of the drugs know where the rental car was going so he could retrieve the drugs later?

If drug dealers had secreted drugs in an unknowing defendant's suitcase, there would have been no guarantee that the suitcase would not have been stolen or lost by an airline or bus operator because the dealers would have no control over the security of the bag.

Some drug couriers will claim that the fact that they granted permission for investigators to search their carry-on luggage is evidence they had no knowledge it contained contraband. Investigators can counter this claim by explaining that through training and experience they know that drug couriers firmly believe that if they give consent (1) the police will believe they are innocent and have nothing to hide, (2) the investigators won't take the time to go through an entire bag looking for drugs because they are lazy, or (3) the investigators will have no chance of locating the drugs because they are so well concealed.

Fingerprint evidence showing the defendant handled the contraband defeats this defense. Telephone numbers, addresses, or other writings or documents the defendant possessed that tie him to known drug traffickers also should always be explored. The method the defendant used to purchase his bus, train, or plane ticket may be indicative of those used by past drug couriers. Further, the use of a polygraph as an interrogation tool may work well if the defendant believes the machine can detect him lying about his knowledge of the contraband.

Investigators should never pass up the opportunity to search someone who has given them consent to do so. It may be a bluff that needs to be called.

SUMMARY

Criminal defense attorneys are ethically bound to defend their clients by all legal means. Some have been creative in their attempts to remove their clients from their legal dilemmas. Defense attorneys are only limited by their imaginations.

In conspiracy trials, defense attorneys have used a variety of tactics to help their clients. One of these is a claim that the client withdrew from the conspiracy before any substantive crimes occurred. This defense shields the defendant from any crimes committed by the coconspirators after the withdrawal.

Another tactic is a claim that the investigators and prosecutor acted in such an outrageous manner during the investigation and prosecution that the client warrants an acquittal or dismissal of the charges.

A multiple-defendant tactic is when one of the defendants on trial changes his plea to guilty and accepts full responsibility for the crimes to protect the other members of the conspiracy. He claims that his codefendants had nothing to do with it. This defense usually arises after the codefendants threaten the remaining defendant or his family with harm if he does not essentially take the blame for them.

The entrapment defense, a popular defense in drug trials, occurs when the defendant claims that he was not predisposed to commit such a crime, that it was the undercover investigator or informant who planted the idea. Presenting evidence that the defendant has engaged in drug trafficking in the past usually defeats this defense.

Investigators also may encounter a defense in which the attorney merely claims that his client is not the person named in the indictment.

Some defense attorneys have gone so far as to produce unscrupulous so-called expert witnesses who, for a fee, will testify to anything that will undermine the credibility of the evidence, tactics, or methods used by the police. Many of these witnesses embellish or outright lie about their qualifications in order to become qualified expert witnesses in court. Investigators should thoroughly investigate the backgrounds of these experts when their testimony contrasts the known facts of a case.

Defense attorneys have long attacked case investigators and the methods they use in conducting investigations. Investigators and prosecutors often end up being put on trial instead of the defendant. This ploy is used to distract the jury from the evidence of the case by attempting to portray the prosecution team as being either dishonest or incompetent or both.

Some defense attorneys may assert that their client actually is a terrorist, drug dealer, or gang member, as the indictment alleges. They add, however, that their client was involved in an entirely different conspiracy that is not the basis for this particular trial. A carefully crafted indictment listing all the facts of the conspiracy investigation usually will nullify this type of defense.

Some defendants merely claim they had no knowledge that there was contraband in the suitcase they possessed or in the car they were driving. Defense attorneys will maintain their clients' innocence and ignorance. Gathering the facts and locating physical evidence such as fingerprints and any documents that may tie a defendant to other known criminals can defeat this defense. The criminal background of the defendant may be sufficient to dilute the defense attorney's contention that his client was unwittingly used by others to transport and conceal drugs or other contraband.

If investigators are aware of these types of probable defenses, they can best plan their investigations to defeat them before they arise.

CHAPTER 9

Extrajudicial Renditions

INTRODUCTION

The *American Heritage Dictionary of the American Language* (4th ed.) defines rendition as "the act of rendering; especially, the act of surrender, as of fugitives from justice, at the claim of a foreign government." Typically these renditions are conducted through a formal extradition process specified in a treaty between the United States and the country where the fugitive is in custody or may be residing. An *extrajudicial rendition* is one in which the formal extradition process is circumvented or otherwise avoided, often without the consent or knowledge of the government where the fugitive is located.

For a variety of reasons, many nations do not live up to their treaty obligations when it comes to the extradition process. Due to endemic corruption or political reasons, many nations will either stall the process or take no affirmative action to bring a fugitive into custody. Other countries are powerless to extradite a fugitive because existing extradition treaties do not cover the charges for which the defendant has been indicted. Still other countries have such a long and drawn-out formal extradition process that it could take many months, if not years, for the host country to make a legal decision about extraditing a fugitive, especially if the suspect is a national of that country. Some nations do not allow the extradition of their citizens to another country under any circumstances. Other countries would rather deport or otherwise expel a captured fugitive back to the country where he maintains citizenship, rather than the United States. This forces the process to begin all over again.

An example is when a Pakistani national who has been indicted in the United States is located in France. The United States will seek a *provisional arrest warrant* for the man's arrest and will provide the French government the formal extradition request through its embassy. Instead of honoring the extradition request, France may opt to deport the fugitive back to Pakistan rather than extradite him to the United States in order to maintain good relations with Pakistan.

In this example, performing an extrajudicial rendition would eliminate the possibility of the fugitive being alerted that he is wanted in the United States and would prevent his deportation to his home country, where he may be able to further avoid being arrested or facing a formal extradition process.

The U.S. Marshals, the Drug Enforcement Administration, the FBI, and other agencies have used this investigative technique for many years. It has proven to be highly effective in delivering fugitives to U.S. courts for trial because, in effect, it circumvents the arduous formal extradition process. Because of the controversial nature of the action, it is sometimes conducted without the knowledge, assistance, or consent of the government where the fugitive is located. Using the technique of extrajudicial rendition sometimes risks straining relations between the United States and other governments; however, it is permissible under U.S. law because it doesn't matter to the courts how a defendant got to the United States to answer his indictment and stand trial. How he arrived to stand trial has no bearing on the defendant's indictment, guilt, or innocence.[1] State and local investigators should not attempt to conduct these renditions without first coordinating with federal law enforcement officials for their assistance and guidance.

THE FORMAL EXTRADITION PROCESS

Extradition is the formal removal of a person from one country to another to prosecute him or to impose a sentence on him as the result of a criminal matter. Many extradition treaties between the United States and other countries list only specific crimes for which a person can be extradited, which prevents some countries from extraditing fugitives who have not committed these crimes. Many countries will not extradite their own nationals to the United States. Others will not extradite fugitives to the United States unless they are American citizens. Some countries will not extradite someone to the United States if they stand the chance of receiving the death penalty, or even life in prison without the possibility of parole. Mexico is such a nation.

When a conspiracy investigation reveals that a suspect is living in a foreign country, federal agents should immediately consult with the U.S. attorney's office that has venue over the matter to determine if an extradition treaty exists between the United States and the country where the fugitive has been located. If an extradition treaty exists and the crime the suspect has been indicted for is covered by it, the first step is for the U.S. attorney's office to immediately seek the suspect's indictment by a federal grand jury, if this has not already taken place. If the federal grand jury indicts the suspect, he immediately becomes a fugitive, and a federal arrest warrant is issued for his arrest.

Whether or not a fugitive is in custody, a decision must be made about whether to seek a provisional arrest warrant for the defendant's arrest, along with a request for the defendant's formal extradition to the United States. If a formal extradition request is made, the defendant's indictment and transcripts of the agents' testimony before the grand jury will eventually become attachments to the request. The decision to seek formal extradition normally will be based on the following factors:

1. **Is the fugitive a citizen of the United States or of the nation where he currently resides?** Many countries are reluctant or are prohibited from extraditing their own nationals to another country to stand trial; however, they are much more receptive to extraditing or deporting an American back to the United States. The likelihood of a successful extradition increases significantly if the fugitive is a citizen of the United States.

2. **How long will the extradition process in the country where the fugitive has been located take?** Many nations have long, drawn-out legal processes that will require that U.S. embassy staff members attend many court proceedings. Sometimes the process is so complicated that it may require the hiring of a local attorney to represent the U.S. government during the legal process. After long periods of time, witnesses become unavailable, memories fade, and interest in the case wanes. The longer it takes to deliver a fugitive to the United States, the greater are the odds of acquittal or dismissal of the criminal charges against the defendant. The time necessary to deliver the fugitive to the United States may make it infeasible to go to trial.

3. **What is the level of cooperation the United States is likely to receive from the foreign nation in both apprehending the defendant and honoring the treaty obligation to extradite the defendant?** The relationship between the United States and the foreign country in question can be so poor as to render the request for formal extradition meaningless. Even some friendly nations will not extradite a fugitive if he faces the possibility of receiving the death penalty if convicted, even if the fugitive is a U.S. citizen. The U.S. attorney's pledge to not seek the death penalty in the matter may overcome this restriction. Still other countries may not extradite a person to stand trial if a comparable law in that country does not exist. Some nations may apprehend the fugitive, but then set bail so low that he is immediately released from jail and once again is on the run.

4. **Once a fugitive is apprehended, is there a chance that corrupt foreign government officials will be paid off to allow the defendant to either escape or to win a favorable court ruling denying the U.S. government's request for extradition?** Many parts of the world have corrupt government officials who, upon learning the defendant's identity, will locate him for the purpose of soliciting a bride in return for allowing him to remain free.

   There are many countries that have a well-deserved reputation for endemic corruption, and special care has to be taken when dealing with them. Corrupt officials can explain why a fugitive is never arrested or why the extradition process becomes endless.

   Even if corruption is not an issue, some nations' law enforcement entities are either underfunded or they lack resources or the will to pursue the fugitive within their borders. Often, financial assistance is required to directly assist the police in apprehending the fugitive and holding him until U.S. authorities arrive.

5. **In light of the answers to the previous questions, is an extrajudicial rendition a viable option, or is it the only option?** Investigators must weigh the use of this technique against the probable outcome of any formal extradition request. Further, they must factor in the likelihood of success in using the technique before, during, or after requesting the fugitive's formal extradition.

PERFORMING EXTRAJUDICIAL RENDITIONS

An extrajudicial rendition can be performed in several ways: The fugitive is taken by force, with or without the permission of the host country, and is transported immediately to the United States; the fugitive is arrested by a cooperative host nation and immediately deported or otherwise expelled directly to the United States; or the fugitive is prompted in some way to travel to a cooperative nation, usually through the use of a ruse or subterfuge, for the purpose of having him detained and expelled directly to the United States.

Another option is for a cooperative country to locate a fugitive and have him deported to his home country so formal extradition can commence. However, if the fugitive's home country is ripe with corruption or has an arduous extradition process, this option is the least desirable.

Many successful extrajudicial renditions are performed when a fugitive believes it is safe for him to transit through or to certain nations without encountering U.S. agents, who he knows want to arrest him. Through intelligence gathered by informants or other means, agents may learn that the fugitive intends to travel outside his home country for either business or pleasure. Once it is confirmed that he will be traveling, a realistic assessment of the likelihood of receiving the travel country's cooperation must be made.

In extreme cases, U.S. agents either pay informants or others to bring a fugitive to the U.S. border or elsewhere so he can be arrested, or agents go after the defendant themselves. The latter will *always* require the cooperation of the host country to shield the agents from criminal liability and to give a promise that formal extradition hearings will not be conducted after the fugitive's arrest.

As an example, in 1985, DEA special agent Enrique Camarena was kidnapped outside his office at the U.S. Consulate in Guadalajara, Mexico, by marijuana traffickers he was investigating. He was held at an isolated ranch house for several days, where he was tortured and questioned about ongoing DEA operations and investigations his office was conducting. His body, and that of an informant, were later found partially buried in secluded locations.

The investigation into special agent Camarena's death was intense. It revealed that a Mexican medical doctor named Humberto Alvarez Machain had been present during the torturing and interrogation and that the doctor had administered amphetamines intravenously to Camarena to keep him from becoming unconscious during the nonstop beatings he sustained through the days. When the United States informally asked for

Dr. Alvarez's extradition to stand trial for agent Camarena's murder, Mexico refused. After months of fruitless diplomatic negotiation, the DEA arranged to have confidential informants "deliver" him to the Mexican border with Texas, where he was immediately arrested and transported to Los Angeles to stand trial in federal court.

Dr. Alvarez's defense attorney argued strenuously that DEA agents had kidnapped his client, violating the extradition treaty with Mexico, and that this outrageous government conduct should prevent the United States from trying him for the offense. The district court judge agreed, and the government appealed to the U.S. Court of Appeals for the Ninth Circuit, which upheld the lower-court ruling. The government appealed to the U.S. Supreme Court, which decided *U.S. v. Alvarez Machain* (504 U.S. 655 [1992]).

The Supreme Court ruled that violating a provision of a formal extradition treaty *did not* preclude the United States from having jurisdiction over a subject. The justices affirmed the notion that it did not matter how a defendant came to be in the United States to stand trial; the fact was that he was in the United States and eligible to stand trial. (See Appendix C for the entire ruling of this Supreme Court case.)

In the Court's decision, the justices cited another case in which the Court ruled that "... There is nothing in the Constitution that requires a court to permit a guilty person rightfully convicted to escape justice because he was brought to trial against his will."[2]

Even though the ruling validated the DEA's method of bringing Dr. Alvarez to justice, the U.S. Justice Department clamped severe restrictions on these types of extrajudicial renditions.

The questions that must be answered in determining the viability of any extrajudicial rendition are

- Does intelligence exist suggesting that the defendant either plans, or may be otherwise willing, to travel to a different foreign country?

When information is received that a fugitive may travel to a different foreign country, agents should immediately make a realistic assessment to determine the likelihood of a successful rendition from that nation. The first step should be contacting the U.S. embassy where the fugitive may be traveling. If the embassy has a resident FBI special agent, called a **legal attaché** or **legat**, or a DEA representative, called a **country attaché**, he or she can provide agents with a best estimate on the chances of receiving full or partial cooperation from the country's police officials. If there is neither an FBI nor a DEA representative at the embassy, the **regional security officer** (RSO) is qualified to act for them. He or she also will know the local police officials and can give an honest opinion on how they will react to such a plan. RSOs are U.S. diplomats who are special agents of the **diplomatic security service** and have substantial law enforcement and foreign relations experience.

Agents should explain the situation to these officials and ask them if their police contacts would be willing to detain the fugitive until arrangements can be made to transport the person to the United States. If this technique has never been tried in that country, the requesting agent should travel to the country and meet with the RSO or other U.S. law enforcement representative. They should pay a personal visit together to the head of the appropriate foreign law enforcement agency that would handle the matter.

When making such a request, it should be to the police agency head. Many foreign police departments are managed like their military, and innovation and decision making are discouraged within the rank-and-file members. Many lower-level police officials will automatically reject the notion of detaining someone, with or without an arrest warrant, and will not entertain the possibility of releasing a fugitive to U.S. authorities. These same lower-echelon officials will not take the issue up their chain of command. All of this is avoided by contacting the director of the foreign police agency directly. The personal relationship a U.S. embassy representative has with the host country police officials will usually make the difference between the foreign police agency acting or not acting on the request.

The agency head should be informed about the urgency of the matter and the fact that the fugitive is a third-country national, meaning he is neither a national of the United States or of the country in question. He should be assured that the fugitive will be dealt with fairly once he arrives in the United States.

He also must be guaranteed that no publicity or disclosure of the police agency's cooperation will be made known without his permission. Many nations do not want to be seen as openly cooperating with U.S. authorities for a variety of complicated reasons. Some fear criticism from other nations if they are perceived as being subservient to the United States or as being willing to grant any request the United States may ask of them. Foreign police officials also fear harsh criticism from their own citizens and members of their government if they deport or otherwise expel someone without benefit of a judicial review.

The agency head should be provided with a copy of the federal arrest warrant, along with the affidavit in support of the arrest warrant or grand jury transcripts detailing what crimes the fugitive is suspected of committing. He should also be told that a U.S. representative to Interpol will also be sending him a copy of an international arrest warrant. The agency head should always be advised that this technique in apprehending fugitives has been successful on many occasions in other parts of the world. (More information on Interpol is given later in the chapter.)

- If the fugitive has no plans to travel to another country, is there an opportunity for an informant or an undercover agent to arrange a business meeting with the fugitive in a friendly country for the sole purpose of arresting him?

International terrorists and drug traffickers frequently travel in the course of doing business. Many are aware of extrajudicial renditions, and will avoid traveling to countries they believe may cooperate with the United States. Others are not on guard.

If an undercover agent or informant is involved in an investigation, he may be able to arrange a meeting with a fugitive in a country that is willing to detain and then deport the fugitive to the United States. Agents should consult with the U.S. embassies located in several of these cooperative countries before the meeting is discussed with the fugitive so options of where to conduct the meeting can be presented to the fugitive.

As an example, an informant working with DEA has received several shipments of drugs in the United States from a Mexican drug trafficker. The DEA knows that Mexico will not deliver a fugitive to the United States without benefit of a formal extradition request.

The informant telephones the trafficker and says he wants to pay him for the drugs he has already received, as well as pay him in advance for another shipment. The trafficker is also told that there is another long-term future business deal the informant wants to discuss, but he will only discuss the matter in person and not on the telephone. The informant also tells the trafficker that he is uncomfortable bringing large amounts of money into Mexico, but he is willing to take the money to another country to pay him. He suggests several countries and tells the trafficker he can vacation with him when their business is completed. The informant says he will reimburse the trafficker for his travel expenses when they meet, to compensate him for his trouble.

The trafficker may agree to travel to another country to collect money owed to him. Making substantial amounts of money is why he is in the business. He also may be intrigued by a future substantial drug deal or may be looking forward to having a free vacation.

- Can the case agent or informant, through ruse, give the defendant a good reason to travel?

Agents and their informants can create a ruse, or subterfuge, for the fugitive to travel. An informant or undercover agent can tell the fugitive that he has inside information that the authorities are about to arrest him where he is and that he should immediately move to a safe haven. The "safe haven" the informant suggests should be a country the fugitive believes is unlikely to cooperate with U.S. authorities. However, it should also be part of the plan that the fugitive will have to transit through another country in order to reach his destination. This country should be highly cooperative, creating the opportunity to capture the fugitive.

The informants or agents can further entice the fugitive to travel by saying they or a trusted driver will meet him at the international airport of this safe haven and take him to safety in an apartment or ranch they own.

As an example, a fugitive decides to seek safe haven in a country that will not cooperate with the United States. He knows that, due to flight schedules, he has no choice but to make a temporary stop at a country that will cooperate. The authorities in the country the fugitive transits through locate and detain him at their international airport. Based on information provided by the United States, the police and immigration authorities tell him he is going to be expelled as an "undesirable," due to his criminal history. They detain him long enough that he misses the last flights to his destination and home country, and they place him on a flight to the United States, where Immigration and Customs enforcement agents arrest him.

- Is the government of a normally uncooperative country willing to turn a fugitive over to a third country that will cooperate fully with U.S. authorities?

Each country is different in the way they handle such situations. Solid police contacts will often make the difference between a foreign police agency cooperating with U.S. authorities or refusing to cooperate. Foreign policy issues such as continued or pending U.S. foreign aid sometimes play into the decision made by the police authorities.

Because there is usually no specific police policy governing this type of enforcement operation, the country involved may have the flexibility to act on the U.S. government request. The police authorities may be willing to act on a request that will take a relatively short period of time and that will not require housing the fugitive until U.S. agents arrive to pick him up. Taking a fugitive from one plane and placing him on another may be perceived as a reasonable request they will grant.

Foreign law enforcement officials may not be willing or able to lawfully arrest or detain a fugitive in their country at the behest of the United States, but they may be willing to expel him to a country that is willing. Thus, a fugitive may find himself removed from an airplane and placed on another that will either be going directly to the United States or to a country that will put him on another outbound flight to America.

As an example of a successful extrajudicial rendition, an undercover DEA agent knew that no extradition treaty existed between the United States and Bolivia. During undercover negotiations in Bolivia for the delivery of a large amount of cocaine in the United States, DEA agents told the head of the drug trafficking organization that the money for payment of the cocaine was with someone at a hotel in Panama City, Panama, and that he had been instructed to only release the money to the organization head.

The trafficker flew to Panama to meet the man supposedly holding the money for the cocaine. When he arrived, Panamanian authorities detained him as a suspected drug trafficker and lodged him in jail until other DEA agents could arrive. Once they were in position, the Panamanian authorities deported the Bolivian national, not to Bolivia, but to the United States on the first flight to Miami, Florida. Unknown to the trafficker, there was a DEA agent occupying the seat on the airplane next to him who arrested him for conspiracy to distribute drugs in the United States when they arrived in Miami.

Extrajudicial renditions work both ways. An example of a successful extrajudicial rendition took place between the United States and Thailand. The Thai government asked that one of its own nationals, then residing in California, be sent back to his home country to stand trial for attempted murder. The government of Thailand was investigating the attempted assassination of their king and had determined that one of the coconspirators was illegally in the United States, having overstayed his tourist visa. Acting on the Thai request, DEA and Immigration special agents located and arrested the man and placed him on a flight back to Thailand without the benefit of an extradition hearing. The DEA country attaché in Tokyo, Japan, informed authorities at the international airport that the Thai fugitive would be changing planes to Bangkok. The Japanese authorities ensured that the fugitive was placed on his connecting flight to Bangkok, where authorities took him into custody. The man was later executed.

Still another example of a variation of extrajudicial renditions was when a detective for the Los Angeles County Sheriff's Department asked a local police department to detain a man who was wanted in Mexico for murder. The man was located and detained, but not arrested. When the detective arrived at the police department, he took custody of the fugitive, a Mexican national, and drove him to the Mexico border, where he was turned over to Mexican authorities in exchange for a U.S. citizen wanted in Los Angeles County for murder.

Extrajudicial renditions come in many forms, and they have been highly effective in bringing fugitives to justice.

INFORMANT DEBRIEFINGS AND OTHER INTELLIGENCE

A thorough debriefing of informants with knowledge of a fugitive is necessary to recognize any possible opportunity to deploy this technique. Many fugitives are globe-trotters who enjoy their illegal earnings. They frequently travel to major sporting events and beach or ski resorts, and engage in other forms of recreation. Travel to any of these places or any special event may provide agents with an opportunity to arrest a fugitive.

Informants can also create an opportunity or a reason for a fugitive to travel. An informant can inform the fugitive that he has a potential customer who wants to meet him in person to discuss a substantial drug deal or other illegal future transaction. Alternatively, the fugitive may suggest a meeting between himself and others to discuss future criminal activity. The informant may not realize that this is important and must be reminded that information about the fugitive's travel plans is an important piece of intelligence information he needs to relay to agents for possible action.

The following are questions to ask an informant or anyone else who is knowledgeable about the personal habits and background of the fugitive to identify possible opportunities to capture him.

1. Is the defendant owed money from a past drug transaction or other illegal activity? Will he travel to collect the money?

2. Is he so desperate for a loan that he's willing to travel somewhere to receive it?

3. Is there a wedding, first communion, confirmation, or funeral coming up soon in his family that he intends to attend? Where?

4. Does he have a sick relative in another country he plans to visit?

5. Is the fugitive himself suffering from an illness that will require medical attention in another country? If so, what is his condition, and when and where will he be traveling?

6. Does he normally travel to a foreign country during certain holiday periods such as Easter, Christmas, or Ramadan?

7. Is the defendant an avid sports fan who plans to travel to attend a World Cup football game, the Olympics, or other similar event? Who is his travel agent?

8. Does the defendant have girlfriends or paramours who reside in other countries? Would he be willing to travel to meet a female who would like to meet him?

9. Is he an avid gambler who may travel to different casinos around the world?

10. Is the fugitive an avid sightseer? Does he have any plans to visit any tourist havens in the future? Can the informant suggest that he travel to see a particular sight located in a friendly country?

11. Is the fugitive a sexual deviate? Will he respond to e-mail inquiries about sexual encounters with children in other countries?

Not all informants will know all or even some of the answers to these and other questions, but asking them to remain alert about any information concerning the fugitive's planned travels could ultimately lead to his arrest.

Disgruntled employees, former girlfriends and paramours, and coconspirators already in jail may all have reasons to give agents insights about the personality and habits of a fugitive. One of these people may even be willing to assist agents in arranging for the fugitive to travel to a location where he can be arrested.

SETTING THE TRAP

Through creativity, investigators may find a way to convince a fugitive to leave his safe abode and travel to another country so they may arrest him. An informant or undercover agent may be able to give the fugitive false information that may prompt him to travel. Alleging that the local police are close to apprehending him or creating someone who wants to meet him to discuss future illegal transactions in which he stands to make a substantial amount of money may be sufficient for this purpose.

The use of Internet e-mail has proven helpful in easy communication between different parties. An agent may consider initiating a "relationship" with the fugitive via e-mail to lure him to another country, supposedly for a sexual encounter or other purpose. This type of technique must be well rehearsed and well thought out before it is attempted.

The informant or undercover agent posing as someone else on the Internet should have several countries in mind before suggesting where the fugitive should travel for a meeting. These countries should all be known to cooperate with the United States, either through a formal extradition treaty or through their willingness to do an extrajudicial rendition.

If the fugitive is willing to travel based on a ruse or other reason, investigators must answer the following questions before taking any unilateral action:

1. **Have agents researched if an extradition treaty exists with the country the fugitive is willing to visit?** Coordination with the local U.S. attorney's office to learn the particulars of any extradition treaty that exists between the United States and the country in question is the best source of this information. Agents should be aware that extradition treaties between the United States and some countries may not cover the fugitive's particular offense. In that case, an extrajudicial rendition may be the only alternative.

2. **Does the U.S. embassy in the country in question have representatives from the FBI, DEA, Immigration and Customs Enforcement, Secret Service, or any other federal law enforcement agency?** These federal criminal investigators know their counterparts best. They can give an honest and

accurate assessment of the possibility of the foreign country cooperating in an extrajudicial rendering and the likelihood of its success.

   If there is no federal law enforcement representation, is there an RSO at the embassy? The RSO can provide invaluable information about the foreign national police and introduce investigators to authorities in a position to assist in the matter.

3. **How long will the country in question hold the fugitive before they are required to release him? Will they detain him until U.S. law enforcement officers have an opportunity to arrive?** The time period a foreign fugitive can be detained varies from country to country. Some nations will immediately notify the foreign fugitive's embassy or consulate at the time of his arrest. Some may not make notification at all, depending on the circumstances and the type of request they receive from the U.S. embassy. Each country is different, and its legal system must be examined to familiarize agents with what to expect when asking for assistance.

4. **In the opinion of knowledgeable U.S. embassy personnel, will the host nation detain a fugitive and deport or expel him to a third country?** This question probably cannot be answered unless the country has had some experience in these matters. The agents are, in essence, asking that the country bend the rules to help the United States apprehend a fugitive from justice. Many countries will immediately cooperate, whereas others might hesitate. Every case must be handled individually, and no two outcomes are likely to be the same.

5. **If the country will cooperate with U.S. authorities, will it hold the fugitive long enough for agents or deputy U.S. marshals to arrive to transport him to the United States?** Agents must immediately make arrangements for their personnel to travel to the country in question to present their case to the authorities and transport the fugitive back to the United States themselves, if necessary. Some destinations may take more than two days to reach, and the cost of such transportation must be factored into the operation.

6. **What commercial flights offer either nonstop service to anywhere in the United States or the fewest possible stops?** It's important for agents to make travel arrangements that will return the fugitive to the United States in the quickest possible time with the fewest number of stops. Many countries will not allow a fugitive to be transported through their country for fear of him requesting political asylum. The asylum laws of these countries may require them to honor the request pending a formal hearing. If such a request is made, it would temporarily prevent the fugitive from further travel until the asylum issue is resolved. Some countries with liberal asylum laws may allow transit with certain conditions. These conditions may include that the fugitive never leave an airplane or that the airplane park in an area that is away from the passenger terminal. Agents are advised to avoid, if possible, transiting through those countries that may have to grapple with the asylum issue.

U.S. embassy staff in the country in which the fugitive is detained will coordinate with law enforcement or immigration authorities at the local embassies of those countries where the fugitive may be transiting. They are in the best position to gauge what the reaction will be when a fugitive who is being escorted to the United States arrives in their country. U.S. embassy staff members may be required to be present at each location where the fugitive changes planes en route to the United States.

7. **Does the fugitive warrant being transported to the United States by military aircraft?** Department of Defense (DoD) resources have been used on many occasions to transport fugitives to the United States. Military bases have been used to house fugitives while they are awaiting other transportation. Using DoD assets requires permission from top managers at the Pentagon, which may require several days to obtain. Using the military avoids all the problems of transiting through countries where the fugitive may ask for political asylum. The U.S. embassy representative who is assisting agents should be the point of contact with any transportation request from the military.

8. **Is the country in question a member nation of the International Criminal Police Organization (Interpol)?** Most countries are members of Interpol and will cooperate with U.S. investigators when possible. U.S. Interpol representatives should coordinate with the Interpol representatives of the countries where the fugitive will be traveling. A certified copy of a U.S. arrest warrant can be express shipped to them, as well as a fax copy for their use.

INTERNATIONAL CRIMINAL POLICE ORGANIZATION

The International Criminal Police Organization (Interpol) has 181 member nations and acts as a conduit for criminal information pertaining to fugitives, drug trends, financial crimes and money laundering, stolen art, vehicles, terrorism, and other crimes that reach far beyond the boundaries of any single country.

Interpol helps coordinate joint operational activities of the member countries, making available know-how, expertise, and criminal intelligence.

Interpol considers the apprehension of fugitives to be one of its most important fields of endeavor. Interpol circulates electronic notices containing identifying data and judicial information about wanted criminals to its membership. It created what is known as a **Red Notice**, sometimes referred to as a **Red Warrant**, that is recognized by a number of countries as having legal value to serve as the basis for a provisional arrest warrant. Interpol offers its membership direct, automatic search facilities, and it responds to inquiries about wanted persons. Interpol encourages its member countries to be proactive in the hunt for international fugitives. It correctly recognizes that fugitives undermine the criminal justice system of each nation when they are not brought to justice.

Each member nation has national police officials who are designated as its representatives to Interpol. These representatives are responsible for coordinating all requests for assistance from Interpol with police agencies within their country. In the United States, many federal law enforcement agencies such as the FBI, the DEA, the U.S. Marshals Service, and the Secret Service have Interpol representatives in Washington, D.C.

Although some countries may act to detain a fugitive at the request of the United States, most of these will demand to see an Interpol Red Notice as verification that the fugitive is wanted in the United States. If a Red Notice is not available, or time does not permit, a letter or notice from a U.S. representative to Interpol may be used as a substitute. The exact requirements will be determined by officials of the nation being asked to detain the fugitive, who is or soon will be in their country.

In lieu of either a copy of a Red Notice or a certified copy of a U.S. arrest warrant, a U.S. embassy may be willing to supply the foreign law enforcement counterpart with a letter or diplomatic note. These documents will request that the government detain the fugitive until a certified arrest warrant can be obtained. In some extreme cases when action is needed immediately, a high-ranking U.S. diplomat may make a personal appeal to the leadership of the police forces of the foreign nation to act.

As an example, in 1995, Pakistani authorities in Islamabad detained Ramzi Ahmed Yousef, the mastermind of the 1993 New York City World Trade Center bombing, after being alerted to his whereabouts by RSO and DEA special agents. Although Yousef carried a Pakistani passport, he was removed to the United States to stand trial without benefit of a formal extradition process.

This was accomplished through a personal appeal by U.S. Ambassador John Mongo to the Pakistani minister of the Interior. Yousef was spirited out of Pakistan on a U.S. government aircraft within twenty-four hours of his detention. He was later convicted for the World Trade Center incident as well as a conspiracy to down twelve U.S. airliners simultaneously over the Pacific Ocean. Evidence of that plot was located in the guesthouse room where he was arrested, and it also was allowed to leave the country.

All of this was accomplished without the benefit of a certified copy of an arrest warrant, a Red Notice, or any other documents at the time of the request, although they were later provided. Pakistani authorities took action and waived all extradition hearings as a result of the direct appeal by the ambassador. Without his personal intervention, the Pakistani authorities would not have acted, Yousef might still be a fugitive today, and thousands of lives might have been lost if his plot to place bombs on twelve different airliners had not been foiled.

In 1997, FBI special agents accompanied by Pakistani authorities arrested Pakistani national fugitive Mir Amil Kanzi in Quetta, Pakistan, near the Afghan border. FBI special agents were allowed to immediately take him back to the United States to stand trial for the murder of two CIA employees that took place outside CIA headquarters in 1992. Once again, the Pakistan government, as a political favor to the United States, waived the formal extradition process. This decision also allowed Pakistan to be rid of a high-profile international terrorist suspect from within its borders.

In another example, in the mid 1990s, a DEA informant in Harrisburg, Pennsylvania, had been advanced twenty-five kilograms of southeast Asian heroin, supposedly for resale in the United States. After seizing the heroin, the informant arranged to meet the Pakistani drug trafficker who had furnished the heroin. The sole purpose of the meeting was to arrest the trafficker. The man refused to meet the informant in the United States, fearing that he would be arrested. He stated that he was aware that the DEA might attempt to arrest him in the United States or a third country. He said there was "only one place in the world" he would meet the informant to receive payment for the heroin: Dubai, United Arab Emirates. At the time, no extradition treaty existed between the United States and the United Arab Emirates.

The resident agent in charge of the DEA's Karachi, Pakistan, Resident Office, who was responsible for all drug-enforcement-related matters on the Saudi Arabian peninsula, personally contacted the chief of the Dubai police force. After learning about the situation, the chief said that because the trafficker had not violated any laws of the United Arab Emirates, he was powerless to act; however, as a police officer, he felt compelled to detain the man.

After consulting with his prosecutor, the chief agreed to cooperate with the DEA. The chief requested that he receive an Interpol Red Warrant to justify his actions. The DEA Interpol representative in Washington faxed a copy of the U.S. arrest warrant along with a formal request to detain the fugitive. The DEA case agent and another special agent immediately traveled to Dubai with the informant and arrived before the trafficker.

When he arrived in Dubai, the Pakistani drug trafficker met with the informant in a hotel room that was wired for audio and video, and he solidified the DEA case by making admissions about being the ultimate source of the twenty-five kilograms of heroin. Once the admission was captured on audio- and videotape, the police detained the man and took him before the local prosecutor.

After three days, the prosecutor released the man back into the custody of the police because no crimes had been committed in the United Arab Emirates. The police in turn released the fugitive immediately to the awaiting DEA agents, who placed the fugitive on a commercial airliner back to the United States. The fugitive pled guilty in federal court and was sentenced to life in prison.

In these examples, personal intervention by members of a U.S. embassy or consulate made the difference in apprehending these significant criminals. Documentation from Interpol made the police officials feel comfortable and more willing to act.

Style Over Substance

As strange as it may seem, some foreign law enforcement officials are more impressed with the packaging of a request from the United States than the actual request.

As an example, a DEA special agent wrote a letter to the law enforcement agency of a South American country asking that they furnish him with documents that would be useful during an international drug investigation. The initial request was not acted on; however, it was never denied.

The agent sent a second letter, this time with a broad red ribbon on one side, along with an embossed seal of the United States embedded in red wax. The request was immediately honored, and the agent received the documentation he requested without changing the nature of the request.

Investigators should keep these small things in mind when dealing with various nations throughout the world. Culturally, these types of additions to any formal request may have significant meaning and give the aura of importance.

This type of ornamentation normally appears on the cover sheet of a diplomatic note from a U.S. embassy when it is presented to a foreign ministry asking that a fugitive be apprehended and extradited. The attorney general of the United States signs formal extradition requests. A simple request for documents is an insignificant request when compared with a request for formal extradition; however, giving it the same appearance commands attention in many countries.

Showing Appreciation

Once a fugitive is safely in the hands of U.S. agents, they should always follow up by showing their sincere appreciation to the foreign law enforcement officials who assisted them in the capture.

Presenting the foreign government officials with anything uniquely American, or unique to the U.S. law enforcement agency(ies) involved in the request, will solidify relations in the future. A simple plaque, certificates of appreciation, baseball hats with their agency's initials embroidered on them, uniform patches, pens, T-shirts, or any other article with a department's badge or logo on it will pay dividends for agents the next time.

SUMMARY

A rendition is when one country surrenders a captured fugitive to another country where he is wanted. Most renditions are completed through the formal extradition process. Other renditions are accomplished through extrajudicial means, sometimes without the consent or knowledge of the government where the fugitive is located.

The formal extradition process is complex, in that it is an international matter laid out in treaties between the United States and many other nations. Not all countries have extradition treaties with the United States, and those that do may not have a treaty that covers crimes of conspiracy or other substantive crimes. These formal extradition processes are time-consuming and require the full cooperation of the nation where the fugitive is located. For a variety of reasons, many nations do not live up to their treaty obligations, or the police and judicial forces of a country may be corrupt. These two factors may delay or eliminate the ability of agents to have a fugitive returned to the United States for trial. This is when an extrajudicial rendition may be necessary.

An extrajudicial rendition can be performed in three ways: (1) A fugitive is taken by force, with or without the permission of the host country; (2) the fugitive is arrested and deported to the United States while traveling through another country; or (3) he is prompted to travel to a specific location, usually through the use of a ruse or subterfuge, so he can be arrested and immediately returned to the United States.

When investigators learn that an international fugitive is planning to travel to another country, they need to coordinate with the U.S. embassy. Many embassies have representatives of the FBI, the DEA, Immigration and Customs Enforcement, the Secret Service, and other agencies who will provide contacts and guidance in such an endeavor. All renditions must be handled through an embassy whenever time and circumstances permit. Skillful diplomats can often receive the full cooperation of the host country in doing favors for the United States. The 1993 World Trade Center bomber, Ramzi Yousef, and Mir Amil Kanzi, the murderer of two CIA employees outside CIA headquarters in 1993, were turned over to the United States by the government of Pakistan without any formal extradition process.

Good intelligence gathered through informants and other means may alert agents when and where an international fugitive may be traveling. Many times a fugitive can be prompted to move from his safe haven to a place where he is vulnerable to arrest. Often an informant can provide a good reason for the fugitive to travel by making him believe he will be meeting someone to discuss moneymaking opportunities. Other fugitives will travel to meet women, handle money affairs, attend sporting events, relax, or for other reasons. The objective is to learn when an international fugitive will be traveling and to where, so coordination with foreign police authorities can be made in aiding in his capture.

The International Criminal Police Organization (Interpol) encourages the capture of fugitives and facilitates their arrests for their 181 member nations. Interpol will verify the existence of arrest warrants, provide copies of Red Notices, and provide intelligence information about the probable whereabouts of international fugitives.

Accomplishing an extrajudicial rendition is an extraordinary event. Investigators should always show their sincere appreciation to those foreign national police officers involved in such an undertaking.

NOTES

1. Federal agents should always check their current department's policy before attempting to perform an extrajudicial rendition.
2. *Frisbie v. Collins,* 342 U.S. 519 (1952).

CHAPTER 10

Overview of Terrorism

INTRODUCTION

Investigators changed with dismantling, disrupting, or investigating the activities of terrorist organizations, be they international or domestic, must be cognizant of their motivations, structure, and financing.

No one definition of terrorism has been universally accepted. The United States has defined terrorism in Title 22 United States Code 2656 f(d) as "premeditated, politically motivated violence perpetrated against noncombatant targets by sub-national groups or clandestine agents, usually intended to influence an audience."[1]

Whether motivated by politics, religion, or hatred, terrorism has existed for hundreds of years. It has been used as a means of achieving political success when other methods have failed.

Conventional wisdom is that political terror is a new and unprecedented phenomenon. However, Marco Polo had this description circa 1298 in *The Old Man of the Mountain*: (He) "kept his assassins bemused with potions and numbers . . . of the most beautiful damsels in the world." The "potions" were believed to be hashish. Today, Palestinian suicide bombers are recruited with the promise of immediate access to heaven, where they will be rewarded with seventy-two virgins and an afterlife in bountiful fields of milk and honey. They also are promised compensation and stipends for their families left behind. Their actions have prompted consistent, immediate retaliation by the government of Israel, which in turn, has prompted revenge killings. This cycle continues today.

Many terrorist organizations derive partial funding from nations sympathetic to their cause. As an example, Iran has been shown to sponsor the terrorist group Hizballah, which operates out of Lebanon and has the goals of "liberating" Jerusalem and ultimately eliminating Israel.

Conventional wisdom also dictates that if state sponsorship of terrorism were eliminated, terrorist incidents would drop dramatically. If terrorist organizations were no longer sponsored by governments, the number of incidents would not drop dramatically, if at all. Stopping state-sponsored terrorism only drives these organizations to obtain money by other means, often through the sale of drugs. The nexus between international drug and terrorist organizations has clearly been established, not only in Pakistan, Afghanistan, and the Middle East, but also in South America and Southeast Asia. Charity fronts to solicit cash donations, allegedly for victims of violence in the Middle East, have been discredited and exposed as successful means of raising funds for terrorist organizations.

More conventional wisdom says that modern technology poses no greater terrorism threat than in the past. However, with strides in technology, terrorist organizations now have the means to securely communicate with coconspirators through encrypted e-mail, satellite telephones, cellular telephones, fax machines, personal communication devices, and the like. Terrorists also have been known to use cell phones to remotely detonate explosive devices.

As of January 2003, thirty-six terrorist groups had been designated by the U.S. secretary of state as foreign terrorist organizations (FTO), in accordance with section 219 of the Immigration and Nationality Act, as amended by the Antiterrorism and Effective Death Penalty Act of 1966. It is unlawful to provide funds or other material support to a designated FTO. Representatives and certain members of designated FTOs can be denied visas or excluded from the United States. Further, U.S. financial institutions are legally compelled to block funds of FTOs and their agents, and they must report the blockage to the U.S. Department of the Treasury. Investigators should recognize that members and sympathizers of these organizations are active participants in conspiracies when they violate these provisions. Here are the thirty-six designated FTOs:

- Abu Nidal organization (ANO)

- Abu Sayyaf Group (ASG)

- Al-Aqsa Martyrs Brigade

- Armed Islamic Group (GIA)

- 'Asbat al-Ansar

- Aum Supreme Truth (Aum) Aum Shinrikyo, Aleph

- Basque Fatherland and Liberty (ETA)

- Communist Party of Philippines/New People's Army (CPP/NPA)

- Al-Gama'a al-Islamiyya (Islamic Group, IG)

- HAMAS (Islamic Resistance Movement)

- Harakat ul-Mujahidin (HUM)

- Hizballah (Party of God)

- Islamic Movement of Uzbekistan (IMU)

- Jaish-e-Mohammed (JEM)

- Jemaah Islamiya (JI)

- Al-Jihad (Egyptian Islamic Jihad)

- Kahane Chai (Kach)

- Kurdistan Workers' Party (PKK, KADEK)

- Lashkar-e-Tayyiba (LT)

- Lashkar I Jhangvi (LJ)

- Liberation Tigers of Tamil Eelam (LTTE)

- Mujahedin-e Khalq Organization (MEK or MKO)

- National Liberation Army (ELN)—Colombia

- Palestine Islamic Jihad (PIJ)

- Palestine Liberation Front (PLF)

- Popular Front for the Liberation of Palestine (PFLP)

- Popular Front for the Liberation of Palestine–General Command (PFLP–GC)

- Al-Qaeda

- Real IRA (RIRA)

- Revolutionary Armed Forces of Colombia (FARC)

- Revolutionary Nuclei

- Revolutionary Organization 17 November (17 November)

- Revolutionary People's Liberation Party/Front (DHKP/C)

- Salafist Group for Call and Combat (GSPC)

- Sendero Luminoso (Shining Path or SL)

- United Self-Defense Forces/Group of Colombia (AUC)

Many of these groups operate throughout the globe and have interacted and conspired with each other to conduct terrorist acts against the United States and its allies.

MOTIVATION FOR TERRORISM

Those who chose terrorism as the means to achieve their goals have many reasons for doing so. No single reason seems to stand out from the others, and many organizations have several objectives when they conduct a terrorist act.

Spreading Fear. The most common goal terrorists have when planning any event is to create fear. They know that by making people fearful, they can lessen their confidence in their established governments. Terrorists believe that by creating enough fear they may eventually lead to a population to support the terrorists, demands in order to end the cycle of violence they are experiencing.

Publicizing a Cause. Terrorist organizations realize that a violent terrorist event can prompt international media coverage, focusing attention on their particular causes and concerns.

Advancing a Cause. Terrorist organizations have used violence and terror to advance their causes for many years. Their goal is to wear down the opposition in order to achieve political gain.

Revenge. Terrorists often seek revenge for successful government operations conducted against them.

TRANSNATIONAL TERRORIST ORGANIZATIONS

Transnational terrorism is international in scope because members of the terrorist organization freely cross international borders to plan and carry out their violent acts. International terrorism commonly involves citizens from more than one country acting in concert with other conspirators.

The events of September 11, 2001, made many Americans acutely aware of terrorism, in general, and the al-Qaeda organization and its leader, Osama bin Laden, in particular. Until then, most Americans viewed terrorism as a law enforcement problem, as a price that was paid for being the world's only superpower. They never thought any terrorist organization would make a serious attempt to achieve its lofty-but-unreachable goal of destroying or seriously damaging the United States militarily, economically, or politically.

The vast majority of Americans and their leaders had an awakening with the attacks on the World Trade Center and the Pentagon that late summer's morning. Suddenly Osama bin Laden and the al-Qaeda network jumped from being a nuisance to being the world's most wanted war criminals, posing an immediate threat to the security and well-being of the nation.

The World Trade Center had been attacked with a vehicle-improvised explosive device by members of al-Qaeda led by Ramzi Yousef in February 1993. That attack left six people dead and more than 1,000 injured. Yousef's intent was to topple one 110-story tower into the other, laying them flat across lower Manhattan, which he hoped would cause the deaths of 250,000 people.

While Yousef was being transported by helicopter to a detention facility over New York, a federal agent remarked to him that the Trade Center towers were still standing. Yousef replied to the effect that if he had twenty or thirty thousand more dollars, he would have been able to build a larger bomb, and the towers would have fallen as planned.

Yousef is considered by many to have been one of the architects of the attacks on September 11, 2001.

In 2002, transnational terrorists, including al-Qaeda, conducted 199 attacks, a reduction of 44 percent from the previous year. Although 725 people worldwide were killed that year by international terrorists, that figure represented a significant reduction from the 3,295 deaths in 2001, which included the events of September 11.

A total of 2,013 persons were wounded by terrorists in 2002, down from 2,283 people wounded the previous year.

THE AL-QAEDA NETWORK

Also known as the Qa'idat al-Jihad, the al-Qaeda terrorist organization is the best-known and most feared international terrorist network. It is comprised of dedicated and trained Sunni Muslims whose present goal is to firmly establish a worldwide Islamic government. Al-Qaeda, in Arabic, means "the base." It is led by a council headed by Osama bin Laden (sometimes spelled Usama Bin Ladin) that decides what major terrorist operations to fund and take place. Bin Laden's top lieutenant is believed to be Ayman al-Zawahiri, a pediatrician who heads the Egyptian Islamic Jihad and who is believed to be the network's ideological adviser. Al-Qaeda is the terrorist group most likely to conduct another attack on U.S. soil. In order to be effective against it, investigators must have some basic understanding about its make up and must realize that attacking it as an ongoing conspiracy is the only logical way to dismantle and disrupt this organization.

Osama bin Laden established al-Qaeda in the late 1980s to bring together Muslims against the then Soviet Union during its war in Afghanistan. Bin Laden, a wealthy son of a Saudi Arabian construction magnet, personally helped to finance, recruit, train, and transport Sunni Islamic extremists to Afghanistan to provide assistance to the Afghan resistance. With the defeat of the Soviet army, bin Laden then focused his efforts on expelling the United States from the Saudi Arabian peninsula and establishing his worldwide Islamic state. Al-Qaeda intends to achieve its goal by conspiring with allied Islamic extremists groups in an effort to overthrow governments it deems to be "non-Islamic."

In February 1988, Osama bin Laden issued a *fatwa*, or religious edict, known as the "World Islamic Front for Jihad (holy war) Against the Jews and Crusaders," which stated that it was the duty of all Muslims to kill U.S. citizens, civilian or military, and their allies everywhere. Because of the presence of Ayman al-Zawahiri, al-Qaeda is known to have merged with the Egyptian Islamic Jihad (Al-Jihad) in June 2001. Al-Qaeda is also known to be in concert with at least the following terrorist organizations for logistical and funding support:

- Egyptian Islamic Jihad

- Jamaat Islamiyya (Egyptian based)

- The Libyan Islamic Fighting Group

- Islamic Army of Aden (Yemen based)

- Lashkar-e-Taiba and Jaish-e-Muhammad (Kashmir based)

- Islamic Movement of Uzbekistan

- Salafist Group for Call and Combat and the Armed Islamic Group (Algerian based)

- Abu Sayyaf Group (Malaysian and Philippine based)

Bin Laden and his followers are true believers in the jihad and are not likely to cease their operations voluntarily.

Al-Qaeda's Activities

The list of the attacks known to be linked to al-Qaeda is growing. In addition to planning, organizing, and funding the events of September 11, 2001, which resulted in the deaths of approximately 3,000 people when al-Qaeda hijackers crashed two commercial airliners into the World Trade Center, another into the Pentagon, and another in a field in Pennsylvania, the network has been identified as being involved in a late 2002 bombing of a hotel in Mombassa, Kenya, that killed 15 and injured 40 others.

One of al-Qaeda's top lieutenants, Khalid Shaikh Muhammad, was arrested in Rawalpindi, Pakistan, after the kidnapping and murder of *Wall Street Journal* reporter Daniel Pearl in 2002. He is the uncle of the 1993 World Trade Center bombing mastermind, Ramzi Ahmad Yousef.

Law enforcement authorities identified al-Qaeda as supporting a nightclub bombing in Bali, Indonesia, in October 2002, in which 180 people, mostly Australian tourists, were killed.

Al-Qaeda was also identified as being responsible for an attack on U.S. military personnel in Kuwait in October 2002 that killed one soldier and injured another.

Al-Qaeda directed a suicide attack on the merchant vessel *Limburg*, a French-owned and operated oil tanker, off the coast of Yemen in October 2002 that killed one and injured four.

On April 11, 2002, al-Qaeda carried out a firebombing of a synagogue in Tunisia that killed nineteen and injured twenty-two others.

In October 2000, al-Qaeda directed a suicide bombing of the USS *Cole* in the port of Aden, Yemen, that killed seventeen sailors and injured another thirty-nine. After floating an explosive-laden boat alongside the Navy destroyer, the men onboard detonated the explosives, causing over a billion dollars in damage to the destroyer in addition to the deaths of the sailors. The valiant efforts of the crew prevented the ship from sinking.

Al-Qaeda is responsible for the suicide truck bombings of the U.S. embassies in Nairobi, Kenya, and Dar es Salaam, Tanzania, that killed at lease 301 individuals and injured 5,000 others. The vast majority of the dead and injured were Muslims. (See Appendix D for details.)

Al-Qaeda claims to have shot down two U.S. Army Blackhawk helicopters and to have killed other soldiers in Somalia in 1993, in an incident that was the factual basis for the book and movie, *Blackhawk Down*. Many experts believe that bin Laden saw the U.S. response to this event as weak and felt that sustained casualties would force the United States to cut and run. Al-Qaeda further claims to have conducted three bombings that targeted U.S. troops in Aden, Yemen, in December 1992.

Disrupted Al-Qaeda Operations

The al-Qaeda terrorist network has also been linked to other events that, if they had been successful, would have caused the deaths of hundreds of persons, including Pope John Paul II and President William J. Clinton.

In 1994, after an accidental fire in a run-down Manila apartment rented by Ramzi Yousef and a coconspirator while they fashioned an explosive device they intended to use to assassinate Pope John Paul II during his visit later that year, Philippine authorities seized a laptop computer that exposed the plans. The laptop also had detailed plans to kill President Clinton during his visit to the Philippines early the next year, along with another plan to simultaneously down a dozen U.S. commercial airliners crossing the Pacific Ocean. Yousef named the plan Operation Bojinka, which is Serbian–Croatian meaning "big noise."

In February 1995, based on information provided by a "walk-in" informant who had been recruited by Yousef to participate in Operation Bojinka, U.S. State Department Diplomatic Security Service and Drug Enforcement Administration special agents and DEA Foreign Service national investigators in Islamabad, Pakistan, led Pakistani authorities to a guest house where they arrested Yousef. He was within a few minutes of leaving Islamabad by bus for the city of Peshawar, near the Afghan border, where he would have assimilated into the community undetected.

The guest house was later determined to be owned by Osama bin Laden, and Yousef's uncle, Khalid Shaikh Muhammad, was in the guest house at the time of his arrest.

Evidence uncovered by DEA and Diplomatic Security Service special agents at the guest house showed that Yousef planned to set off bombs on the airliners by using digital watches as timers attached to battery-operated toy police cars, which would be the ignition sources. Other evidence included published timetables of U.S. airliners, soldering irons, electronic diodes, and other items necessary to fashion bombs. A *Newsweek* magazine was found opened to an article detailing law enforcement efforts to track Yousef's movements.

Yousef was later tried and convicted in the Southern District of New York for this conspiracy and received a 240-year federal prison sentence. He was later tried for the 1993 bombing of the New York City World Trade Center and received a life sentence.

Ramzi Yousef possessed a fraudulently obtained Pakistani passport at the time of his arrest. He was expelled from Pakistan directly to the United States, without benefit of any judicial review, to stand trial.

Al-Qaeda has also been linked to a conspiracy to set off a large bomb at the Los Angeles International Airport in 1999. This plot was foiled when a U.S. Customs inspector noticed what she thought was explosive material in the vehicle of an al-Qaeda member who was attempting to cross into the United States from Canada.

Figure 10–1   U.S. Customs Special Agents scan destruction at the World Trade Center. *Source:* Courtesy of Bureau of Immigration and Customs Enforcement

Jordanian authorities thwarted an al-Qaeda conspiracy to carry out a bombing operation against U.S. and Israeli tourists visiting their capital for millennial celebrations in late 1999. Jordanian law enforcement authorities arrested twenty eight suspected al-Qaeda members and brought them to trial.

In December 2001, British national and al-Qaeda associate Richard Colvin Reid was stopped by quick-thinking American Airline flight attendants from igniting fuses to explosive material secreted in his shoes while he was on board a Paris to Miami flight. After Reid was subdued, the flight was diverted to Boston. His arrest prompted the Transportation Security Administration to examine most passengers' shoes during routine airline screening procedures at U.S. airports.

The Reid investigation revealed that he had previously conducted surveys of other airlines and different destinations before settling on the Paris to Miami route. He also had used cryptic e-mail messages to communicate with his coconspirators, who encouraged him to continue with the plans even after he was scrutinized by Paris airport officials the previous day. These authorities became so concerned with his presence that the added security scrutiny caused Reid to miss his intended flight. American Airlines paid for his overnight stay until he departed the next day.

Al-Qaeda is credited with attempting to shoot down an Israeli chartered airliner with a Russian-manufactured shoulder-fired surface-to-air missile as it departed the Mombassa,

Figure 10–2 World Trade Center debris field.
Source: Courtesy of Bureau of Immigration and Customs Enforcement

Kenya, airport in November 2002. This incident has prompted U.S. airlines to seriously consider installing antimissile devices on all of their aircraft, which, if adopted, will cost the industry millions of dollars.

Al-Qaeda's Strength

The best intelligence estimates are that al-Qaeda probably has several thousand members and associates. In February 2003, FBI Director Robert Mueller III testified before Congress that several hundred Islamic radicals with links to al-Qaeda were believed to be living in the United States. These terrorists are most likely organized into cells and are awaiting orders to carry out attacks. The deaths and arrests of about a third of the known al-Qaeda senior leaders has conclusively interrupted or delayed some known terrorist plots and probably others that will never be known to law enforcement authorities.

The 2003 war with Iraq has undoubtedly brought more associates to the ranks of al-Qaeda who view the conflict as being religious based. Because al-Qaeda operates in small *cells* their exact numbers cannot be determined. These cells are designed to limit the information any one member of a cell can reveal if he should be caught and interrogated by law enforcement (see Figure 2–2 for details).

Figure 10–3   World Trade Center destruction overview.
Source: Courtesy of Bureau of Immigration and Customs Enforcement

Its ties to numerous other Sunni Islamic extremist groups reinforce the al-Qaeda terrorist network. These groups are known to include the FTOs al-Gama'a al-Islamiyya, the Islamic Movement of Uzbekistan, and the Harakat ul-Mujahidin.

Al-Qaeda's willingness to exercise extreme operational security and to conduct extensive preplanning operations adds to their strength. However, too much preplanning has also led to the downfall of some of their operations. Al-Qaeda is not willing to chance an operation failing. They have shown extraordinary patience until they perceive there is a significantly greater chance of success than failure.

Area of Operations

The al-Qaeda terrorist group is truly a worldwide network. It was based primarily in Afghanistan until late 2001, when U.S. and coalition forces removed the Taliban, the Islamic extremist government in power at the time. Action against the Taliban came as a direct result of the attacks of September 11, 2001, due to its support and alliance with al-Qaeda.

With the onset of the war in Afghanistan and the destruction of the al-Qaeda terrorist training camps there, the network was forced to disperse into even smaller groups,

Albania	Iran	Saudi Arabia
Algeria	Iraq	Somalia
Afghanistan	Ireland	South Africa
Azerbaijan	Italy	Spain
Australia	Jordan	Sudan
Austria	Kenya	Switzerland
Bahrain	Kosovo	Tajikistan
Bangladesh	Lebanon	Tanzania
Belgium	Libya	Tunisia
Bosnia	Malaysia	Turkey
Canada	Mauritania	Uganda
Egypt	Netherlands	United Arab Emirates
Eritrea	Pakistan	United Kingdom
France	Philippines	United States
Germany	Qatar	Uzbekistan
India	Russia	Yemen

Figure 10–4   Countries where Al-Qaeda has been known to operate.

mostly in South Asia, Southeast Asia, and the Middle East. They are known to be on five continents, and not necessarily in nations that have a primarily Muslim population (see Figure 10–4).

External Financial Aid

Osama bin Laden initially financed al-Qaeda through his own personal wealth and holdings while he resided in Saudi Arabia. Since he left that country, he has deployed a variety of means to solicit funding to continue operations.

Al-Qaeda maintains moneymaking business fronts, many of which have been located in the United States, primarily in Detroit and New York. They also solicit and receive outright donations from like-minded supporters and obtain funding from unwitting contributors through so-called Muslim charitable organizations. Efforts by the Department of Homeland Security and other agencies to block al-Qaeda funding have curtailed the group's ability to obtain money.

The DEA has documented Taliban and al-Qaeda members engaging in the sale of heroin in Afghanistan. The Taliban also has received funding through the taxation of opium at various stages of production. United Nations crop-substitution programs have failed miserably there, and the production of opium has returned to prewar levels. There is every reason to believe that Afghan opium is still being used as a means of generating income for Taliban sympathizers and Islamic terrorist organizations, including al-Qaeda.

Terrorists, like drug traffickers, practice the systematic movement of money from one country to another, called the ***Hawala underground banking network***. Its transactions are similar to money wire transfers conducted by banks and other companies such as Western

Union. As an example, al-Qaeda needs to move large amounts of money from one location to another to finance a terrorist event or to provide living expenses for its membership. Al-Qaeda will provide a trusted member of the Islamic community in a country such as Pakistan with the money they need transferred to another country. The Hawala businessman will provide a chit receipt for the funds and will telephone or fax instructions to his contact in the other country to provide cash to the intended recipient, minus his fee. These businesses exist due to the trust earned through religious, ideological, or family ties to the terrorist organization.

These Hawala networks exist wherever high concentrations of Muslims live around the world. No paper trail is ever created, and the funds are difficult to trace.

Al-Qaeda has also been known to purchase diamonds to smuggle from one country to another. The smaller diamonds are substantially easier to smuggle than large amounts of currency, and they also eliminate paper trails.

The Al-Qaeda Training Manual

On May 10, 2000, during a search of al-Qaeda associate Nazih al Wadih Raghie's home in Manchester, England, the Metropolitan Police seized a computer containing a file named "the military series." A review of the translated file showed it to be related to another file named "Declaration of Jihad." The files contained what is now commonly referred to as the *Al-Qaeda Training Manual*.

The contents of the manual are a compilation of material derived from various unclassified military, intelligence, and law enforcement training materials for internal security, guerilla, and covert operations around the globe. Although al-Qaeda is not mentioned specifically, there should be no question that the manual reflects its training doctrine and was taught at the various terrorist training camps that existed in Afghanistan and elsewhere. Captured videotapes of training sessions depict students practicing material found in the manual.

It is believed that hundreds of copies of the manual were distributed on CD-ROM to members of al-Qaeda, primarily paid for by Osama bin Laden.

The manual contains an introduction and eighteen lessons, or chapters, covering topics ranging from recruitment to security, operational planning, and assassination. The following are the main chapter topics in the manual:

Presentation
Introduction
First Lesson—General Introduction
Second Lesson—Necessary Qualifications and Characteristics for the Organization's
     Members
Third Lesson—Counterfeit Currency and Forged Documents
Fourth Lesson—Organization Military Bases, "Apartment Places"—Hiding
Fifth Lesson—Means of Communication and Transportation

Sixth Lesson—Training
Seventh Lesson—Weapons: Measure Related to Buying and Transporting Them
Eighth Lesson—Member Safety
Ninth Lesson—Security Plan
Tenth Lesson—Definition of Special Operations
Eleventh Lesson—Espionage (1) Information-Gathering Using Open Methods
Twelfth Lesson—Espionage (2) Information-Gathering Using Covert Methods
Thirteenth Lesson—Secret Writing and Cipher and Codes
Fourteenth Lesson—Kidnapping and Assassinations Using Rifles and Pistols
Fifteenth Lesson—Explosives
Sixteenth Lesson—Assassinations Using Poisons and Cold Steel
Seventeenth Lesson—Torture Methods
Eighteenth Lesson—Prisons and Detention Centers

The manual is a wealth of insider information for law enforcement and intelligence officers that is rife with religious passages and examples of reasons why Muslims should perform violent acts against "the enemy." In lesson nine, "Security Plan," training in Afghanistan is specifically mentioned.

The "Presentation" page of the manual is telling, in that it illustrates the mindset of people prone to become members of this or other Islamic extremist terrorist organizations.

Presentation

To those champions who avowed the truth day and night. . .
And wrote with their blood and sufferings these phrases. . .

The confrontation that we are calling for with the apostate regimes does not know Socratic debates . . . Platonic ideals. . . nor Aristotelian diplomacy . . . But it knows the dialogue of bullets, the ideals of assassination, bombing, and destruction, and the diplomacy of the cannon and machine-gun.

Islamic governments have never and will never be established through peaceful solutions and cooperative councils. They are established as they (always) have been

By pen and gun

By word and bullet

By tongue and teeth

Law enforcement officers who believe they may be investigating a conspiracy involving al-Qaeda or another Islamic extremist terrorist organization should obtain a copy of the manual, which is available through public and official sources, and learn firsthand the training and philosophy these people most likely have received.

Many of the techniques taught in the lessons of the manual mimic tactics used by international drug organizations to defeat surveillance and detection by law enforcement officers. A sanitized version of the manual can be found on the U.S. Department of Justice Web site.

SUBNATIONAL TERRORIST GROUPS

Subnational terrorist groups operate primarily within a certain geographic area or national boundary. However, they have been every bit as deadly as their transnational counterparts. The now-defunct 17 November terrorist group operated in Greece for nearly twenty-eight years, claiming its first victim, CIA Station Chief Richard Welch, in 1975. Even though it is listed as an FTO by the U.S. State Department, it primarily operated within Greece. The 17 November received its FTO status by virtue of an attack on U.S. embassy personnel, which made it an international terrorist event. The goal of the organization was to institute a communist form of government within Greece. Because of a close-knit organizational structure with few members, they were able to operate freely for a long period of time. The group was foiled after an improvised explosive device (IED) exploded prematurely, injuring one of its members. Greek investigators discovered other weapons and explosives in the member's residence, and other evidence led to the discovery of the other members of the group.

Single-Issue Groups

The *Earth Liberation Front* (ELF) and *Animal Liberation Front* (ALF) advocate violence to supposedly protect the earth and animals from exploitation, cruelty, genetically engineered crops, and the like. They both are close-knit organizations that have caused millions of dollars in property damage to construction sites, laboratories, car dealerships, and other establishments, but they have never intentionally killed anyone to further their cause. However, their methods are designed to invoke terror in their victims and to advance their political agenda. Because these organizations are decentralized and consist of small individual cells, law enforcement has had a difficult time in infiltrating their ranks to gain firsthand, timely intelligence about their activities.

The following description is from the Earth Liberation Front Web site, *earth liberationfront.com:*

> *Meet the E.L.F.*
>
> The Earth Liberation Front is an international underground movement consisting of autonomous groups of people who carry out direct action according to the E.L.F. guidelines. Since 1997 E.L.F. cells have carried out dozens of actions resulting in close to $100 million in damages.
>
> Modeled after the Animal Liberation Front, the E.L.F. is structured in such a way as to maximize effectiveness. By operating in cells (small groups that consist of one to several people), the security of group members is maintained. Each cell is anonymous not only to the public but also to one another. This decentralized structure helps keep activists out of jail and free to continue conducting actions.
>
> As the E.L.F. structure is non-hierarchical, individuals involved control their own activities. There is no centralized organization or leadership tying the anonymous cells together. Likewise, there is no official "membership." Individuals who choose to do actions under the banner of the E.L.F. are driven only by their personal conscience or decisions taken by their cell while adhering to the stated guidelines.

Who are the people carrying out these activities? Because involved individuals are anonymous, they could be anyone from any community. Parents, teachers, church volunteers, your neighbor, or even your partner could be involved. The exploitation and destruction of the environment affects all of us—some people enough to take direct action in defense of the earth.

Any direct action to halt the destruction of the environment and adhering to the strict nonviolence guidelines, listed below, can be considered an E.L.F. action. Economic sabotage and property destruction fall within these guidelines.

Earth Liberation Front Guidelines:

- To inflict economic damage on those profiting from the destruction and exploitation of the natural environment.
- To reveal and educate the public on the atrocities committed against the earth and all species that populate it.
- To take all necessary precautions against harming any animal, human and non-human.

There is no way to contact the E.L.F. in your area. It is up to each committed person to take responsibility for stopping the exploitation of the natural world. No longer can it be assumed that someone else is going to do it. If not you who, if not now when?

People who take independent action based on the ELF Web site are every bit conspirators with other members of this organization. It would be important to show that suspects have visited the Web site in the past or that they possess other material concerning the ELF or ALF, to show a nexus with these organizations.

National Separatists

Spain serves as a good example of a country plagued by an organization seeking a separate state from within its borders. The Basque Fatherland and Liberty (ETA) terrorist organization seeks independence from Spain and a sovereign nation in the Basque region near the French border. For years the ETA has resorted to using car bombs and other IEDs to achieve its goals. These IEDs have caused the deaths and injuries of hundreds of people, but they have not swayed the Spanish government to grant any of their demands.

Although Spain has taken aggressive action to eliminate the ETA, much work needs to be done to completely eradicate them.

The *Irish Republican Army* (IRA) has the goal of separating Northern Ireland from British control and melding it into the Republic of Ireland. For decades, the predominately Catholic IRA has fought with the Protestant British using IEDs and assassinations to achieve its political goals. Much of its funding came from American-based Catholics who, wittingly and unwittingly, donated money for the cause.

Former IRA members are believed to now be conducting terrorist training for members of the Revolutionary Armed Forces of Colombia (FARC). The FARC is responsible for hundreds of murders and kidnappings of American citizens as it struggles to overthrow the established government of Colombia.

Other examples of national separatists include the Palestine Liberation Organization, which has long sought to establish a Palestinian state within Israel, and the Kurdistan

Workers' Party, whose goal is to establish an independent state within the borders of Turkey. Both organizations have used violent terrorist tactics to achieve their political goals.

National separatists view themselves as *freedom fighters* and tend to use just enough violence to bring attention to their causes without alienating supporters.

Religious Extremists

An antiabortion organization that advocates and carries out violence against doctors, their facilities, and employees who perform abortions is an example of a *religious extremist group*. Many members of these organizations profess that they are doing God's work, yet they do not feel remorseful for their actions. They are true believers who feel frustrated by the legal system and the famous *Rowe v. Wade* U.S. Supreme Court decision that essentially legalized many forms of abortion. They see themselves as people who are protecting unborn children, who have no means of defending themselves.

Not all members of antiabortion organizations advocate or practice violence against abortion clinics; however, it stands to reason that people who do perform violent acts most probably were members of these organizations at one time.

Religious Cults

In 1990, David Koresh was the founder of the **Branch Davidians**, a religious cult headquartered at Mount Carmel, outside Waco, Texas. The 1,400-member religious cult showed undying loyalty to him, and members armed themselves with numerous automatic weapons and altered firearms in violation of federal gun laws.

On February 28, 1993, the Bureau of Alcohol, Tobacco, and Firearms (ATF) attempted to execute a federal search warrant at Koresh's compound for illegal or modified firearms. What followed was the most violent episode ever encountered by federal law enforcement authorities at the time. Almost immediately after "knocking and announcing" their intentions to serve the search warrant, the ATF special agents were fired upon. A fierce gun battle began that left four ATF special agents dead and sixteen others injured from gunfire.

The FBI responded to the scene en mass because they have jurisdiction over assaults and murders of federal agents. On April 19, after 51 days of failed negotiations, members of the cult spread flammable material throughout the inner walls of the compound, setting it ablaze. Eighty-five persons, many of them children, died in the fire that some blamed the FBI for starting.

Twelve of the Davidians were later federally indicted for murder and conspiracy to murder federal agents and for federal firearms violations.

Left-Wing Groups

The Weathermen terrorist group was a domestic left-wing radical organization that was a violent offshoot of the **Students for a Democratic Society**. The Weathermen engaged in what they perceived as a revolutionary struggle with a degenerate capitalist society. The group claimed responsibility for the bombing of New York City's police headquarters in 1970, the U.S. Capitol building in 1971, and the Pentagon in 1972, and it was believed to be responsible for many other acts of violence.

The **Baader-Meinhof** terrorist group was a 1970s German-based radical socialist organization that frequently bombed U.S. Army and German government installations with the goal of furthering communism and expelling NATO forces from the country.

Right-Wing Groups

Right-wing domestic terrorist organizations have long existed in the United States. Many, such as skinheads, neo-Nazis, and militia organizations, stem from and are influenced by White supremacist groups such as the Ku Klux Klan. The FBI considers these types of domestic terrorist groups as posing the greatest threat to internal security of the United States.

These right-wing groups are motivated by their hatred of the United Nations, minority citizens, taxes, and the government itself. Many members view themselves to be patriots who have been given the constitutional authority to violently oppose the government.

Timothy McVeigh and Terry Nichols were found responsible for the April 19, 1995, bombing of the Alfred P. Murrah Federal Building in Oklahoma City, Oklahoma, in which 168 people were killed. McVeigh was later executed for his participation in the event. Nichols was convicted and sentenced to life without the possibility of parole. McVeigh said his actions were in retaliation for the deaths suffered at the hands of government agents at the Branch Davidians' compound in Waco, Texas.

Lone Actors

Some left-wing and right-wing terrorists may be **lone actors**, but their intentions are as deadly as any attack carried out by members of a large conspiracy. Eric Rudolph was arrested for the Atlanta Olympics Centennial Park bombing in 1996 that killed 2 and injured over 100. He is also suspected of causing three other bombings at abortion clinics, at least one of which was designed to kill investigating police detectives by the use of a delayed timer on a second bomb. He was finally arrested, and the government is seeking the death penalty for his actions.

Mir Aimal Kanzi, a Pakistani national living in northern Virginia near Washington, D.C., became upset with U.S. foreign policy in the Middle East. In 1993, after purchasing an AK-47 assault rifle, he stood on the street near a left-turn lane servicing the headquarters for the CIA. He opened fire on about a half-dozen vehicles containing CIA employees while they waited for a green light to turn into the facility.

Kanzi fled the United States back to his native Pakistan, where he was eventually arrested by FBI agents and brought back to northern Virginia, where he was convicted of state murder charges and later executed.

Although he acted alone, the U.S. government considered his act a terrorist event because of the status of the victims and the means he used to kill two CIA employees and wound several others.

Criminal Organizations

Throughout U.S. history many criminal organizations have used terrorist-like tactics to achieve their goals. Disputes in the expanding West, border crime by Mexican bandits, gin smugglers during Prohibition, traditional organized crime, and modern drug cartels all have used terror to achieve their goals. Criminal organizations use terrorism as a tactic to deter law enforcement, and they are motivated by profit. The motivation for most terrorist acts is, as we have seen, political.

Modern international drug trafficking organizations have elicited the aid, and partnered with, genuine terrorist organizations, such as the ***Revolutionary Armed Forces of Colombia*** (FARC) and the ***Shining Path*** in Peru. These communist-inspired terrorist groups use money earned from Colombian drug traffickers to further their political agendas. The FARC is responsible for assassinations, kidnappings, extortions, and church bombings using funds derived from cocaine traffickers.

In 2002, elements of the 16th Front of the FARC were indicted in the United States, based on an investigation by the DEA for conspiracy to import and distribute cocaine. This marked the first time that members of a terrorist organization had been indicted for drug trafficking.

Colombian cocaine traffickers have assassinated political candidates and newspaper journalists, have promoted corruption, and have threatened and carried out acts of violence against police authorities who oppose them. At the height of the Medillian cartel, the group secreted a bomb on a commercial airliner to kill an alleged police informant and also killed many innocent passengers when the plane crashed, all to demonstrate the cartel's ruthlessness.

Domestic gang members have brought terror to entire neighborhoods to gain control of territory to sell drugs. These gangs have exercised terrorist tactics to intimidate their drug competitors and customers alike. They have often dealt directly with Colombian and Mexican drug cartels in providing cocaine to manufacture the ***crack*** variety of the drug. These drug gangs are often solely responsible for the manufacture and distribution of crack cocaine and phencyclidine (PCP) in entire cities throughout the United States.

COMBATING TERRORISM

Since the events of September 11, 2001, the United States military has almost exclusively channeled its efforts to fight terrorism around the world. Two terms are often used to describe these efforts:

> *Antiterrorism*. Antiterrorism refers to efforts made to report, assess, and analyze intelligence about terrorists in order to provide forewarning about coming events.
> *Counterterrorism*. Counterterrorism, on the other hand, is the proactive activities of the military or police to capture or neutralize terrorists involved in past terrorist events and in planning for future events.

Combating terrorism requires the combined talents of antiterrorism and counterterrorism organizations. Antiterrorism analysis that is not acted upon is rendered useless, in that activities of terrorists are merely being documented or predicted. Counterterrorism organizations act on information vetted by antiterrorism professionals and take action when and where needed to put terrorists and their leaders out of business. These organizations predominately exist within each branch of the military. Law enforcement has traditionally been used to investigate those responsible for terrorist acts within the borders of the United States. However, more and more proactive enforcement has taken place since September 11, and these efforts have been responsible for the prevention of scores of terrorist acts both domestically and internationally.

Many experts in the field believe that even at the current rate, it will take years, possibly decades, to bring down terrorist organizations operating around the world.

SUMMARY

Investigators charged with investigating terrorist events must be well versed in the different terrorist organizations that operate both domestically and internationally. Terrorists are motivated by politics and religion, whereas criminal organizations are profit motivated. Terrorist groups can be broken into two distinct categories: transnational and subnational. Many domestic terrorist organizations fall under the subnational category.

There are thirty-six foreign terrorist organizations (FTOs) identified by the U.S. Department of State. These FTOs operate predominately in the Middle East, Southeast Asia, and Southwest Asia.

The al-Qaeda terrorist organization, headed by Osama bin Laden, has been known to operate in at least forty-seven countries on five continents. It truly is an international terrorist network. Al-Qaeda has been responsible for numerous bombings and acts of terror, and it has joined forces with other Middle Eastern–based terrorist organizations. An al-Qaeda training manual was seized in Great Britain that detailed the training that many of al-Qaeda's members have received.

There are also numerous domestic terrorist organizations operating within the borders of the United States, including the Earth and Animal Liberation Fronts.

Advancing a cause, garnering publicity, spreading fear, and exacting revenge are all motivations for terrorism. There is a definite nexus between drug and terrorist organizations. Many terrorist organizations gain monetary support through working in concert with international drug cartels, or they sell drugs themselves to finance their activities. Drug cartels have exhibited tendencies to use terrorist-like tactics to intimidate political leaders and police officials in order to continue their criminal enterprises.

Antiterrorism refers to the collection and analysis of intelligence to predict future terrorist events. Counterterrorism refers to the actions of government agencies, usually with the military, to capture and eliminate terrorists operating throughout the world.

NOTE

1. For purposes of this definition, the term "noncombatant" is interpreted to include, in addition to civilians, military personnel who at the time of the incident are unarmed or are not on duty.

SUGGESTED READING

U.S. Department of State. *Patterns of Global Terrorism 2003*. Washington D.C.: U.S. Department of State, 2003.

CHAPTER 11

Overview of Drug Trafficking

INTRODUCTION

Because American conspiracy laws are extraterritorial, federal agencies have been able to indict and prosecute drug traffickers regardless of where they may operate when a nexus to the United States is established. It is one of the most effective tools used by enforcement agencies to dismantle entire criminal organizations.

For conspiracy investigators to be effective in dismantling drug trafficking organizations they must have some basic knowledge about what drugs are, where they originate, and what criminal organizations are most likely to be involved in their manufacture and distribution. For many years heroin, cocaine, and marijuana have been the top three varieties of illegal drugs abused in the United States and elsewhere. Many other drugs have emerged over the past forty years; however, these three have remained as the most popular. *Club drugs*, such as ecstasy, katamine, and gamma hydroxybutyrate (GHB), have become popular at *rave parties* recently, and they illustrate how quickly emerging drugs can take hold of certain segments of the population.

People have used drugs in one form or another for thousands of years. The reason is simple: Drugs make them feel good and alter their sense of consciousness. Unfortunately, the same drugs that provide euphoric effects can be highly physically and/or psychologically addictive. They are illegal to possess, use, or distribute because of the destruction they cause to individual users and to society as a whole. International treaties make drug trafficking a universal crime.

Because most illegal drugs sold in the United States have their origins in foreign countries, drug trafficking conspiracy investigations are automatically international in scope. What differentiates a drug conspiracy case from a traditional criminal investigation is that the identity of at least one suspect is known in a drug case before an investigation is initi-

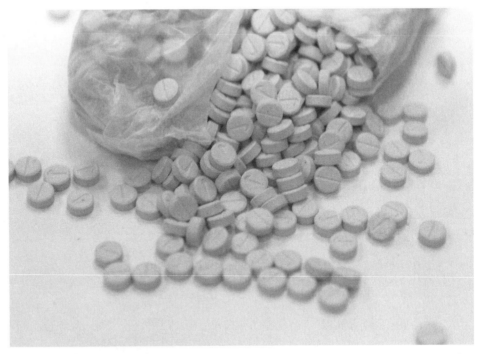

Figure 11–1   Ecstasy tablets.
Source: Courtesy Bureau of Immigration and Customs Enforcement

ated. Absent a chance encounter with a suspect in possession of a large amount of drugs that indicate he is a dealer, most drug cases are initiated based on information provided by a confidential informant. The informant either is or was personally involved in the drug trade, and he most often provides information about drug traffickers to help himself in his personal legal dilemma. Drug conspiracies, like terrorism, are proactive cases that are investigated *as the crime occurs.*

Drug trafficking is a multibillion-dollar industry that is practiced worldwide. Because of conspiracy laws, money launders of the ill-gotten gains of drug traffickers can find themselves personally liable for, and coconspirators of, drug trafficking organizations (see Pinkerton, Chapter 1, theory of vicarious liability for details).

Investigators must know what drugs come from which different parts of the globe. This knowledge offers clues to the identities of the nationalities, ethnic groups, and organizations that may be trafficking drugs in their areas of responsibility.

A common investigative technique used in drug cases is the use of undercover agents. Most after-the-fact cases do not afford the police an opportunity to introduce an investigator undercover to gather firsthand, timely information. Drug conspiracy cases are the exception, and the technique has proven highly successful, although dangerous.

Figure 11–2   Money seized from drug dealers.
Source: Courtesy Drug Enforcement Administration

SOURCE COUNTRIES OF POPULAR ILLEGAL DRUGS

Colombia

The most prolific drug traffickers in the world are from South America's oldest democracy: Colombia. Unquestionably the primary sources of cocaine in the world, Colombian traffickers also have expanded to the heroin trade. Colombia produces the most-abused variety of heroin found in the United States, predominately in the Northeast.

Cocaine trafficking organizations initially relied heavily on Bolivia and Peru to supply coca bush leaves (an essential ingredient for cocaine) to feed their cocaine processing laboratories; however, over the past decade they have stepped up production of their own coca bush to eliminate the need to rely on foreign production. The amount of cocaine produced annually in Colombia is staggering. Three-hundred-ton seizures in the past have had no impact on world wholesale prices. The vast majority of the finished cocaine hydrochloride finds its way through well-established smuggling routes in North America and Europe. Law enforcement authorities worldwide seize only a fraction of the cocaine produced in Colombia.

When cocaine use declined heavily in the United States in the early 1990s, shrewd Colombian traffickers expanded their market to Europe. Until then, cocaine had been virtually unseen in Western Europe while America's streets had been flooded with it. Now multiton seizures in Europe are commonplace.

Drug conspiracy investigators need to recognize that when cocaine is seized in their jurisdiction, the ultimate source of supply, and the top leadership of the conspiracy, are in Colombia. The cocaine most probably has been smuggled into the country from the interior of Mexico by organizations managed by Mexican-national drug traffickers.

Colombian heroin is one of the purist and most potent in the world. The Drug Enforcement Administration (DEA) manages a **Heroin Signature Program** that chemically analyses heroin seized in the United States. DEA chemists can identify heroin that is unique to Colombia, as well as to other source countries.

The DEA also operates the **Domestic Monitoring Program**, in which user amounts of heroin are purchased for qualitative laboratory analysis to determine purities. Street dosages at high levels of purity are indicative of a large supply of heroin in the United States.

The DEA also maintains a database named **Operation Fountain Head**. Colombian cocaine traffickers routinely place popular logos, symbols, pictures, printed or handwritten letters, or numbers on kilogram packages of cocaine to identify the ownership of the drug. It is common to see scorpions, religious symbols, car logos, and the like on kilogram packages, and these marks may offer clues to the identities of the drug trafficking organizations and the particular laboratories that produced them. Seizing identically marked kilogram packages of cocaine in different parts of the country or the world sheds light on the capacity of a cocaine laboratory and extent of the organization's smuggling abilities.

Most cocaine is now smuggled into the United States through the interior of Mexico after vessels, many of them go-fast boats, have off-loaded their cargo on its shores. Colombian traffickers for years paid Mexican smugglers to transport huge amounts of drugs through that country and then piecemeal it into the United States by land vehicles. Within the last ten years, however, Mexican smuggling organizations have demanded product instead of cash for payment of their services, and they have now grown into formidable cocaine trafficking cartels in their own right. Because Mexico does not produce the raw precursor (coca leaves) to produce cocaine, the cartels must rely on Colombia for their finished product.

Mexico

Besides having the distinction of being the main conduit of cocaine into the United States, Mexico has been a longtime source of marijuana, heroin, and methamphetamine. Because of their long partnerships with Colombian drug traffickers, Mexican criminal organizations have grown into large and powerful criminal organizations. Corrupt police and government officials, including the military, have aided them. Although corruption has waned in recent years, it often explains why drug traffickers have remained largely untouched by the Mexican judicial system.

Black tar heroin is produced exclusively in Mexico and exported to the United States, where it has been popular primarily on the West Coast and in the southern border states.

Figure 11–3   Powdered methamphetamine.
Source: Courtesy Drug Enforcement Administration

Most of the marijuana grown in Mexico is also smuggled into the United States, almost always by land. Because the Bureau of Immigration and Customs Enforcement (ICE) only has the resources to inspect approximately 2 percent of incoming cargo, it is obvious why Mexico is the main conduit for a variety of drugs entering America. With increased emphasis on terrorism prevention, ICE has recently improved its capacity to inspect cargo entering from Mexico.

At one time outlaw motorcycle gangs controlled the methamphetamine market; however, Mexican drug organizations undercut these gangs and now produce the vast majority of methamphetamine abused in the United States. Although many clandestine high capacity methamphetamine laboratories can be found throughout the United States, they are usually manned, supplied, or somehow connected to Mexican national traffickers. One of the essential ingredients of methamphetamine is ephedrine. It is no longer manufactured in the United States, but it can be found as the main ingredient in over-the-counter cold remedy tablets, so the demand for pseudoephedrine has increased significantly for Mexican methamphetamine laboratory operators. Many of the pseudoephedrine tablets entering the United States are predestined for use in these laboratories, and they are supplied by Lebanese nationals living in Canada who are thought to have connections with terrorist organizations in the Middle East.

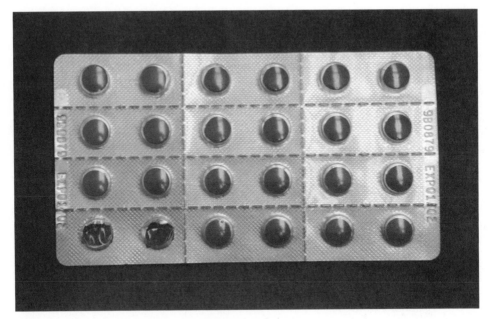

Figure 11–4   Blister package of pseudoephedrine.
Source: Courtesy Drug Enforcement Administration

Bolivia and Peru

These two countries supply almost 30 percent of the coca bush needed by Colombian traffickers to manufacture cocaine. Criminal organizations from both of these countries have aspired to compete directly with Colombian cocaine traffickers, but they only control a small portion of the total market.

Much of the coca bush produced in these countries is used for domestic consumption. Peruvians and Bolivians have chewed the coca leaf for centuries to ward off the effects of high altitude sickness.

U.S. eradication efforts in these countries have had an effect on the total amount of coca leaf produced annually.

Golden Triangle

Thailand, Burma, and Laos comprise the area known as the Golden Triangle. Second only to Afghanistan, the growing regions of these countries produce an enormous number of *Papaver somniferum L.*, or opium poppy plants, to fuel heroin laboratories in Southeast Asia. The growers are powerful enough to employ private armies to protect their fields from government intervention.

Thai nationals are proud of the flourlike heroin they produce, and they place their particular multicolored brand name logos on the plastic packaging containing the drug. **Double-Uoglobe, Tiger**, and **Lucky** are just a few of the established brand names. Thais sell heroin in **units** that are 700 grams in weight, as opposed to the traditional kilogram (2.2 pound) amounts. About 5 percent of heroin abused in the United States comes from Thailand. The market share was once as high as 20 percent; however, Colombian heroin has captured much of the market previously held by Thailand.

Thai nationals are the primary traffickers of heroin and marijuana produced in the Golden Triangle. A popular variety of marijuana grown and marketed in the region is known as **Thai Sticks**. The marijuana, however, could originate in Cambodia, Laos, or Vietnam, but many of these nationals lack the contacts and sophistication to sell large tonnage of the drug. Thai Sticks are predominately sold by Thai nationals.

With the popularity of methamphetamine abuse in the United States, Thais have recently begun exporting methamphetamine tablets there after realizing huge sales success in Southeast Asia, Korea, and Japan.

Thanks to training and lobbying by the DEA, Thailand passed a conspiracy law in the late twentieth century and has enjoyed some success in dismantling drug organizations.

Golden Crescent

Afghanistan, Pakistan, and Iran make up the **Golden Crescent** region of Southwest Asia. Before the U.S. Global War on Terrorism, Afghanistan was the largest opium-producing nation. Since the war, production has returned to almost prewar levels. Eradication efforts and crop-substitution programs have failed to reduce the country's opium production. About 90 percent of the opium produced in Afghanistan is smuggled to Turkey, where heroin laboratories supply addicts in Western Europe and Great Britain. Only a small percentage of opium produced in the region is converted into heroin for domestic consumption in Afghanistan, Pakistan, and Iran. From 5 percent to 20 percent of heroin processed in this area makes its way to the United States, and most of this is controlled by Pakistani traffickers.

Drug lords, as they are known in Pakistan, mostly live and operate in or near the semi-autonomous Northwest Frontier Province of the country. Many of these drug lords are powerful tribal leaders with close ancestral ties to Afghanistan. They also are known to employ private armies to protect them from law enforcement efforts by the Pakistan government.

Afghanistan and Pakistan produce the largest amounts of **hashish** in the world. Hashish is the collected resin of the marijuana plant that is molded into what are called **plates**. Because of the large production of hashish, very little marijuana is left for domestic consumption and none is exported. Most of the hashish produced in the region is exported to Europe, Canada, and the United States.

Canada

As previously mentioned, a large source of pseudoephedrine comes from Canada. Also, a relatively new variety of Canadian marijuana grown in British Colombia, known as

B.C. Bud, has grown extremely popular in the United States. Canadian traffickers have been known to exchange equal amounts of cocaine for their premium marijuana. The *tetrahydrocannabinol* (THC) content of B.C. Bud makes it one of the most potent varieties of marijuana produced anywhere in the world.

Europe

Every week, millions of methylenedioxy-*n*-methylamphetamine (MDMA), or *Ecstasy*, tablets are manufactured in Europe, primarily in Belgium, Germany, and the Netherlands. Most of these *designer drugs* are distributed in the United States through bars and rave parties.

Ecstasy is sold wholesale in 1,000-tablet increments known as *boats*. Although the primary users of the drug are Caucasian, many non-Whites are also responsible for selling the drug. Mexican drug traffickers have recently begun to sell large amounts of Ecstasy in an attempt to capture a portion of the market. Israeli organized crime syndicates are heavily involved in the importation and distribution of Ecstasy in the United States and elsewhere.

Ecstasy tablets, which are also known simply as *X*, are aspirin-sized tablets that come in many colors. Almost all bear a particular logo identifying the manufacturer. Cartoon characters, automobile trademarks, windmills, and stars are just a few of the hundreds of logos found on seized Ecstasy tablets from Europe.

United States

The United States has long been a source country for marijuana and *Lysergic Acid Diethylamide* (LSD). LSD abuse has significantly dropped since the 1960s, but it can still be found. The drug is almost exclusively manufactured in the San Francisco Bay area of California, but it can be found in other areas of the country as well.

A potent variety of marijuana known as *sin semilla*, Spanish for "without seeds," is grown in California. Indoor growing operations of marijuana can be found anywhere in the United States, as well as open marijuana fields in national forests and on private property. Domestic marijuana growers and wholesale traffickers and smugglers tend to be Caucasian. Illegal Mexican aliens who are hired by the traffickers tend many of these fields.

Drug agents frequently subpoena utility bills of residences where marijuana indoor growing operations are suspected. These bills tend to be much higher than the average residential bill for the same neighborhood, due to the amount of electricity and water used in growing marijuana without the benefit of natural sunlight.

Phencyclidine (PCP) is a powerful animal tranquilizer that is marketed almost exclusively by Black traffickers to other Blacks. The chemicals are relatively easy to obtain, and the required laboratory operation is much less sophisticated than with other clandestinely manufactured drugs. The bulk of PCP production takes place in Los Angeles, and it is flown or driven to large urban areas throughout the country. There is no demand for PCP outside the United States.

Figure 11–5   Loose marijuana.
Source: Courtesy Drug Enforcement Administration

Katamine, a popular animal tranquilizer used at rave parties, is usually diverted or stolen from legitimate sources in the United States and sold to customers who frequently purchase Ecstasy.

Another rave party favorite is the clear liquid **Gamma Hydroxybutyrate** (GHB). It is easily manufactured with a common industrial cleaner and is frequently domestically made for consumption with Ecstasy at rave parties. It is also known as **Liquid X** and **Great Bodily Harm**. GHB is also a known "date rape drug" that is used by sexual predators to render their victims unconscious.

USE OF CONFIDENTIAL INFORMANTS IN DRUG CONSPIRACIES

Confidential informants (CIs) are a necessary part of drug law enforcement. They are frequently used to introduce an undercover agent to drug traffickers in order to make a *controlled buy*, or purchase of drugs to be used as evidence of a suspect's drug dealing.

Drug CIs are also some of the most difficult to manage and control. Drug conspiracy investigators must attempt to discover what is motivating a particular informant to provide information to the police. Misjudging an informant's motive can create tremendous control problems and can easily jeopardize any drug conspiracy investigation. Investigators must ask themselves why anyone would want to provide information that potentially could result in their injury or death at the hands of the traffickers they betray.

Motivations

When asked, many CIs will express their reason(s) for giving information to the police; however, they are not always truthful. The number one factor that motivates most informants to provide drug intelligence is being caught in a drug conspiracy themselves. Others speak of seeking repentance for past crimes when, in reality, they want to play the role of a lifetime by being involved in something exciting to them. These egotistical informants are the most uncontrollable because they have a preconceived notion of how the police operate. Informants have been known to replicate what they have read in a book or have seen in a movie, only this time, they are the main characters.

Other informants seek approval from an authoritarian figure, such as a police investigator. These people have never had any positive reinforcement, and they seek it from their police handler for a job well done.

Informants motivated by making money are by far the most cooperative and controllable because they know they must deliver in order to receive compensation.

An informant with perverse motives may be seeking information from the police on the targets of their investigations or the methods used in investigating drug conspiracies. They may also supply information to divert scarce resources from where they are needed. Informants have been known to offer their services to drug traffickers for the purpose of identifying undercover officers and learning police tactics. Drug traffickers have threatened informants if they did not obtain this information for them.

The courts and the public view informants as being incredible, devious, and underhanded. Their information must always be corroborated. All contacts CIs have with drug traffickers, either by accident or design, must be documented. Investigators should always insist that informants record their telephone conversations with the targets of the investigation for verification purposes.[1]

If a meeting between an informant and a drug dealer cannot be recorded, a recorded follow-up telephone conversation will help corroborate what was said at the unrecorded meeting.

Informants can never be trusted, and investigators should not socialize or otherwise have contact with them except for official business. The mishandling of informants has cost many investigators their jobs, livelihoods, and reputations.

CIs who will not follow the direction of their police handlers should not be used. These informants place themselves and investigators in unnecessary danger when they do not follow their handlers' directions.

Ideally, informants should only be used to introduce an undercover agent to a member of a drug conspiracy so he or she can independently identify other conspirators. Unfortunately, this is seldom the case because the traffickers only trust the informant, not the undercover agent.

Because most informants are required to have almost daily contact with the targets of any drug conspiracy investigation, it is almost inevitable that the drug traffickers will discover they were working for the police. Police investigators must take steps to protect informants from any retaliation the conspirators may contemplate. Limiting the exposure of an informant to the conspirators will increase the chances that his cooperation will be unrealized.

Covert Operations

The most frequently used technique in investigating ongoing drug conspiracies is covert operations. Whether an informant or a police investigator is the undercover operative, valuable information about suspect identities and the activities of a drug conspiracy can be gathered using this technique. The use of a police officer should always be the first choice when an operation is contemplated, however frequently a CI must be relied on.

Many experienced drug traffickers are satisfied with their current customer base and are reluctant to meet new people. This can sometimes be overcome if the conspirators are in need of someone possessing a special talent to reach or maintain their goal. A thorough debriefing of an informant may reveal a conspirator's need for a money launder, truck driver, boat captain, pilot, or enforcer. This knowledge may provide an opportunity to introduce an undercover police officer or another informant to infiltrate the organization.

Investigators contemplating participating in an undercover operation must be prepared. They should possess the necessary undercover documents, vehicle, living quarters, credit cards, telephone numbers, and cover story to be convincing to the traffickers. Attempts to introduce an undercover police officer into a drug conspiracy should not be attempted until he or she is fully prepared both physically and mentally. Undercover work is the most dangerous aspect of drug conspiracy investigations.

Controlled Deliveries

A highly successful investigative technique in learning the identities of drug conspirators is through what is known as a **controlled delivery**. As an example, an express delivery service notices that a damaged package contains a controlled substance and notifies the police. Investigators should immediately take steps to deliver the package to the addressee for the purpose of identifying and arresting him. Time is crucial because most delivery services offer computerized tracking of packages and their scheduled delivery.

Investigators can obtain a court order to place an electronic device inside the package that will alert them when it has been opened. An undercover officer can disguise himself as an employee of the delivery service and deliver the package while other investigators have the delivery address under surveillance. Once the electronic device notifies them that the package has been opened, they have the authority to retrieve the package because drugs are still inside. Once the location is secured, the suspect is arrested and asked to cooperate in expanding the investigation. Some states allow for a search warrant in anticipation of the controlled delivery being successful. If this is not possible, an application for a search warrant can still be made; however, the drugs should be removed from the package before it is delivered. At this point, at a minimum, an arrest warrant for the addressee should be requested.

Controlled deliveries are conducted both domestically and internationally. By virtue of treaties, many nations cooperate with the United States and each other in the use of this investigative technique.

Other Considerations

Drug dealers maintain meticulous records of their transactions. These **pay and owe sheets**, as they are called, usually contain code names for customers, and they document the amount of drugs the dealers received from their source of supply and how much of their inventory has been sold, advanced, or lost. Some of these codes are sophisticated and others are not. The FBI can provide expertise in code breaking and can give expert testimony in any court proceedings concerning their examination.

Some drug dealers record their sales data on disguised files on their computers. When police are searching a residence or business as a result of a court-authorized search warrant, all computers and paper files should be seized. Computers should not be turned on because they can be rigged to erase themselves if a particular procedure is not followed. Only specially trained forensic laboratory personnel should retrieve the data from any computer hard drive that is seized.

Drug conspirators also frequently rent private garage space to store records, drugs, weapons, and money. If keys to safe-deposit boxes, padlocks, or any other items such as garage rental receipts are located, they should be seized, and steps should be immediately taken to search these places as well.

Other documents in a trafficker's home or business may lead to the identity of other conspirators. Airline tickets, rental car receipts, income tax returns, address books, and phone directories should all be seized for future analysis.

SUMMARY

In order to effectively investigate drug conspiracies, investigators must have some working knowledge about the illegal drug business. They must know where illegal drugs originate and what nationalities are most likely involved in their smuggling and distribution. They should know, for example, that most cocaine comes from Colombia and that it is smuggled through the interior of Mexico and into the United States. Heroin found in the United States most frequently comes from Colombia, Mexico, Thailand, and Pakistan. Marijuana is cultivated around the world, including Canada, but a significant portion is grown in the United States for domestic consumption. The club drug Ecstasy originates in Europe, and other designer drugs have domestic roots.

Investigators should realize that most drug conspiracy cases originate from information derived from confidential informants. Informants have different motivations for providing information to the police, and investigators should not take anything an informant tells them on face value. Informants are inherently unreliable, and their information must always be corroborated.

The use of undercover agents is a frequent investigative technique in drug conspiracy investigations. Investigators contemplating performing an undercover role must be mentally and physically prepared for such a dangerous assignment.

Controlled-delivery investigations are another proven investigative technique in drug conspiracy cases. This is when a package containing drugs is delivered by police to the addressee so they can arrest him. Evidence gathered at the address often leads to the identities of other members of the conspiracy.

When conducting searches investigators should be aware that drug traffickers will document their sales of drugs either on paper or through the use of personal computers. These items should be seized for thorough analysis by a qualified forensic examiner.

Whenever receipts for private storage garages or safe-deposit boxes are found, efforts should be made to search them for additional contraband and drug profits.

NOTE

1. Investigators should check legality with their local prosecutors before recording consensual telephone conversations.

SUGGESTED READING

Lee, Gregory D. *Global Drug Enforcement: Practical Investigative Techniques*. Boca Raton, FL: CRC Press, 2003.

CHAPTER 12

Gang Profiles: Crips and Bloods

INTRODUCTION

There are literally thousands of street gangs operating within the United States. They are comprised of every race and ethnicity, but they have many things in common. Understanding how gangs operate will assist police officers when they conduct gang-related conspiracy investigations. Recognizing the characteristics all gangs possess will give investigators a logical course of action when investigating crimes perpetrated by gang members. Many wanna-be gangs often follow the leadership displayed by well-established criminal organizations such as the Crips and Bloods, and they will exhibit many of the same characteristics.

The *Crips* and *Bloods* are two predominately Black, violent, national gangs that planted their roots in the streets of south-central Los Angeles in 1989. They have been highly successful in the drug trade in Southern California, and they have stretched their tentacles to other major cities across the United States, where their goal is to control the drug trade. Murder and other crimes of violence associated with drug trafficking have increased wherever these gangs emerged.

As a result of the local success of the Crips, other gangs formed to combat their increased influence in the drug trafficking arena. These gangs merged to become the Bloods, an alternative to the Crips, and they originated from Compton, California, a suburb of Los Angeles. The Bloods and Crips made gang warfare commonplace, and drive-by shootings were used most often to spread violence on the streets of Los Angeles County.

The Crips and Bloods are loosely aligned with the *Folk Nation* and *People Nation* of Chicago, respectively. These are rival gangs that exhibit an all-for-one and one-for-all mentality, with unquestioned devotion among gang members. Membership in these organizations is for a lifetime. Those who do not subscribe to this code of ethics, or who otherwise violate orders of the leaders, are punished by anything from performing manual labor to death.

GANG IDENTIFIERS

The Crips adopted the color blue as their identifying symbol and extensively used the word *cuzz*, short for cousin, to identify other members of the organization. Other dark colors are worn as well, but the wearers' intent is to make their affiliation to the gang obvious to others. Some Crip gang members wear virtually everything blue they can find, including blue shoes, shoelaces, and the like. In contrast, the Bloods do the same with red, which symbolizes blood. Innocent persons wearing either predominately red or blue are sometimes mistaken as rival gang members and are killed by the other gang's members for simply unwittingly wearing the opposite gang's *colors*. Clothing accessories such as blue or red handkerchiefs, belts, and hats are commonly worn by these gangs to further show their affiliation with either the Crips or Bloods.

Bloods can be identified by tattoos of two burned dots over a single burned dot, which symbolizes a dog's paw, because many Bloods refer to themselves as such. Bloods also frequently wear the jersey of the Chicago Bulls professional basketball organization.

Both gangs extensively use *monikers*, or street names, in lieu of members' given names. Many gang members do not know the true names of the other gang's members, only their monikers. These monikers often appear on graffiti found on walls marking gang territory in a given geographic area. The first letter of the gang member's first name is often used as part of the moniker, such as T-Bone or C-Breeze. Often, these gang members will sport tattoos of their street moniker.

Bloods and Crips view themselves as gangsters, and they act like such. Many have taken monikers such as Capone, Baby Face, and Scar Face.

The gang members are so devoted to their own organizations and so opposed to rivals that even while talking to other fellow gang members, or *homeboys*, Crips will avoid using the letter B and Bloods will not use the letter C. An example of communication might be saying "bigar" for cigar, and "cooze," for booze. These gang members also display contorted hand signals to communicate membership or affiliation with others. The Bloods *flash* gang signals to one another. A gang member curls his thumb and index finger until they meet to form a circle. The three remaining fingers are extended to their fullest, and the hand is placed against the stomach area, palm of the hand face down, with the thumb and index finger touching the stomach. Next, the hand is moved in a circular motion, turning the palm of the hand face up, touching the little finger and the wrist to the mid-stomach area.

Most gang members range from 15 to 35 years old. The youngest members seem to be the most violent as they attempt to show their worthiness to the gangs.

Investigators should be cognizant that these gang members are so devoted to their gangs that they view fellow gang members as extended family members.

Graffiti is an important means of communication within gang communities. Because graffiti is often used to mark territory controlled by a particular gang, the mere crossing out of a particular graffiti marking represents a significant challenge to the rival gang, which often results in violence or death. Gang investigators can often predict future violent action between gangs when they observe newly created graffiti or the crossing out of existing graffiti on walls within their communities.

FRIENDS AND ENEMIES

Crips will ally with other gangs that denounce the Bloods, and Bloods will ally with gangs that denounce the Crips.

Independent gangs that ally with the Crips must denounce the gangs affiliated with the People Nation, and those affiliated with the Bloods must denounce the Folk Nation gang. These different gangs become either allies or enemies of the Crips and Bloods, which creates further tension and violence. Literally hundreds of individual gangs across the country will sometimes change their affiliation with either the Crips or the Bloods, and they need to be monitored by local law enforcement intelligence units.

STRUCTURE OF THE ORGANIZATIONS

There does not appear to be any centralized leadership in either the Crips or the Bloods. Both gangs, especially the Crips, are made up of "sets" that operate within specific geographic locations. Examples of these include the Compton Crips, which has about 20 sets, and the Hoover Crips, which has about 10 sets, both located in Los Angeles County. The East Coast Crips have many more sets. Each of these sets has leadership from within, but none of them is accountable to any one individual or group of individuals acting like board members of a corporation. There are about 200 documented Crips gangs and 70 Bloods gangs within Los Angeles County alone. The Crips and the Bloods rely on the Folk and People Nations, respectively, for logistical and other support in their criminal enterprises.

Sets also are located in many other large U.S. cities. These sets are comprised of four individual types of gang members: hard-cores; associates; peripherals; and want-to-bes.

The *hard-cores* are exactly what the name implies. These are the members who talk, act, and dress in traditional gang colors while committing criminal acts.

Associates identify themselves as being connected with a particular gang or set, but they seldom become involved in routine gang activity. These people usually provide moral and logistical support, such as supplying drugs to the gang for retail sale.

Peripherals do not have specific roles within the gangs, however are called upon to perform specific criminal activity when increased manpower is required for a particular operation.

A *want-to-be* is someone who identifies himself as a member of the Crips or Bloods even though he probably is not in that gang, usually in an attempt to gain influence in an area that is not controlled by the gangs. Want-to-bes adopt similar characteristics of the gangs and wear their particular gang's colors. These want-to-bes are a pool of future recruits within the actual gangs with which they affiliate. To show their worthiness for gang membership, many of these people can commit more dangerous acts than the actual gang members.

Within each set, three groupings of members are found. An *old gangster* is usually one of the founding members of the set and is one of the hard-cores. *Baby gangsters* (BGs) and *tiny gangsters* (TGs) comprise the younger, juvenile members of the sets. The older gang members, who are sometimes referred to as *shot callers*, maintain control of the BGs and TGs within their particular sets.

Although the Bloods are predominately Black, they have begun to accept other ethnic groups into their organization. Hispanics, Whites, and Chinese members have been identified as Bloods members. These individuals have been known to engage in drug sales, car thefts, robberies, rapes, extortion, and murders.

The Bloods leadership within New York City has been identified as:[1]

- *First Superior (The leader)*. Oversees the set and acts as the disciplinary officer.

- *Second Superior*. Assists and advises the First Superior; carries out the First Superior's duties in his absence.

- *Minister of Defense*. Provides strategies and information to the First Superior for the operations of the set.

- *Minister of Information*. Provides information concerning the set and its enemies.

- *Head of Security*. Provides weapons and discipline to all members of the set.

- *Commanding Officer*. Dictates orders as specified by the Superior.

- *Captain*. Disseminates orders to Lieutenants.

- *Head Lieutenant*. Assists and advises the Captain and carries out his orders in his absence.

- *Lieutenant*. Ensures the principal soldiers carry out orders issued by the captain.

- *Principal Soldier*. Follows orders from Lieutenants and carries out the set's battles.

In general, every Blood's function is to keep "banging" at all times. No one Blood member is considered to be better than another. Each member considers himself to be a soldier, putting in "work" (fighting) and maintaining the superiority of all Bloods over their enemies, especially the Crips.

The Bloods have also formulated a concept of war, which also reveals their philosophy on life:[2]

- Always listen before you talk, look before you walk, and observe before you stalk.

- In war, you must follow the commands of the higher ranks, who are designated as such because they are more, if not better, informed than you.

- Never make important decisions while angry, because an intemperate nature can cause one to run into a brick wall. Allow time to rationalize.

- What is pain to a warrior is but a privilege. Pain, and handling pain, are measures of a warrior, for to know victory is to know defeat.

- The injuries that you inflict upon the enemy should be considered such vicious acts of terrorism that the damage inflicted causes the enemy to never consider revenge.

- Never allow the enemy to live in your midst because one day he may rise up to re-pay you for the mistake.

- One must be a fox to recognize a trap and a lion to fight and intimidate the enemy.

- The best defense is oftentimes a good offense.

- There is no greater sin in war than ignorance.

- War has no room for diplomacy; war is outright vicious.

- Beware those around you who shout out the most yet find time to talk during conflict. These individuals will reason with the enemy.

- In war, strive to render the enemy harmless, disrupt the enemy's alliances, and attack before you are attacked.

- Silence and observation are major weapons in defense.

- During war, or peace, never allow your priorities to be misguided.

RECRUITMENT AND INITIATION

The bylaws of the Crips and Bloods demand that there be an aggressive approach to recruitment. Both gangs demand loyalty above all, and they require a "prospect" to demonstrate his courage and worthiness as a potential gang member. Often, these prospects are required to commit a violent crime, be assaulted, or to play Russian roulette in the presence of other gang members to show their sincere desire to join the gang. This manner of recruitment may be designed to ensure that no police officers infiltrate the groups.

Initiation into the Crips is most commonly described as **walking the line**. Here the prospect is required to walk with his hands behind his back between two lines of fullfledged gang members while they beat and kick him. If he should fall on one or both knees before reaching the end of the line, he must start the process over again.

A way to gain acceptance into the Bloods is for a prospect to participate in a **Bloodin**, in which he must either spill his own or someone else's blood during a violent act. Fighting, slashing, assaults against law enforcement officers, rapes, robberies, and group sex with a woman are all examples of Blood-in activities.

In New York City, Bloods have demonstrated a propensity for violent attacks against unsuspecting victims. Usually, victims are slashed across the face with little or no warning of the attack. Bloods have been identified in Brooklyn's Crown Heights, Queens' Far Rockaway, and Manhattan's 11th Street areas.

VIOLENT PRISON BEHAVIOR

Prisons throughout the United States are populated with both Crips and Bloods. Correctional facilities have experienced numerous problems with these gang members, who continue their criminal activities behind prison walls.

When placed with the general prison population, Crips and Bloods routinely assault, kill, sodomize, and otherwise victimize non-gang members. They quickly establish their own turfs within the prisons and do not hesitate to attack correctional officers and staff.

They are major sources of drugs and other contraband within the prisons. Correctional officers learned quickly that they must separate these two groups of gang members within the same facility in order to maintain some semblance of normalcy.

The graffiti created by these gang members sometimes give clues about upcoming murders and assaults against non-gang members or staff.

Visitors of gang members are usually other gang members or associates. Sign-in rosters of these visitors may produce leads to coconspirators involved in crimes committed within the correctional facilities.

These gang members have spawned prison gangs such as the **Consolidated Crips Organization** (CCO) and the **United Blood Nation** (UBN). The growth of these organizations is expected to continue as more Crips and Bloods are introduced into prison populations. CCO and UBN members are frequently involved in violence directed against other ethnically oriented gang members.

In New York City jails, the Bloods have developed a particularly violent reputation. In 1997, they were responsible for over half of the stabbings and slashings that occurred throughout the NYC Department of Corrections.

SUMMARY

An understanding of these rival Los Angeles–based street gangs, their characteristics, and their illegal activities will enhance an investigator's abilities to recognize the potential risks of investigating conspiracies involving them.

The Crips and Bloods street gangs emerged from their roots in Los Angeles in 1989 to become national gangs, perpetrating violent crimes that usually involve the drug trade.

They have distinctive dress that identifies them as members of their particular organizations. Crips wear many blue articles of clothing and accessories, whereas the Bloods wear many pieces of red clothing. Gang members have formed code words and signals identifying themselves as members or associates of a particular gang. They all exhibit an all-for-one and one-for-all attitude.

The Crips have aligned themselves with the Folk Nation, whereas the Bloods have aligned themselves with the People Nation. Both are violent street gangs in Chicago.

Both gangs have an organizational structure that somewhat mimics the military, in that certain gang members hold positions of responsibility and carry military titles. These gangs require prospective members to undergo violent initiation rituals to prove their worthiness.

Members of these gangs are steadily being incarcerated at correctional institutions throughout the United States. They are organizing within prison walls, not only for their own protection, but also to perpetrate crimes against non–gang members. They are responsible for the majority of the drugs and weapons found within many penal institutions.

NOTES

1. Information from a New York City Department of Correction intelligence brief, based on material confiscated from gang members.
2. Ibid.

CHAPTER 13

Terrorism Conspiracy Case Study

INTRODUCTION

The following case study illustrates how law enforcement investigates conspiracies committed by terrorists. Chapters 14 and 15 depict actual conspiracy investigations conducted against drug traffickers and gang members.

The purposes of these case studies are to demonstrate the investigative techniques that are deployed during a conspiracy investigation and to show how the application of the law can bring down entire criminal organizations. Alternatives for handling situations also are explored.

This first case study concerns the historical conspiracy investigation of the terrorists who were responsible for the September 11, 2001, hijacking of four U.S. commercial aircraft that were crashed into the World Trade Center in New York City, the Pentagon, and a field in Pennsylvania. It is completely factual. Much of the information is derived from open media sources and unclassified FBI publications.

CONSPIRACY TO COMMIT AIR PIRACY AND TERRORIST ACTS AGAINST THE UNITED STATES

No country has ever experienced anything like the events of September 11, 2001. The United States had received its share of international terrorist attacks overseas, but only once domestically—in 1993 when Ramzi Yousef masterminded the original attack on the World Trade Center's twin towers in which six persons were killed and one thousand Americans were injured. The country had been fortunate in that attack because the twin towers did not collapse, but a new breed of terrorists willing to die in the process of attacking America has emerged.

Figure 13–1   World Trade Center destruction.
Source: Courtesy Bureau of Immigration and Customs Enforcement

Nineteen hijackers died on the four flights commandeered that day, but one terrorist failed to die for his cause only because he had come under FBI scrutiny while at a flight school and had been arrested and incarcerated on immigration violations prior to the attacks.

Zacarias Moussaoui, a French citizen of Moroccan descent, came to the FBI's attention when it received reports from his flight instructors that he was intensely interested in learning how to fly and steer a commercial airliner, but not in takeoffs or landings. Because he could not be tied to any specific crime or ongoing conspiracy, he was arrested and held on various immigration violations pending further investigation, and he remained in custody on September 11, 2001. After the World Trade Center and other attacks, the FBI focused its attention on Moussaoui, and he later was indicted in the Eastern District of Virginia as the so-called "20th hijacker." He is a devoted Muslim and self-proclaimed disciple of Osama bin Laden, the leader of the international terrorist network al-Qaeda. It was the most intensive historical conspiracy investigation ever conducted by the FBI.

The United States was on a heightened state of alert at the time of the attack. In early August 2001, national security advisers warned President George W. Bush that Osama bin Laden's operatives could be planning to hijack a U.S. jetliner as part of an effort to free Sheik Omar Abdel-Rahman, a blind Egyptian cleric serving a life sentence for conspiracy to blow up the World Trade Center and other New York landmarks. The indirect warnings were vague and nonspecific. A flight instructor had earlier informed the Phoenix, Arizona, FBI office about Zacarias Moussaoui's odd request for training, but none of this information made sense until the attacks occurred.

No one can say for certain when an agreement was reached to destroy the World Trade Center and the Pentagon, and probably the White House or the U.S. Capitol building, if United Airlines Flight 93 had not crashed in Pennsylvania. However it is obvious that the hijackers had reached an agreement, and now it was the FBI's job to determine if Moussaoui had been a party to that agreement. The government's theory was that Moussaoui was the 20th hijacker, who only missed his fateful flight because he was in jail for immigration violations at the time of the attacks.

The FBI uncovered the required overt acts necessary to convince a federal grand jury of Moussaoui's involvement. Appendix B contains Moussaoui's indictment for his alleged participation in the crimes, and it details each overt act in which he and the others are known to have participated. In the following is a compilation of overt acts committed by the dead hijackers, as well as some by Moussaoui that were uncovered during the FBI investigation and reported in both official and open news sources.

On August 12, 2001, 33-year-old Mohammed Atta, the Egyptian-born leader, supervisor, and manager of the other hijackers, prepared for a trip to Las Vegas after returning from a ten-day final planning session in Spain. During his Las Vegas stay he was known to drink alcoholic beverages heavily and to have women at his disposal, despite being a devote Muslim.

The FBI believe Atta was the primary al-Qaeda operative in the United States, as well as one of the pilots of American Airlines Flight 11, which crashed into the north tower of the World Trade Center.

In 1982 he moved to continue his studies in Germany, which is well known as a base for al-Qaeda operatives. In 1985, Atta had enrolled in an architecture program at Cairo University, a school known for having radical Muslim students.

After graduation, Atta became involved in terrorist-related activity, including a purchase of chemicals used in bomb making in early 2000. He was known to travel frequently. It is believed Atta attended terrorist training camps in Afghanistan.

He eventually settled in Florida sometime in 2001 to attend flight training at Huffman Aviation in Venice, Florida, and later at SimCenter, Inc., in Opa-locka, Florida, and the Palm Beach Flight School in Palm Beach. People who met Atta described him as, among other things, stoic and focused.

On August 13, 2001, Atta arrived in Las Vegas, flying first class on an America West flight from Washington, D.C., the same class of travel he would use on September 11. Atta most probably used the trip as an opportunity to review airport security screenings, to carefully watch flight attendants, and to observe the locking mechanisms on the cockpits, which were used on most U.S. airliners at the time.

Another conspirator, Hani Hanjour, and at least two other hijackers were also in the city, staying at an Econo Lodge, off the Las Vegas Strip. They paid the hotel bill in cash, probably so they would not create any paper trail of their transactions and travel.

Hanjour, a Saudi national, is believed to be the primary pilot who plunged the hijacked American Airlines Flight 77 from Dulles International Airport into the Pentagon. He trained at the CRM Airline Training Center and Sawyer School of Aviation in Arizona and at the Freeway Airport in Maryland.

CRM Airline Training instructors told the FBI that Hanjour was studying for his private pilot's license. They described him as a bad student who never did his homework, missed flights, and displayed no commitment. Federal Aviation Administration (FAA) records revealed that in 1999, someone with his same name received an FAA commercial pilot's license. It is unclear if this was the same person. Commercial pilots can fly for compensation, but they cannot carry passengers, only loads.

Hanjour's family told the FBI that he had become a changed man, more serious and introverted, after returning to Saudi Arabia from the United States. They said he called them about eight hours before the September 11 attacks, but he did not say where he was and never mentioned the United States.

On August 12, 2001, Zacarias Moussaoui arrived in Minnesota from Phoenix, Arizona, to begin flight school, paying $6,300 in cash. The money is believed to have been provided via wire transfer by Mohammed Atta while he was in Europe.

Moussaoui trained on a Boeing 747 flight simulator at the Pan Am Flight Academy in Eagan, Minnesota.

FBI headquarters had received, but not yet acted on, a warning memo from its office in Phoenix about possible al-Qaeda members using American flight schools to train terrorists.

On August 14, 2001, the National Security Agency and the Central Intelligence Agency both noted that there was an unusually high amount of "chatter" in electronic intercepts of known al-Qaeda figures, but no specific targets or dates were mentioned.

On the same day, Atta flew coach from Las Vegas to Fort Lauderdale, Florida, on a Continental Airlines flight with a stopover in Houston, Texas. Atta might have used this flight to experience the anticipated numbers of passengers and the resistance the conspirators might encounter on the day of the hijackings.

Moussaoui's lack of flying skills alarmed his instructors at the Pan Am Flight Academy in Minnesota. The next day, the academy's program manager called the FBI, expressing the fear that, because of his serious lack of concern about anything but the basic fundamentals, Moussaoui might be planning a hijacking. This information was reported to FBI headquarters, which failed to tell their Minnesota office that their Phoenix Field Division had reported similar information.

Hanjour returned to San Diego, California, from Las Vegas after meeting with Atta. He had conducted numerous check flights (flights that student pilots take with an FAA examiner on board the plane in order to obtain a license) in both Nevada and Arizona in rented single-engine planes.

On August 16, 2001, Atta rented a single-engine Piper Arrow at the Palm Beach, Florida, flight training school.

This same day Moussaoui was taken into custody by the FBI in Minnesota and held on immigration charges. During the arrest and subsequent search of his apartment, the FBI confiscated two knives and several flight manuals for a Boeing 747. Also confiscated was a notebook in which two German telephone numbers were written, along with the name

Ahad Sabet. They also found a computer disk containing information related to aerial pesticides, a piece of paper referring to handheld Global Positioning System receivers, a pair of fighting gloves, and a pair of shin guards.

The FAA issued a warning on August 16 that terrorists could use cell phones, key chains, and pens as possible weapons in order to hijack a commercial airliner.

On August 17, 2001, Atta returned to the Palm Beach flight training school with an unidentified man of Middle Eastern descent. At the same time, Ziad Samir Jarrah, a 33-year-old Lebanese national, prepared for a check flight in a single-engine plane at a Fort Lauderdale flight school. He had already received flight training at Huffman Aviation in Venice, Florida. He was later believed to have piloted United Airlines Flight 93, which was headed to the Washington, D.C., area before it crashed in Pennsylvania. It has been speculated that his target was either the U.S. Capitol building or the White House.

Jarrah had enrolled in Huffman Aviation in 2000, and he was commended as an excellent pilot. On April 23, 2001, he rented an apartment in Hollywood, Florida. He was issued a Florida driver's license on May 2, 2001. In late August, Jarrah and Atta attempted to use online facilities at the Longshore Motel in Hollywood. The motel manager remembers that the two men claimed to be computer engineers from Iran who were visiting from Canada to find jobs. However, after becoming dissatisfied with the service they were receiving, Atta and Jarrah left, angrily saying, "You don't understand; we are here on a mission!"

Two days before the attack, Jarrah telephoned his father with an urgent request for $2,000. The father complied.

On August 19, 2001, FBI headquarters was warned by Supervisory Special Agent Coleen Rowley in the Minnesota office that Moussaoui could be a possible terrorist seeking to hijack a plane. FBI headquarters now began to circulate a memo from Phoenix FBI Special Agent Kenneth Williams, who warned that al-Qaeda operatives might be training at U.S. flight schools and recommended that the bureau undertake a nationwide canvassing of such schools.

Coleen Rowley later became one of three people named as *Time* magazine's "2002 persons of the year," in part for her courage in bringing FBI shortcomings in this matter to the attention of upper management.

Further investigation revealed that on August 20, 2001, Nawaf Alhazmi rented a car from a Jeep dealership in Wayne, New Jersey. Alhazmi, a Saudi national, was admitted to the United States as a nonimmigrant within one month of a meeting in Malaysia, and he appears to have overstayed his period of authorized time, making his status illegal on September 11. A flight instructor at Sorbi Flying Club, in San Diego, California, where Alhazmi took lessons in 2000, said Alhazmi and fellow student and hijacker Khalid Almihdhar were interested in flying large planes, like Boeings. Alhazmi was a presumed pilot of the hijacked American Airlines Flight 77.

Almihdhar, 26 years old, was believed to be either a Saudi or Yemeni citizen. Just after New Year's Day 2000, he and Alhazmi met in Kuala Lumpur, Malaysia, with Tawfiq bin Atash, a senior aide to Osama bin Laden and a principal suspect in the attack on the USS Cole in Yemen. On August 21, 2001, the CIA transmitted information about Almihdhar to the FBI and the Immigration and Naturalization Service, and Almihdhar's name was placed on the INS watch list because of suspected bin Laden ties on August 24, 2001. However, he had already entered the United States.

Almihdhar bought an American Airlines Flight 77 ticket six days before the attack. Investigation linked Alhazmi to Osama bin Laden on several fronts, and he is considered by the FBI to be a major coconspirator in the September 11 attacks.

After his arrest, the Minnesota FBI office requested permission from its headquarters to seek a search warrant for Zacarias Moussaoui's computer. This permission was denied due to probable cause concerns.

FBI headquarters later denied that this request to seek a search warrant for Moussaoui's computer, in hindsight, was something that should have been done. (*Note:* Supervisors dealing with terrorism investigations should direct their subordinates to consult with their local prosecutor for his or her opinion about the likelihood of locating a judge who will grant search authority in any similar situation.)

Investigators discovered that on August 22, 2001, Fayez Ahmed, also known as Fayez Rashid Ahmed Hassan Al Qadi Banihammad, used his Visa card to withdraw $4,900 in cash, which had been transferred to his Florida bank account the day before from an account in the United Arab Emirates. He would later be on board United Airlines Flight 175, which crashed into the south tower of the World Trade Center. His pilot's license bore an address for a flight school in Tulsa, Oklahoma, however the school did not have any record of him ever attending.

In 1995, Ahmed attended the U.S. Defense Language Institute in San Antonio, Texas. His father last spoke with him in March 2001, when he told him he was leaving the country with a relief organization, but he did not say where he was destined.

Also on August 22, Ziad Jarrah purchased an antenna for a Global Positioning System device and other equipment, along with the schematics for a Boeing 757 cockpit.

French intelligence reported to the FBI on August 23, 2001, that Zacarias Moussaoui had al-Qaeda connections and he had recently traveled to Afghanistan.

The CIA sent out an alert that prompted the FBI in New York to look for Khalid Almihdhar, who had listed the New York Marriott on his immigration form.

Neighbors saw Almihdhar and others at an apartment in San Diego practicing on a computer simulator program for 757 aircraft.

The following day, Almihdhar established an American Airlines customer profile, in which he paid cash for a flight originating at the Baltimore/Washington International Airport.

The next day, using the same American Airlines profile number that had been established by Almihdhar the day before, Majed Moqed, a Saudi national, reserved a ticket for American Airlines Flight 77 through the American Airlines Web site. Moqed flew into Washington, D.C., on a United Flight from London. He carried a tourist visa in his passport. On September 5, 2001, he purchased his ticket for American Flight 77, which later plunged into the Pentagon.

On August 26, 2001, Almihdhar flew to Baltimore and bought a ticket with cash for American Airlines Flight 77 on September 11. He is known to have worked out twice at Gold's Gym in Laurel, Maryland, with fellow hijackers of American Airlines Flight 77.

The same day, Waleed Alshehri, another Saudi national, booked his flight on American Airlines Flight 11, using a Visa card to pay for the ticket and giving a Hollywood,

Florida, address. Alshehri had a commercial pilot rating for single- and multiengine aircraft. He was also a certified flight instructor. On June 21, Alshehri had moved into the Homing Inn in Boynton Beach, Florida, with his brother, Wail Alshehri, and fellow American Airlines Flight 11 hijacker, Satam Al Suqami. AA Flight 11 was flown into the north tower of the World Trade Center.

Nawaf and Salem Alhazmi booked their flights on American Airlines 77 through *www.travelocity.com* on August 27, 2001, charging them with a Visa card. Salem Alhazmi was a Saudi national who had no record of receiving flight training in the United States or elsewhere. He opened a bank account in June 2001 with the help of his brother, Nawaf, after arriving in the United States with fellow hijacker Abdulaziz Alomari. Salem Alhazmi was admitted into the country as a nonimmigrant visitor and was in a lawful status on September 11. He spent time working out with four of the other American Airlines Flight 77 hijackers at Gold's Gym in Laurel, Maryland.

Reservations for one-way e-tickets for Fayez Ahmed and Mohand Alshehri, another Saudi national, for United Airlines Flight 175 were mailed to their apartment in Florida on August 27.

The FBI cannot find any record of flight training for Alshehri, nor is there any family linkage between Mohand Alshehri and hijackers Waleed and Wail Alshehri. Little was discovered about Mohand Alshehri's involvement in the actual attacks. Agents discovered a witness who saw him in January 2000 with fellow hijacker Hamza Alghamdi, renting a private post office box at Mail Boxes Etc. in Delray Beach, Florida, that was paid up for one year.

Hamza Alghamdi, 30 years old, was believed to be a Saudi national. He died aboard United Flight 175 when it crashed into the south tower of the World Trade Center. He obtained a Florida identification card on June 26, 2001, and received a driver's license the following day. No record was ever found of him receiving any pilot training. About this time period, he was living at the Delray Beach Racquet Club, in Delray Beach, Florida. He may have been a brother of, or somehow otherwise related to, Ahmed or Saeed Alghamdi, his fellow hijackers.

On August 28, 2001, Mohammed Atta made a reservation for American Airlines Flight 11 using his Visa card, and he returned to Fort Lauderdale from Baltimore on US Airways.

Saudi national Satam Al Suqami, 25 years old, also booked a reservation for American Airlines Flight 11; however, he paid cash. No record was ever located of him receiving any flight training. He entered the United States on May 26, 2001. He received a Florida identification card on July 3, along with fellow hijacker Wail Alshehri. They both listed their addresses as the Homing Inn in Boynton Beach, Florida.

Al Suqami registered for a monthlong membership at the Delray World Gym in Delray Beach on July 1, 2001.

Another Saudi national, Adbulaziz Alomari, booked a seat on American Airlines Flight 11 using *www.AmericanAirlines.com*. No record can be located of him receiving flight training. He was identified by a witness as the person accompanying Mohammed Atta on the morning of September 11 on a Colagan Air flight from Portland, Maine, to Boston's Logan International Airport. Why he and Atta went to Portland to begin their trek to Boston is still a mystery. They may have perceived airport security in Portland to be less vigilant than what they might have encountered in Boston.

Saudi national Wail Alshehri had arrived in the United States from Saudi Arabia, leaving behind a suicide note. He also never received any flight training. His responsibilities during the hijacking appear to have been to provide the muscle for the operation. He earned a Bachelor of Arts degree in physical education, and U.S. officials suspect that he was one of the hijackers who attended Osama bin Laden's camp for combat training. His father claimed he had mental problems.

Also on August 28, Ziad Jarrah checked out of the Pine Del Motel in Laurel, Maryland. The FAA issued a warning about possible violence against U.S. carriers flying in and out of Israel, but there was no mention of any domestic threat.

Ahmed Alghamdi and Hamza Alghamdi reserved one-way tickets for United Airlines Flight 175 on August 29, 2001. Ahmed Alghamdi would later be aboard Flight 175. He was a Saudi national who possibly received nonflight training at a U.S. Naval Air Station in Pensacola, Florida. He was admitted into the United States as a nonimmigrant student but overstayed his limit and was an illegal alien on September 11. He studied engineering at Umm al Qura University in Mecca, Saudi Arabia, but suddenly left for Chechnya in 2000 without notifying his family. They never heard from him again. The fact that he traveled to Chechnya offers a clue that he may have been an Islamic fundamentalist who wished to participate in a jihad.

Saudi national Ahmed Al Haznawi, 20 years old, purchased a ticket for United Airlines Flight 93, which would eventually crash in Pennsylvania. Cockpit voice recorders confirm that passengers on the plane resisted the hijackers, possibly forcing the plane to crash rather than continue. Many of the passengers knew about the attacks at the World Trade Center from calls made to friends and relatives from the plane immediately after the hijacking.

Al Haznawi also had no record of ever receiving flight training. He obtained his Florida driver's license along with Saeed Alghamdi on July 10, 2001. A videotaped suicide message he made in March 2001 was later aired on al-Jazeera Television on April 15, 2002.

Also on August 29, FBI agents in Minnesota appealed their denial from Washington to seek a search warrant for Zacarias Moussaoui's personal computer.

FBI agents later determined that on August 30, 2001, Mohammed Atta purchased a utility tool kit that contained a knife.

Ziad Jarrah worked out at U.S. 1 Fitness Center in Dania, Florida, where he had been taking one-on-one lessons in street fighting and defense tactics with instructor Bert Rodriguez.

Hamza Alghamdi moved into the Crystal Bay Motel Apartments in Deerfield Beach, Florida, on August 31, 2001.

On September 2, 2001, Khalid Almihdhar, Hani Hanjour, and Majed Moqed obtained weekly guest passes at Gold's Gym in Greenbelt, Maryland. Nawaf Alhazmi only obtained a day pass.

Also that day, United Arab Emirates national Marwan Al-Shehhi, 22 years old, inquired about purchasing a cell phone at a shopping mall in New Jersey. Agents later determined he had received flight training at the Huffman International Flight School in Venice, Florida, and at the Aero Precision Flight School in Punta Gorda, Florida. He is believed to be either Mohammed Atta's cousin or nephew through his Egyptian mother's lineage. Al-Shehhi accompanied Atta as they traveled throughout the world. He began his flight training with Atta at the Huffman flight school in July 2000. According to fellow students,

Al-Shehhi and Atta told them that Atta was a member of the Saudi royal family and Al-Shehhi was his bodyguard. FBI agents believe that it was Al-Shehhi who was the primary hijacker–pilot who skillfully made the left bank of United Airlines Flight 175 into the south tower of the World Trade Center.

Banking records examined by FBI agents revealed that on September 3, 2001, in Hamburg, Germany, Atta's former roommate there, Ramzi Binalshibh, received $1,500 by wire transfer from the United Arab Emirates.

On September 4, 2001, the FBI notified the FAA about the FBI's interest in Zacarias Moussaoui.

FBI agents later learned that on this same day, Hani Hanjour and Salem Alhazmi moved out of their Paterson, N.J., apartment. Further, all of the American Flight 77 hijackers were now in Baltimore and were seen exercising at Gold's Gym.

Mohammed Atta sent a FedEx package on this date to the United Arab Emirates, paying in cash.

FBI agents later discovered that on September 5, 2001, Mohammed Atta was in Washington, D.C., where he attempted to rent an apartment at 4000 Tunlaw.

The future American Airlines Flight 77 hijackers worked out again at Gold's Gym on the same day. The FBI and CIA also met with French officials in Paris regarding Zacarias Moussaoui and a possible planned attack on the U.S. embassy there.

Ahmed Alnami and Saeed Alghamdi flew to Newark, New Jersey, from Fort Lauderdale. Alnami was a Saudi national who had no flight training record. Agents later discovered that on May 28 he arrived in the United States on a Virgin Atlantic flight from London to Miami. The INS admitted him as a nonimmigrant visitor and he was one of the few hijackers who had legal status on September 11.

The investigation of Saeed Alghamdi, presumed to be a 31-year-old Saudi national, could not locate any record of flight training. The FBI and the INS originally mistook him for a Saudi Air pilot named Said Alghamdi, who received military aviation training in the United States. However, a records check with the Florida Department of Motor Vehicles revealed that Saeed Alghamdi was issued a state identification card on July 10, 2001. It was later determined that he lived with Hamza Alghamdi at the Delray Beach Racquet Club in Delray Beach in the middle of June 2001. He was aboard United Airlines Flight 93 on September 11.

Also on September 5, Ziad Jarrah and Ahmed Al Haznawi paid cash for tickets to Newark, New Jersey, from Passage Tourism in Fort Lauderdale.

Airline records later obtained showed that the entire group of men who hijacked United Airlines Flight 93 headed to Newark from Fort Lauderdale on this date. The FBI also later learned that Atta's former roommate in Germany, Ramzi Binalshibh, left Hamburg on September 5 for Madrid, Spain, and then, it is believed, went on to Afghanistan.

FBI agents discovered that on September 6, 2001, Satam Al Suqami and Abdulaziz Alomari flew from Florida to Boston's Logan International Airport, where they are believed to have conducted surveillance on security procedures.

Further, on the same day, Fayez Ahmed wired $8,055 back to an account in the United Arab Emirates.

The following day, September 7, 2001, Ziad Jarrah and Ahmed Al Haznawi flew from Fort Lauderdale to Newark, New Jersey.

The FBI later determined that on September 8, 2001, Hamza Alghamdi left the Crystal Bay Hotel Apartments in Deerfield, Florida, and Mohammed Atta wired a total of $7,860 to Mustafa Ahmed in the United Arab Emirates.

Agents also discovered later that an unidentified Arab male retrieved a package sent on September 4 by Mohammed Atta from the FedEx office in Dubai, United Arab Emirates.

After coordinating with local law enforcement officials, the FBI learned that on September 9, 2001, Ziad Jarrah was cited by a Maryland state trooper for speeding 90 miles per hour on a 65-miles-per-hour portion of Interstate 95. He was not arrested.

Further hijacker activities on that day included Marwan Al-Shehhi's return of a rented automobile to Warricks Rental Car in Pompano Beach, Florida. He asked the attendant if he could use his credit card to pay for the car instead of Mohammed Atta's card, which was used to secure the vehicle. He also wired $5,000 to the United Arab Emirates that day.

Two unknown hijackers were later determined to have stayed at the Charles Hotel in Cambridge, Massachusetts.

Mohammed Atta arrived in Boston and rented a car from Alamo Rent A Car at Logan International Airport.

Waleed Alshehri wired $5,000 to Ahamad Mustafa in the United Arab Emirates.

The day before the hijackings occurred, Atta and Abdulaziz Alomari checked into the South Portland Comfort Inn in Portland, Maine, and were seen at the local Pizza Hut. They were also seen at a Key Bank drive-up automatic teller machine (ATM), a Fast Green ATM, and at a local Wal-Mart department store.

Agents also later learned that an electronic message posted that day by an unknown author in a Yahoo! financial chat room read: "to the deapest part called the center of the earth by this weekend, northeast region will be destroyed new providance soon to fall apart."

Agents further learn that Marwan Al-Shehhi and three others checked into the Milner Hotel in Boston and inquired about prostitutes.

Also on September 10, the National Security Agency picked up two intercepts: "Tomorrow is zero day" and "The match begins tomorrow." They are not transcribed until September 12. It will never be determined if the intercepted messages, if translated earlier, could have prevented the tragedy.

At 7:45 A.M., September 11, 2001, American Airlines Flight 11 out of Boston en route to Los Angeles with 92 passengers aboard was soon under the control of hijackers Sataam Al Suqami, Abdulaziz Alomari, Wail Alshehri, Waleed Alshehri, and Mohammed Atta. At 8:45 A.M. it was flown into the north tower of the World Trade Center.

At 7:58 A.M., a second airliner originating from Logan Field in Boston, United Airlines Flight 175, with 65 passengers destined for Los Angeles, was taken over by hijackers Marwan Al-Shehhi, Hamza Alghamdi, Ahmed Alghamdi, Mohand Alshehri, and Fayez Ahmed. It was flown into the south tower of the World Trade Center at 9:05 A.M.

American Airlines Flight 77, also bound for Los Angeles with 64 passengers, departed Dulles International Airport in northern Virginia at 8:10 A.M. It was soon under the control of terrorists Salem Alhazmi, Nawaf Alhazmi, Khalid Almihdhar, Hani Hanjour, and Majed Moqed. Witnesses, many of whom were employees of the Drug Enforcement Administration at its headquarters, saw the plane make a wide circle over Crystal City, Virginia, and

Figure 13–2   The Pentagon shortly after attack.
Source: Courtesy U.S. Army

veer toward the Pentagon, striking it at ground level. The impact rattled the twin 12-story
DEA buildings and caused fire alarms to go off.

At 9:42 A.M., United Airlines Flight 93 departed Newark, New Jersey, for San Francisco, California, with 44 passengers aboard. It traveled as far west as Ohio before making
a U-turn and crashing in a rural area in Stony Creek Township, Pennsylvania, southeast of
Pittsburgh, at 10:03 A.M., after hijackers Ahmed Al Haznawi, Saeed Alghamdi, Ahmed Al-
nami, and Ziad Jarrah struggled with the passengers. Many of the passengers had telephoned relatives to tell them what was happening, and they had been told about the World
Trade Center attacks. Because this flight only had four terrorists on board, the FBI speculated that Zacarias Moussaoui would have participated in this hijacking if he had not been
arrested earlier for immigration violations.

FBI agents at the Pennsylvania crash site located pocketknives, box cutters, and duct
tape. A female flight attendant's body had her hands bound with a plastic band.

The methods used to uncover the overt acts committed by the hijackers included the
recovery of physical evidence, interviews with witnesses and relatives, phone toll analysis,
analysis of records from financial institutions, and the use of public and private sources of
information.

Figure 13–3   The Pentagon on fire.
Source: Courtesy U.S. Army

Few, if any, of the overt acts committed in furtherance of the conspiracy were criminal in nature. Even the duct tape, box cutters, and pocket knives the hijackers carried onboard had been screened through airport security before they boarded the planes, and were within the law at the time.

The hijackers were dedicated and meticulous in their planning. Their flight training and lifestyles were well funded by al-Qaeda through money wire transfers, primarily from the United Arab Emirates. Much of this money was later shown to have originated from a series of charitable front organizations operating in the United States and elsewhere, as well as from the wife of the Saudi ambassador to the United States. Several hijackers actually wired thousands of dollars back to the United Arab Emirates because they knew they wouldn't need it after September 11.

The FBI investigation revealed that all of the hijackers entered the United States legally. Of the nineteen who died, only three were out of status for minor INS violations while they resided in the United States, and most of those were for overstays when visas expired. When they arrived, three of the hijackers had business visas, fifteen had tourist visas, and one had a student visa.

Fifteen of the hijackers were from Saudi Arabia, two were from the United Arab Emirates, one was from Lebanon, and one, the apparent cell leader Mohammed Atta, was from Egypt.

Eleven of the hijackers had Florida driver's licenses or state-issued identification cards. The others had Virginia driver's licenses.

Several hijackers had multiple pieces of identification from several states, some of which were obtained fraudulently. These frauds were some of the few criminal acts committed by the hijackers during their entire time in the United States.

Four hijackers received traffic tickets for moving violations. Nothing in their behavior during their interactions with the police aroused any suspicions. The hijackers apparently were coached on remaining calm in the face of U.S. authorities.

The hijackers used twenty-four U.S. bank accounts, three of which were shared. They used five credit cards, none of which were stolen. They received the financial backing for their plan from overseas. Up to twelve international financial accounts were used. Wire transfers were sent from overseas to the hijackers in the United States. Transfers were kept well under $10,000 so they would not arouse suspicion. None of the hijackers had a job in the United States.

Through public and private records, the FBI determined that the hijackers used ninety-five known phone instruments to communicate. These included cell phones and pay phones. They used hundreds of prepaid calling cards, which are difficult to trace unless they are found on a suspect's person. They almost always used these cards to call overseas, and, based on telephone subscriber information, they did not contact any suspected al-Qaeda supporters in the United States.

Through the power of subpoena, the FBI obtained telephone tolls and determined that the hijackers collectively called Syria fifty-three times, Saudi Arabia twenty-eight times, Germany twenty-five times, United Arab Emirates sixteen times, Egypt twelve times, Lebanon ten times, Yemen seven times, Morocco four times, France two times, Israel once, Jordan once, Sudan once, and Oman once.

Generally, the hijackers traveled in pairs and lived with each other. They used publicly accessible Internet service, mostly through Internet cafes. No storage media, laptops, or desktops belonging to the hijackers were ever recovered except from Zacarias Moussaoui.

The conspiracy to hijack aircraft in the United States and use them as weapons of mass destruction may have originated in Germany as early as 1996. Three of the hijackers studied together in Hamburg, along with other conspirators. They possessed no documents indicative of a terrorist plot.

Each hijacked flight had at least one hijacker on it who knew how to fly the plane. The hijackers received their flight training in the United States. It is believed that they received formal training in hijacking aircraft in al-Qaeda training camps in Afghanistan, and possibly Iraq, and were then quickly sent out of the country after completing the training to avoid U.S. detection.

Each flight had some hijackers seated close to the cockpit. With the exception of American Airlines Flight 77, on which two hijackers sat in seats 12 A and B, all of the hijackers sat in either first or business class.

"Legal" weapons and restraints, including duct tape and plastic pull ties, were brought onboard and used, and these, coupled with the hijackers' own physical strength, were enough for the hijackers to take over three of the four airplanes. Several hijackers were known to have taken karate lessons, and many worked out at health clubs regularly.

The FBI determined that American Airlines Flight 11 left Boston for Los Angeles at 7:45 A.M. The plane, a Boeing 767, crashed exactly one hour later into the north tower of the World Trade Center. It had ninety-two people aboard, seventy-six passengers, two pilots, nine other crew members, and five hijackers. During that sixty-minute flight, an attendant managed to telephone someone to advise them that one of the five hijackers, Sataam Al Suqami, had stabbed one of the passengers.

An audio recording on board the plane showed that the hijackers never revealed their intention of crashing the plane into a building. In fact, they made statements to calm the passengers' fears, such as at 8:24 A.M., one of the hijackers said, "We have some planes. Just be quiet and you'll be okay . . . if you make any moves, you'll endanger yourself and the airplane."

There is speculation that the hijacker–pilot on United Airlines Flight 175 purposely waited for the first plane to crash into the north tower of the World Trade Center in order to draw in media attention to record the crashing of the second plane into the south tower. Someone on board the plane was able to make a call indicating that the two pilots had been killed and one flight attendant had been stabbed.

At 8:41 A.M., someone keyed the airplane's radio and said, "stay in your seats," presumably to the passengers. United Flight 175 had a total of sixty-five persons on board, including fifty-one passengers, two pilots, seven other crew members, and the five hijackers. The destruction of the two World Trade Center towers killed almost three thousand people.

American Airlines Flight 77 left Dulles International Airport in northern Virginia at 8:10 A.M. for Los Angeles. The hijackers are known to have checked into the flight between 6:22 A.M. and 7:52 A.M. It crashed at 9:39 A.M. into the southwest portion of the Pentagon in Arlington, Virginia, killing 184 people. It had sixty-four persons on board, including fifty-three passengers, two pilots, four other crew members, and the five hijackers.

The first indication there was something wrong was when the plane made an unauthorized turn at 8:45 A.M.

Evidence suggests that rehearsals of the hijackings were conducted.

The hijackers hid "in plain view," altering their appearance to fit into society. They shaved their beards, drank alcohol, went to strip clubs, and sought prostitutes.

The FBI found a handwritten letter in Arabic at three different locations, including in Mohammed Atta's suitcase, in a vehicle left in a parking lot at Dulles International Airport, and at the crash site of United Airlines Flight 93 in Stony Creek Township, Pennsylvania. The letters read in part:

> "Examine your weapon before departure . . ."

> "When the storming begins, strike like heroes who are determined not to return to this world."

> "Take prisoners and kill them . . ."

> "Your last words should be, There is no God but Allah. Mohammed is his messenger."

It is apparent that the nineteen hijackers agreed to conduct the air piracies for the purpose of using the airplanes as weapons of mass destruction. The letters are physical evidence that an agreement took place. The numerous overt acts the hijackers committed were all designed to further the goal of the conspiracy. The actions of the hijackers, such as taking flying lessons, becoming physically fit, being schooled in fighting tactics, making wire transfers, and having telephone contact with countries known to be havens for terrorists, are all excellent examples of overt acts.

These overt acts were discovered through the investigative process. The FBI immediately checked the manifests of the airliners to discover associations between those on each plane, as well as their associations with other passengers from other airliners.

One way of establishing an association is through telephone toll records. The hijackers' phone numbers were shown to be calling each other, which confirmed that a relationship existed between them. Telephone calls to overseas locations possibly helped identify other members who supported the conspiracy. They might have revealed the source of the funding used to pay for flight training and the living expenses of the hijackers.

Much of the information given here came from extensive interviews of neighbors, friends, and associates of the hijackers. Their perceptions might have been helpful in determining the motivation behind such acts, and they might have identified other unknown members of the conspiracy.

The entire investigation provides insights into the planning, cunningness, and methods of operation of the al-Qaeda terrorist network. Hopefully these insights will prevent a reccurrence of this or any other terrorist event aimed at the United States or elsewhere.

CHAPTER 14

Drug Trafficking
Conspiracy Case Study

INTRODUCTION

International drug smuggling organizations can be large and complex. The organizers, supervisors, and leaders of these organizations are often sophisticated and make significant efforts to avoid detection. Many of the overt acts they commit are not criminal in nature, but for those that are, attachment of liability to these crimes can be made against each member of the organization if they were a member of the conspiracy at the time the crimes were committed.

The following case study illustrates how such a drug smuggling organization managed to avoid detection for over 12 years, and how it had access to funding, equipment, and drug suppliers to facilitate the criminal enterprise.

CONSPIRACY TO IMPORT CONTROLLED SUBSTANCES INTO THE UNITED STATES

The telephone rang at DEA Special Agent Lee's home at 5:10 A.M. on a Wednesday morning in the late summer of 1988. Lee had only been at the Monterey, California, DEA office for 10 days, and he had spent most of the time acquainting himself with the area and meeting detectives from the police departments in the county. He didn't realize he was about to become involved in a case that would take him and others two and a half years to complete. It would be a case in which fifty-five of the sixty-two identified suspects would be federally indicted in the Northern District of California. Of the fifty-five defendants, forty-nine would plead guilty, four would be found guilty at trial, one would die before going to trial, and one would remain a fugitive. It would be one of the largest and most complex drug-importation conspiracies in the agency's history, spanning from California to Fiji, Papua New Guinea, Thailand, other parts of Southeast Asia, and Hawaii.

In the phone call, an officer at the U.S. Coast Guard Station in Monterey told Lee that Santa Cruz County sheriff's deputies had discovered a boat off-loading what looked to be tons of marijuana onto a private camping area called Red, White, and Blue Beach, a secluded area in northern Monterey Bay that was surrounded by lettuce and artichoke fields.

When it was apparent that law enforcement had arrived in the area of the off-loading, the boat, a fifty-foot fishing vessel, shoved off, and the Coast Guard was looking for it in Monterey Bay.

Because Santa Cruz County fell under the responsibility of the DEA's San Jose Resident office, Lee said he would notify them in the morning, and he asked to be kept apprised of the search developments.

Detective Steve Robbins of the Santa Cruz County Sheriff's Department was notified early in the morning of what had transpired. Robbins, a law school graduate, had extensive experience in drug investigations.[1] He dressed and went to the scene of the off-loading. He met other deputies, who said that six persons were in custody and they had seen at least twenty to thirty off-loaders fleeing the area on foot in all directions. A cursory check of the area by Detective Robbins revealed numerous abandoned vehicles—mostly pickup trucks of every size and description, many of which had camper shells attached. There also were papers, trash, surfboards, notes, beer bottles, camouflage netting, flashlights, electronic equipment, and what was later determined to be about nine tons of marijuana, half of which had been neatly packed into the camper shells of the pickup trucks. Most of the trucks had air shocks to help disguise the weight they were hauling, and all the camper shells either had curtains or blinds to keep out prying eyes.

Detective Robbins was told that a citizen witness was walking along the beach around 2:30 A.M., on a night lit by a full moon, when he encountered scores of people who were removing large, black, waterproof sail bags and cardboard boxes from the fishing vessel, which was anchored about a hundred meters off the shore facing the small cove. The boat had its engines running to fight the waves pushing it onto the beach. People were removing the sail bags and boxes from the boat and floating them to shore on surfboards, rubber rafts, Zodiac inflatable crafts, and anything else that would float. Robbins could see a line of pickup trucks waiting nearby that had not yet been loaded with the bags. It was apparent that after a truck had been loaded, it had been driven to a dirt roadway leading to picturesque California Highway 1 about a quarter mile away, where it was parked.

The witness told Robbins that he walked back to the campgrounds, where he dialed 9-1-1 from a public telephone and talked with a Sheriff's Department dispatcher. It was later determined that this public telephone was the only one located within a five-mile radius of the secluded beach.

The dispatcher initially transferred the telephone call to the Monterey Coast Guard Station, thinking the matter was under its primary jurisdiction. When the coastguardsman heard the circumstances, he immediately transferred the call back to the Sheriff's Department because the off-loading was still in progress.

It so happened that several members of the street narcotics enforcement team were at the county jail just finishing booking prisoners when the dispatcher informed them by telephone about the witness's observations. She knew that the deputies were at the county jail and that there were no other patrol units available to respond to the Red, White, and Blue Beach. The fact that she informed the street narcotics deputies by phone, instead of radio, would catch the suspects by complete surprise. It was later discovered that the leaders of the smuggling operation had police scanners to monitor the Santa Cruz County Sheriff's Department, as well as other local and federal law enforcement agencies operating in the area.

The street narcotics team, led by former Santa Cruz County Sheriff's Sergeant Terry Parker, formulated a plan with patrol deputies to interdict the suspects and to not use radios before making contact with the suspects.

Two deputies responded from the county jail to the beach in separate marked vehicles. When they turned onto the dirt entrance to the beach, they encountered a pickup truck parked next to a large Ryder rental cargo van, facing opposite directions. A motor home was parked a few yards away. As the deputies got out of their vehicles, the driver of the pickup truck facing the deputies drove toward them at high speed, sideswiping one of the deputy's cars, and then turned north on California Highway 1. One deputy pursued the pickup truck while the other deputy wisely stayed behind to detain the other suspects. The diversionary tactic used by the driver, who was later identified as Michael Mendez, one of the conspiracy leaders, did not work.[2]

As the pursuit ensued, the deputy said he observed Mendez throw papers that resembled those found from a steno notepad out the window. Only after the last papers were tossed out of the vehicle and left to the mercy of the wind did the driver stop, at which time he was promptly arrested without incident.

Other responding deputies arrived on scene and saw the multitude of people fleeing in all directions. The driver of the Ryder rental truck, Charles Goodyear, and four others were captured in addition to the fleeing driver. The motor home was unoccupied.

Once the suspects were in custody, the deputies discovered the huge amount of marijuana on the beach, along with the abandoned marijuana-laden vehicles lined up bumper to bumper.

The deputy originally involved in the pursuit retraced his chase and recovered many pages that Michael Mendez had ripped out of a notebook. Robbins's examination of the pages revealed probable nicknames, code words, unrelated numbers, obvious telephone numbers, sketches, and other markings that appeared related to the identities of the off-loaders. Words such as "Team A" and "Red Team" were written, along with telephone numbers to what turned out to be cellular, residential, and motel telephone numbers in the area.

An examination of the motor home, which served as the smuggler's command post, revealed it contained optical and electronic equipment, including a police scanner tuned to every police department in the county as well as the military police at nearby Fort Ord, the DEA, the FBI, U.S. Customs, and the U.S. Coast Guard. If the original responding deputies had been notified by their sheriff's radio as opposed to the telephone, all the off-loaders would have been warned by the occupants of the motor home and certainly would have departed with the marijuana.

The enormity of the event cannot be understated. As the sun rose, it was apparent that this was a cleverly planned, sophisticated operation that required enormous manpower and logistics to accomplish. It was obvious to Detective Robbins that this group of off-loaders had done this before.

Each of the abandoned vehicles was searched for marijuana, other items of evidence, and registration papers. Some of the registered owners lived as far away as Carlsbad, California, which was about 425 miles south. In his haste to escape on foot because the deputies had blocked the only roadway, Michael Mendez's brother, Brian, had abandoned a briefcase that was found on the passenger front seat of a heavy-duty pickup truck. In it were several thousands of dollars in cash and his wallet with his driver's license.

Santa Cruz County Sheriff's Department crime laboratory technicians arrived and took charge of the massive crime scene. They spent many hours collecting and later processing the items left behind for fingerprints and other items of physical evidence. Deputies began the arduous task of picking up almost ten tons of marijuana that was to be stored until time of trial.

While conducting the crime scene examination, the deputies were surprised to find an off-loader hiding in the underbrush next to abandoned boxes and sail bags of marijuana. Apparently he did not have time to escape after the original deputies arrived.

Detective Robbins opened one of the black, waterproof sail bags to see that it contained approximately fifty individually plastic-wrapped kilogram-sized packages of marijuana. Each kilogram-sized package was double hermetically sealed. Sandwiched inbetween the two plastic shields was a white four-by-six-inch sheet of paper with the printed likeness of a greenish gold Chinese dragon and the words "Golden Dragon" printed on top. The case was quickly dubbed by the same name.

In the meantime, the Coast Guard had been busy. They had scoured Monterey Bay and had boarded several boats matching the general description of the one seen by the witness, and some that didn't. At 9:43 A.M., they finally found a fifty-foot fishing vessel named the *Pyrgos* that was registered in Alameda, California, that had two scruffy looking men who looked as though they had been out to sea for at least a month. Onboard the *Pyrgos,* Coast Guard officials found about three tons of marijuana packaged identically to the marijuana found on Red, White, and Blue Beach.

The Coast Guard arrested the two men and towed the vessel to the Monterey Station. They notified Special Agent Lee, who was now at work, as well as the U.S. Customs Service, who responded with a dozen agents to collect the marijuana and interview the two men.

U.S. Customs Special Agent Robert Barr, in the presence of DEA Special Agent Lee and Special Agent Wayne Amedy of the U.S. Coast Guard Intelligence and Law Enforcement Branch, advised the captain of the boat, John Meyer, and his engineer, Rex Henderson, of their rights. Both men acknowledged they understood their rights and waived having an attorney present. They were interviewed separately.

According to Meyer, he was a financially broke fisherman who earned more selling small amounts of marijuana on the side than by fishing. He said he had received a telephone call a month before from a Kenny Johnson, whom he described as a longtime friend. Johnson told him how he could make a lot of money. Johnson said he was offering Meyer and a

Figure 14–1   "Golden Dragon" logo on kilogram package of marijuana.

partner of his choosing a chance to earn $100,000 each by smuggling a load of Thai marijuana into the United States. Meyer said he told Johnson he'd think about it. About a week later, Johnson called him back and wanted an answer. Johnson sweetened the deal by saying that if he or his partner should be arrested, their families would receive a $40,000-a-year stipend for every year they spent in jail so long as they kept quiet about the other participants in the smuggling operation. Meyer said he then agreed to participate and would be contacting his partner. Johnson told Meyer to contact a man named George Carollo in Alameda to obtain the boat that would be used in the smuggling venture.

Meyer said he immediately called Rex Henderson to see if he was interested in being his engineer on the trip. Henderson agreed, and the two men traveled to Alameda to see Carollo.

Figure 14–2   Sheriff's deputy inventorying seized marijuana.

Figure 14–3   Sheriff's deputy with seized marijuana.

Figure 14–4   Fishing vessel *Pyrgos* after being seized by U.S. Coast Guard.

When they arrived at the dock in Alameda, Carollo showed them the boat, a fifty-foot fishing vessel that could hold about fifty tons of fish. He pointed out sophisticated navigation and radio equipment on board, and he loaded the boat with a month's worth of provisions and said there were 8,000 gallons of diesel fuel in the tanks.

Carollo had Meyer sign a fake lease for the boat, and Meyer was instructed to say he had leased the boat from Carollo and to say he had no prior knowledge of the smuggling activity.

On the date of their departure, approximately one month before Meyer and Henderson were arrested, two other men Carollo had hired to assist them met them at the dock in Alameda. Meyer and Henderson described the men as having no boating or sailing experience, and they said they only knew the pair as "Jake" and "The Russian," who had a heavy accent. Neither man ever identified himself by any other names during the entire month's journey to retrieve the marijuana and return with it to California.

Carollo gave them a set of radio codes and told them to broadcast on a particular radio frequency at a rendezvous point some distance east of Hawaii. There, they would be met by another vessel that would transfer the marijuana to them. While they talked, a young Hispanic male drove up and loaded about 200 custom-made, black, waterproof sail bags onto the boat. Carollo said the bags were to be used to store and protect the marijuana once it was transferred from the other vessel.

About two weeks later, Meyer, Henderson, Jake, and the Russian reached the rendezvous point about 400 miles east of Hawaii and contacted the other vessel via radio as instructed. The next morning, the other vessel arrived with two men and a woman aboard. The captain of the second vessel introduced himself as "Willie;" however, the other two never identified themselves by either name or moniker.

Meyer and Henderson both described Willie as being a consummate sailor. They had the impression the woman was his girlfriend, but they did not know the relationship between them and the other man, who spoke with a thick German accent.

For the rest of that day and all through the night, they transferred the thousands of individual rectangular-shaped kilogram packages of marijuana contained inside boxes from Willie's boat to the *Pyrgos*. Many of the boxes were opened to place the marijuana into the 200 black, nylon, waterproof sail bags. Each sailing bag contained about fifty kilograms. That evening they celebrated by smoking marijuana and eating steaks the woman prepared. Exhausted, they rested for the next day's sailing.

During their conversations with Willie, he told them the three of them had been arrested in Papua New Guinea and had spent several days in jail before making bail.

Henderson said the Russian told him that he and Jake collected money for Carollo that he earned from selling marijuana in the San Francisco Bay area.

When they finally arrived in Monterey Bay, a man in a twenty-two-foot boat who was acting as their pilot to guide them to the Red, White, and Blue Beach met them. Once close to shore, they anchored and were soon surrounded by inflatable boats, surfboards, and other flotation devices used by the numerous off-loaders to remove the sail bags and boxes containing the marijuana. This went on for several hours, until the man in the smaller boat told them that there was too much marijuana for the trucks to handle. He instructed them to go back out to the bay and wait to be contacted the following night, when the off-loading would continue. Before they departed, Jake and the Russian got into one of the smaller boats and were taken to the beach.

About 9:40 in the morning, the Coast Guard cutter came alongside their vessel and boarded it. The crew found the marijuana and arrested them, towing their fishing vessel to the Monterey Coast Guard Station on the opposite side of the bay.

Meyer and Henderson said they didn't have any other information about the importation scheme, and they denied knowing any other people who were involved other then those they mentioned.

While the questioning was going on, coastguardsmen and Customs agents removed approximately three tons of marijuana from the fishing vessel and placed them in a large truck, where they were transported to the DEA's temporary office at the Monterey County Sheriff's Department for safekeeping. When Lee briefed his supervisor, Resident Agent in Charge Martin London, at the San Jose Resident Office about what had transpired, London immediately assigned him as the case agent. The contacts Lee had made and the informants he had interviewed to initiate new cases in Monterey would have to be held in abeyance pending the outcome of this investigation.

The following day, Special Agent Lee drove to the other side of Monterey Bay to the Santa Cruz County Sheriff's Department, where for the first time he met Detective Robbins and an inspector for the Santa Cruz County District Attorney's office named Charles "Stoney" Brook, one of the most tenacious and thorough investigators Agent Lee had ever met. Brook, a partially bald former Marine with a trimmed mustache who celebrated the Corps' birthday by cutting cupcakes with a bayonet, said the district attorney wanted to prosecute every person possible who was involved in this case.

Detective Robbins said that his boss, the Santa Cruz County sheriff, had also personally called the U.S. attorney for the Northern District of California and demanded that he federally prosecute each suspect identified in the investigation.

Once Customs Special Agent Barr and Coast Guard Special Agent Amedy arrived, the five of them began to sift through the voluminous amount of evidence that was gathered from the beach and piled into Brook's small office. Each of the off-loaders arrested at the scene had requested an attorney and had refused to cooperate.

It became apparent that no one agency was going to successfully investigate this case. Although the primary jurisdiction fell with the DEA, Lee welcomed the help of the others, and an ad hoc task force was suddenly created.

All members of the task force received permission from their supervisors to conduct the investigation for as long as it took and to devote their full-time efforts to the case.

The initial step was to sort out what leads needed to be followed. The owners of the vessels and the vehicles abandoned on the beach had to be found. Persons whose names or monikers were found on the pages discarded by Michael Mendez had to be fully identified, located, and interviewed. Subscriber information for telephone numbers called by the Mendez brothers had to be obtained, and a detailed analysis of toll numbers called by these subscribers would have to be made by DEA intelligence analysts from San Francisco.

Two of the alleged off-loaders arrested in the confusion that night had retained attorneys who insisted their clients were victims of circumstance. They were willing to take polygraph examinations to exonerate themselves. A Customs agent later administered the tests, and both were determined to be truthful when they said they were merely walking by as the police were attempting to round up people. It was the polygraph examiner's opinion, based on the exam, that they had absolutely no knowledge that the off-loading was occurring. After a consultation with the Santa Cruz County District Attorney's Office, they were immediately released from jail and no charges were filed against them.

An examination of the evidence found on the beach made it clear that between thirty and fifty people probably were involved in the smuggling scheme. The task force members had their work cut out for them.

During the course of the next two and a half years, the registered owner of each vehicle abandoned on the beach was identified, located, and interviewed. In almost all cases, they were arrested after being interrogated.

About one in five suspects arrested admitted to participating in the off-loading operation. Each of these admitted conspirators could reveal, on average, five names of other people who also participated as off-loaders. When each block of five people were finally located and interviewed, on average, one of them would reveal the names of five additional off-loaders at the scene. Of those interviewed, one of them would know five others, and so it went until more than 50 persons were positively identified as having participated in the off-loading of the *Pyrgos*.

Each person essentially told the same story. They had been contacted anywhere between a few months and a few days before the off-loading and had been asked if they wanted to earn $25,000 for a night's work. They were told what specific motel to check into in Santa Cruz the night before and what street corner to stand at that evening so they could quickly jump into a pickup truck and be driven to a secluded redwood-sided house with a large wooden deck on an acre or more of flat land in an area of the Santa Cruz Mountains called Bonny Doon. There, Michael Mendez made individual and team assignments and issued them inflatable rafts, surfboards, and other equipment that would be used in the off-loading. None of the off-loaders knew all of the others involved, but they all knew Michael or Brian Mendez. None of the lower-level conspirators had information about the source of the supply of marijuana or any of the Mendez brothers' distributors, customers, or facilitators. None had any conception of how the money generated from the sales of the marijuana was to be stored or laundered.

What the task force needed now was someone who could tie all the players together, someone who knew the other supervisors, managers, and decision makers of the scheme, someone who could identify the ultimate source of the marijuana and who had insight into the money trail. Such a person was found when an off-loader mentioned that he saw a man he knew as John Quizenberry at the Red, White, and Blue Beach.

When Quizenberry was finally arrested, he was stunned. He had successfully conducted or facilitated the importation of over 100 tons of marijuana and hashish over the past decade. Once arrested, he immediately retained private counsel and soon agreed to cooperate with the task force members.

At his attorney's law office in downtown San Francisco, Quizenberry made his proffer to investigators to determine what he could provide in the way of investigative leads in this case. Quizenberry was a well-groomed, good-looking man who was college educated and had no criminal history. He was also well traveled. He had visited most continents in his marijuana smuggling ventures and had spent a significant amount of time at world-renowned resorts in Bali, Fiji, Tahiti, the Bahamas, and other places to avoid U.S. law enforcement and enjoy the spoils of his illegal trade.

Lee told Quizenberry, who was nervously seated at a conference table across from Lee, Robbins, and Brook, that he hoped he would be completely truthful in the initial interview. Lee explained that he had conducted many proffers and that there had never been an occasion when a defendant told the entire truth the first time. He hoped Quizenberry would be the first.

Quizenberry's attorney took exception to Lee's notion that his client would be anything but truthful, and after he vented a while, the interview commenced. Quizenberry spoke in generalities and mentioned names that the task force members had already heard. After two frustrating hours, the meeting concluded and the investigators drove back to their respective offices about 100 miles away. When Lee arrived at the DEA office, there was a phone message from Quizenberry's attorney to call him back immediately. When Lee did, the attorney apologized, saying that shortly after the investigators left, Quizenberry admitted to him that he had held back vital information in the identification of some of the people involved in the conspiracy. The attorney did not want to jeopardize a reduction in sentence for his client so soon, and he wanted to arrange a second meeting. A meeting was set for the following day at a hotel room in Santa Cruz, near where Quizenberry lived.

Over the next three days, Lee, Robbins, Brook, Amedy, Barr, and U.S. Customs Special Agent David Wales participated in the debriefing of Quizenberry about every aspect of the case and about his past smuggling experiences. None of the investigators had ever seen anyone cooperate as fully as Quizenberry.

Quizenberry was shown the notes Michael Mendez threw out his truck window, as well as other papers, notes, and photos of individuals who had previously been identified. Quizenberry was able to name almost all the persons whose nicknames appeared on papers discarded by Mendez or that were found in the motor home. Nicknames such as "Mel," "Ron," "Tarzan," "Tim," "TT," "BLT," "Boo-Boo," "Bergie," "Wayno," and "Jeff" were recognized by Quizenberry, who was able to identify a total of 41 persons he personally knew were involved in the smuggling operation either as off-loaders, supervisors, or investors. He was able to describe what each individual's specific role was in the conspiracy. He had had personal contact with many of the people or had personally recruited them into them conspiracy. He was able to reconfirm that the two men arrested walking in the area who had passed polygraph examinations had no involvement in the conspiracy.

Quizenberry solidified the investigators' case against Michael Mendez and implicated his two brothers, David and Brian. He said he became involved in the conspiracy when David Mendez contacted him six months before the discovery of the off-load. He said he had been involved in a large number of smuggling operations with the Mendez brothers over the past decade and had used this same off-loading site at least twelve times in the past ten years. He said David Mendez owed him and two others $800,000 from a smuggling operation two years prior. David Mendez told him he would make it up to him after he did one last large load of "Thai" marijuana, and he knew he (Quizenberry) had the contacts necessary to supply the drug.

Quizenberry said he met with David Mendez and "BLT" at a Sheraton Hotel in Santa Barbara, California, on about April 14 specifically to discuss the smuggling venture. Quizenberry said the meeting lasted two hours and that he checked into the hotel using his real name. David Mendez instructed him to attempt to obtain as much marijuana as possible for the smallest possible down payment.

According to Quizenberry, Michael Mendez's plan was to have him use his contacts in Thailand to procure ten or more tons of marijuana. The seller would transport the drugs on a Thai commercial fishing trawler to a designated location in the South China Sea, where it would meet a sixty-foot sailing vessel and transfer the load to it. The sailing vessel would then meet with another vessel from Hawaii and transfer the marijuana to it. That vessel would then rendezvous with the fishing vessel *Pyrgos,* from Alameda, that would anchor at the off-load site. Quizenberry said Michael, Brian, and David had decided to smuggle the marijuana this way to keep law enforcement off balance and to keep the crews sharp by requiring them to only travel short distances.

When shown photographs supplied by the California Department of Motor Vehicles, Quizenberry was able to identify numerous registered owners of vehicles that were abandoned on Red, White, and Blue Beach. These were all people he had personally hired for the off-loading operation, and they had been involved in past smuggling operations as well.

Quizenberry said that he flew to Oahu, Hawaii, met with a contact of his named Mark Gutin, and recruited him to be the captain of a sailing vessel to be used in the beginning stages of the smuggling operation. Gutin hired a crew and sailed the vessel to Thailand to transport approximately twelve tons of marijuana to a rendezvous point with a second vessel. Quizenberry recalled that Gutin was to receive $1,300,000 for his participation in the conspiracy.

Gutin advised Quizenberry that he had a friend who owned a sailing vessel that would be suitable to assist in the operation. Gutin and Quizenberry drove to meet with the boat owner, Christopher Kent. After much discussion, Quizenberry decided the fifty-three-foot sailing vessel Kent owned, named the *Askoy*, would be adequate for the operation, and he offered Kent $135,000 for it, which Gutin accepted. According to Quizenberry, he told Kent the vessel was going to be used to fish in the South Pacific; Kent was never told the vessel was going to be used in a marijuana smuggle. This information relieved Kent of any criminal liability because he was not a member of the conspiracy.

Quizenberry returned to California and telephoned Michael Mendez to inform him that he had found a vessel suitable for transporting at least ten tons of marijuana. Michael Mendez said he would travel to Hawaii to give Gutin money for the down payment for the vessel and to determine if it needed any repairs to make it seaworthy.

Quizenberry said that during the next several months, he and Michael Mendez contacted potential investors for the smuggling venture to raise capital to purchase the *Askoy* and the marijuana and to cover other expected expenses associated with the operation.

During this time Quizenberry flew to Reno, Nevada, and met Michael Mendez at the MGM Grand Hotel. While in Mendez's room, Quizenberry turned over to him five cashier's checks, all made out payable to cash in amounts less than $10,000, and about 185 one ounce gold Kugerand coins to be used to purchase the *Askoy*.

Quizenberry said he also personally solicited funds from thirty different individuals to purchase the marijuana from his supply in Thailand. Each of these persons furnished him with between $8,000 and $30,000, for a total that was enough to purchase twelve tons of Southeast Asian marijuana.

In the October preceding his arrest, Quizenberry contacted an Eric Baker, who agreed to act as the navigator on a Thai fishing trawler that would be used to transport the marijuana from the source of supply to a rendezvous point in the South China Sea. Baker also agreed to hire money couriers to transport the cash Quizenberry had collected to Thailand. Quizenberry agreed to pay him $300,000 for performing both jobs. The money couriers Baker hired received $50,000 each for their efforts. Quizenberry said Baker had transported money to Thailand several times in the past and was an expert in doing such things. Baker furnished his couriers with specially designed diver's tanks that had the bottoms machined to screw open so the tanks could conceal money.

Shortly after the money arrived in Thailand and was delivered to the source of supply, Eric Baker called Quizenberry to tell him everything was fine.

Quizenberry traveled through Australia to Thailand, where he met with his source of supply, Phanom Verot. Verot welcomed him warmly because he had done many other transactions with him in the past.

Over the next ten days, Verot smuggled Quizenberry into Cambodia in order to inspect the marijuana he had for sale. Quizenberry described the storage facility as being a 100-by-50-foot concrete slab that had a thatch roof supported by tall columns. He could not say with certainly where the storage site was, other than it was "in the middle of nowhere." He did say that it was close to a river where the fishing trawler could dock and easily be loaded. The marijuana had been removed from the stalks and was piled high in different corners of the concrete slab flooring.

According to Quizenberry, some of the marijuana was rotten and unsuitable. However there was a sufficient amount for his twelve-ton order. He picked out what he thought was the best quality, and he was relieved to learn that two German-manufactured hermetic sealing machines he had shipped to Verot had already been taken to the storage facility. Quizenberry said that to ensure that he received the marijuana he had selected, he ordered over 12,000 four-by-six-inch labels with the depiction of a greenish gold Chinese dragon and *Golden Dragon* written on each. These were the same labels found by investigators at the scene of the off-loading. As Verot's men poured the marijuana into each machine to be sealed in one-kilogram quantities, he placed a label on each package and sealed the marijuana again, forming a double seal with the label sandwiched between the two sheets of plastic, making his marijuana water resistant and easy to identify. It also discouraged Verot from substituting the marijuana he had picked with an inferior variety.

After spending over a week sealing the kilo-sized packages of marijuana, they readied the load for transport to the fishing trawler. Baker, who was assigned to be a passenger on the Thai fishing trawler to oversee the operation, later met Quizenberry when the trawler was being loaded. The trawler departed for its scheduled rendezvous with the sailing vessel *Askoy,* which was being captained by Gutin. Once Gutin received the load, Baker returned to Bangkok and met Quizenberry to tell him that the load was in Gutin's possession.

Quizenberry then left Thailand and returned to Santa Cruz, California, and contacted Michael Mendez to tell him that the transportation of the marijuana was on schedule. Quizenberry said he learned two weeks later from Mendez that the *Askoy* had successfully met up with another sailing vessel he commissioned, named the *Aloe,* and the marijuana had been transferred to it. The *Aloe* was on time to meet with the *Pyrgos,* and Quizenberry knew it was the *Pyrgos* that would be bringing the marijuana to the Red, White, and Blue Beach in Santa Cruz.

The day before the *Pyrgos* arrived in Monterey Bay, Quizenberry met with Michael and Brian Mendez in Santa Cruz to hammer out the final details. They got into a pickup truck driven by Michael Mendez and drove to several locations throughout the city, picking up six or seven other men and transporting them to a secluded home in the Santa Cruz Mountains owned by a Jonathan Warden. Michael Mendez told Quizenberry that Warden's property was surrounded by trees and isolated from the main road and the lot was large enough to accommodate the 50-plus off-loaders when they received their final instructions before the *Pyrgos* arrived.

At the property, Michael Mendez assembled the men into groups and assigned them individual jobs to perform during the off-loading operation. Quizenberry specifically remembered that Michael had written the names of the persons on a steno pad and that he had it with him when they left for the beach. This is the notebook Mendez later tore pages from while he was pursued by Santa Cruz County sheriff's deputies.

After spending about an hour at the house, the off-loaders piled into their camper-shell-equipped pickup trucks and headed toward the Red, White, and Blue Beach. Once there, they deployed to their assigned areas to await the arrival of the *Pyrgos*. Quizenberry said he stayed in the motor home with Michael and the others for several hours during the off-loading, and he had just left for a moment to urinate in the bushes when the sheriff's deputies arrived.

Quizenberry said he fled on foot back to town, where he hailed a taxicab that took him to his residence.

Quizenberry's proffer was a treasure trove of information for the investigators. His testimony would be used to help convict not only the main defendants in the case, but the peripheral players as well. His testimony would also later convince forty-nine of the other defendants to plead guilty to the charges. The investigators knew they had a substantial amount of work to do to corroborate Quizenberry's statement, and they set out on their task.

Investigators went to the different motels identified by Quizenberry where the various off-loaders stayed. They obtained the registration information for guests on the evening in question. The names of each motel's registered guests were given to Quizenberry, who identified those he knew were part of the smuggling scheme. The other names also were run through records maintained by the California Department of Motor Vehicles. DMV provided copies of their driver's license photos, which were also shown to Quizenberry. He was able to identify several others involved whose names he did not know or who had registered under assumed names.

All the registration cards were collected for latent fingerprint and handwriting examination. Some of these coconspirators were later identified through record fingerprints.

The telephone toll information from the home and business telephones of Michael, Brian, and David Mendez, as well as the others arrested on the night of the smuggling operation, was obtained. An analysis of the telephone calls made by these suspects was revealing. Investigators had telephone records that tended to verify and corroborate what Quizenberry had told them. Based partially on when certain phone calls were made, the investigators were able to obtain the exact dates when crucial decisions were reached or when travel arrangements for members of the conspiracy were made.

The investigators also systematically checked with the DMV to identify the registered owner of each vehicle abandoned on Red, White, and Blue Beach. Arrest warrants were obtained for these people. When DA investigator Stoney Brook and Detective Steven Robbins arrived at one of the addresses looking for the registered owner of one of the abandoned trucks, a man who answered the door said that the man in question had recently moved. When asked for his identification, the man produced a California driver's license that differed from the name of the registered owner.

But something struck them as being amiss. When they returned to their office, they reviewed all the photographs provided by DMV and realized that the man they had just talked with had a striking resemblance to the registered owner of the abandoned truck. They were correct in concluding that the man they had seen had assumed the identity of someone else and that he was in fact the true owner of the abandoned vehicle.

Brooks and Robbins immediately returned to the residence to further investigate and discovered the front door ajar. When they entered the residence after announcing their presence, no one was there. They observed that food was cooking on the stove and the interior of the residence appeared as though the suspect had left immediately after they had left the residence the first time.

Further investigation revealed that the abandoned vehicle had recently been purchased from a Ford dealership in Salinas, California. A review of the bank auto-loan records showed that the name of the person who applied for and received the loan from the federally insured bank was the same as the fictitious registered owner. When checking out the information on the loan application, they also discovered that the home and work addresses were fictitious.

When the DMV photograph of the man who received the loan and purchased the truck was shown to Quizenberry, he immediately identified him as a person he knew to be involved in the off-loading.

It was later discovered that the man had applied for a California driver's license using the name of a deceased person who was born about the same year as the off-loader. Because most birth and death certificates are not cross-referenced, the man was able to obtain the deceased person's birth certificate, and he used it to fraudulently obtain a California driver's license.

DEA Special Agent Lee later sought and received a federal indictment for the man, not only for his participation in the smuggling scheme, but also for bank and mail fraud. Mail fraud applied because the California DMV only mails driver's licenses to the address of the applicant. They are not issued at the DMV office where the application is made. Because the frauds were perpetrated to secure a vehicle to be used in the off-loading operation, all other members of the conspiracy at the time were also charged with the offense. The man was later located and arrested.

During the execution of a search warrant at Michael Mendez's home in Santa Barbara, California, Special Agent Lee found a National Geographic publication, *Journey into China,* which had the identical dragon logo that was printed on the labels used by Quizenberry. Also, several hundred thousand dollars in cash was found buried in PVC pipe on the property.

On average, one in five of the defendants arrested agreed to cooperate with the investigators and to testify in court if necessary. The assistant U.S. attorney and the investigators insisted that these cooperating defendants agree to testify in order to receive any legal consideration.

As word got out within the legal community that almost 20 percent of the defendants were cooperating with federal authorities, the investigators began to receive telephone calls from other attorneys who wanted to cut a deal with the government. They also offered to have their clients self-surrender to the investigators at a given time and place.

Investigators discovered that Michael Mendez, who was married, had a paramour rent the motor home he used as his command post at the off-loading site. Quizenberry identified her from her DMV photograph. The same photograph was shown to the rental agent, who verified that she was the woman who had made the deposit for the recreational vehicle and had driven it away.

The assistant U.S. attorney thought it would be almost impossible to charge the woman with conspiracy, not because she wasn't a conspirator, but because the evidence, despite the best efforts of the investigators, was probably insufficient to secure a conviction. No single individual who was cooperating with the government could name her as being charged with the responsibility of securing the motor home for the off-loading operation, nor was she at the off-loading site. After some research, Lee found an obscure, seldom-used law titled *misprison of a felony*. In essence, the woman was guilty of having knowledge of a crime that was about to occur and had failed to report it to federal authorities. The federal grand jury indicted her for this charge, and she pled guilty in federal court.

Special Agent Lee, Detective Robbins, and Inspector Brook traveled to Hawaii to conduct follow-up investigations of that end of the case. They were specifically looking for the two sailing boats used to transfer the marijuana from the Thai fishing trawler to the *Pyrgos*.

They contacted the Maui County Police Department and met with their narcotics detectives. Detectives asked their confidential informants to obtain information about the vessels and the transportation of a large amount of marijuana. Within two days, an informant reported that he had just learned that the owner of the *Askoy*, who was named Helmut Gutin, had just called his wife in Maui and told her he was at the Royal Suva Yacht Club in Fiji.

Lee immediately went to the U.S. Coast Guard in Honolulu to see if they had any contacts in Fiji. A coastguardsman had just returned from a South Pacific law enforcement conference in the Cook Islands and was able to provide the name of the police chief in Suva, the capital of Fiji. The coastguardsman wrote a letter, which his admiral signed, outlining the case and asking the police to merely verify if the vessel was at the club and to provide this information before taking any other action. The letter was faxed to the Fijian police headquarters.

In the interim, Detective Robbins and Special Agent Lee traveled to the big island of Hawaii after county police there located the *Aloe,* the vessel that had rendezvoused with the *Pyrgos* and transferred the marijuana to it. When he arrived, the ship's captain, William "Willie" Harrington, was arrested and later transferred to federal custody in Honolulu.

The next day, the Coast Guard admiral received a telephone call from the Suva police chief, who said that they not only had found the vessel, but had arrested the owner on board and was prepared to take him to the U.S. Embassy.

Lee and Robbins immediately flew to Fiji to meet with police authorities, who had Gutin, a German national, in custody and held at a prison facility.

After coordinating with the Fijian authorities, Lee requested that a coastguardsman travel to Fiji to go over various charts and maps found by the authorities inside the *Askoy* at the time of Gutin's arrest.

Lieutenant Richard G. Brunke, an intelligence officer from Alameda, responded to the request for assistance and arrived in Fiji a few days later. He was able to detect the past travels of the vessel from pinholes in nautical charts and other characteristics only an experienced seaman could ascertain. His expert examination of the charts and log entries verified that the vessel had been involved in the smuggling venture.

Figure 14–5   Sailing vessel *Askoy* after it was seized in Fiji.

    A search of the vessel *Askoy* also found marijuana residue similar to the variety of marijuana seized at Red, White, and Blue Beach.

    After consulting with the assistant U.S. attorney, formal extradition proceedings against the German national were initiated.

    Based on the information provided by Meyer and Henderson, the two men arrested on the *Pyrgos,* Special Agent Lee traveled to Papua New Guinea to pursue the leads. He coordinated with police authorities, and together they seized a hotel ledger documenting that the three crew members of the sailing vessel *Aloe* stayed there overnight before setting sail to rendezvous with the *Askoy.* Lee also determined through his local police contacts that, in an apparent effort to disguise the true identity of their vessel, the smugglers aboard the *Aloe* had paid locals to paint their sailing vessel a different color. The new color matched the description provided by Meyer and Henderson.

A Papua New Guinea customs official told Special Agent Lee that he had arrested the crew members of the *Aloe* after they had docked and gone into a nearby village without presenting visas or documentation to immigration officers. They were lodged in a local jail pending a hearing a few days later when they were released. This discovery corroborated information previously furnished by Meyer and Henderson about the crewmembers of the *Aloe* being arrested. Further, a PNG official was able to give physical descriptions of the crew members that were comparable to those given by Meyer and Henderson.

The investigative team had uncovered a large number of overt acts. These acts included everything from the seemingly innocent purchase of a vessel to meetings with the ultimate source of supply for the marijuana.

In all, sixty-two people had been identified as having participated in the marijuana smuggling conspiracy. Of that number, fifty-five were indicted by a federal grand jury for their roles in the crimes. All but six pled guilty after reaching a plea agreement with the government rather going to trial, and four of the six remaining conspirators were found guilty. The government of Thailand refused to extradite one defendant, the source of supply for the marijuana, and the remaining conspirator died from complications related to the AIDS virus.

Each defendant was convicted of conspiracy to import a controlled substance into the United States. Some of the defendants were found guilty of bank and mail fraud stemming from the defendant who fraudulently obtained a California driver's license through the mail in order to secure a fraudulent bank loan to purchase a truck to be used in the off-loading operation.

The residence used to stage the off-loading operation was the first real property ever seized in the Northern District of California based on its use to facilitate a drug crime. Special Agent Lee filed an affidavit describing how the secluded home in the Santa Cruz Mountains was used to stage the off-loaders with the full knowledge of the owner, who was compensated by the Mendez brothers. A U.S. magistrate judge agreed and ordered the property federally seized under Title 21 of the U.S. Code.

No single conspirator knew the identities of all the other conspirators. Some only knew a few, others knew more. The investigators of the task force were the only ones who knew all the defendants involved.

The Mendez marijuana transportation and distribution organization had been in operation for over 15 years. They had used the Red, White, and Blue Beach to off-load marijuana on at least twelve different occasions over a ten-year period. Other locations included beachfront property Michael Mendez had purchased with his drug profits.

None of the marijuana smugglers viewed his activity as especially devious. They viewed what they were doing as "providing a service" to the marijuana smoking community. The fact that they made millions of dollars in profits through their illegal activity probably motivated them as well.

Thanks to the federal drug conspiracy law, the entire organization was dismantled. Without it, it would have been hard, if not impossible, to secure the convictions of all the members of the conspiracy for their particular roles, even with the testimony of Quizenberry. The ability to attach the crimes committed by all members of the conspiracy to every member proved to be a powerful incentive for them to plead guilty to the crime of conspiracy, rather than take their chances on being convicted of all of the crimes.

NOTES

1. Steve Robbins is now the chief deputy sheriff for operations for the Santa Cruz County Sheriff's Department.
2. No member of the conspiracy is identified by his or her true name. The names of the investigators are their actual names.

CHAPTER 15

Gang Conspiracy Case Study

INTRODUCTION

Gangs and violence are synonymous. Such was the case on Halloween night 1993 in Pasadena, California, when nine juveniles returning home after a party were shot by members of a street gang affiliated with the Bloods criminal organization. Three of the juveniles, who were fifteen, fourteen, and thirteen years old, died in what police described as a retaliatory shooting for the murder of a Bloods-affiliated gang member earlier in the day. The "P-9" gang shooters initially thought their victims were members of the rival Crips gang, but they later learned that they had mistakenly killed children.

CONSPIRACY TO COMMIT MURDER; ATTEMPTED MURDER

About 8 P.M., Reggie Crawford, Edgar Evans, Stephan Coats, and six of their friends arrived at an eighth-grade Halloween party in the central portion of Pasadena, California. About 10 P.M., they started home, stopping at several residences for late-night trick-or-treating. One of the surviving juveniles said that, while they were walking on the sidewalk, a car containing hard-core Bloods slowly drove by, and the occupants gave them what he described as a "hard stare."

As they continued walking in the 500 block of north Wilson Avenue, two men jumped out from behind some bushes in front of them and opened fire with a 9-millimeter handgun and a .38-caliber revolver, hitting six of the juveniles. One of those killed was struck five times with the semiautomatic pistol fire. Another survivor said that one of the men said to his partner, "Now, Blood," before firing at them, a clear indication that the murders were gang connected. One injured victim later told police that one of the deceased juveniles had worn a black bandana. The police knew that this fact alone could have made the shooters believe they were associated with the Crips.

The killings and the shooting galvanized residents of Pasadena's northwest community, despite the fact that they were accustomed to "gangbangers" and their violent activities. The killing of three seemingly innocent children turned many members of the community against the shooters and the gang itself. Although some of the victims were described as "associates" of the Crips gang, the neighborhood remained solidified in its disgust with the shooting.

The Pasadena Police Department launched an intensive investigation. Detective Michael Korpal, who is now a lieutenant in charge of the Technical Services Section, was one of the investigators summoned from his home to respond to the scene of the shootings. Korpal was quickly assigned as the lead investigator, and he, along with other detectives and uniformed police officers, located witnesses, all of whom said essentially the same thing: Two men had been lying in wait, had jumped from their cover behind bushes, had shot the juveniles, and then had run off.

Neighborhood canvasses conducted by detectives located other witnesses who said the shooters ran through backyards and over fences to several waiting vehicles around the corner that fled at a high rate of speed. One witness said that one of the fleeing suspects wore a red bandana on his head, indicative of his affiliation with the Bloods street gang.

Crime scene investigators located fourteen 9-millimeter shell casings, along with three live .38-caliber wad cutters. The presence of the live rounds was indicative of a faulty revolver or of the shooter possibly not being familiar with his weapon because there was no evidence that the weapon had been reloaded due to the lack of expended .38-caliber shell casings.

The City of Pasadena soon offered a $50,000 reward for information leading to the arrests of suspects. Within several days, detectives received about a dozen anonymous telephone calls from persons claiming to have direct or secondhand knowledge about the murders. Many suspects were named but later cleared through investigation. However, the common theme of the calls was that members of the P-9 street gang had committed the shooting in retaliation for the earlier shooting death of fellow gang member Fernando Hodges.

On November 3, Detective Korpal was contacted by a uniformed police officer who had talked with a juvenile concerning a report of someone brandishing a firearm not far from the shooting scene. The juvenile said he had been walking south on Wilson Avenue when the driver of a late 1970s Cadillac pulled in front of him and parked the car. The driver, a male Black about twenty-eight years old had a semiautomatic handgun tucked into his front waistband. The man exited his vehicle and walked up to the witness and asked, "What up, Cuz?" The witness described this as a greeting between Crips gang members. The juvenile said he responded that he didn't "bang," indicating he was not a member of any gang. The man responded, "Good,'cause I don't want to have to smoke your ass like I did your homeboy's the other day." The man then got back into his vehicle and drove away.

The juvenile witness said he had been close to one of the dead victims and he initially hesitated to tell the police anything for fear of being killed himself.

Weeks later, detectives displayed a photo lineup of six suspects to the witness, who positively identified Lorenzo Newborn as the man he saw with the pistol.

Detectives interviewed the surviving shooting victims. One of them said he belonged to the Straight Ballin' Young, or SBY street gang, an affiliate of the Crips. He said that some-one had spray painted the initials "SBY" on a wall at his school. Someone had recently spray painted an X over the B in SBY, which he and the police knew was a common practice in establishing gang territory. The letter B was symbolic of the Bloods. The victim thought that a member of the Crips had crossed the letter out to show dominance of their gang in the area. Even though this particular graffiti had no bearing on the investigation, police knew that an insignificant event like this could later lead to violence by one gang against another to maintain dominance in the area where they thrived. This information did reveal that the shooting victims were essentially in training to become full-fledged gang members them-selves when they became older.

On this same day, the Los Angeles County Sheriff's Department crime laboratory made its preliminary findings on the expended bullet cartridge cases found at the crime scene. The opinion of the firearms examiner was that, based on the markings on the 9-millimeter cases, the firearms manufacturer could be Smith & Wesson, Ruger, or Taurus.

On November 10, a witness contacted Detective Korpal. The witness explained that the previous day her daughter had contacted her at her place of employment about a shoot-ing that had just taken place at their home. Police officers had responded to the scene and had made a report of the incident. According to the witness, her son was a former Crips gang member and was trying to leave the gang lifestyle. He told her that about 8 P.M. on Hal-loween night, he saw Lorenzo Newborn and several other P-9 gang members hiding around shrubbery in the area of Blake and Pasadena Avenue, not far from the scene of the murders. The witness said her son had learned that the P-9s had shot up the area while looking for "Crips to kill." The attack on the witness's home precipitated her call to the police.

Detective Korpal and Officer Derrick Carter later that day contacted the witness's son, who verified his mother's statements and said that Newborn and other P-9 gang members had also visited the home of a friend named "Will" and that they had also threatened him the same night.

Detectives Korpal and Uribe went to "Will's" address, as provided by the witness, and made contact with a man who identified himself only as "Charles."

"Charles" said that he was "Willie's" cousin and that Willie was not home. Charles ad-mitted to detectives that he had been present at a confrontation October 31 at his home, which was located down the street from the witness's residence. According to Charles, he, Willie, and a couple of their friends were inside Charles's house after returning from trick-or-treating about 9 P.M. As the friends exited Charles's house to go home, several male Blacks who had been hiding in some shrubbery confronted them. Charles said he recognized two of the seven or eight men in this group as Lorenzo Newborn and Solomon Bowen, who he knew were P-9 gang members.

Charles said he saw that "Solomon" possessed an unknown type of handgun. As the men circled around him and his friends, several of the men were saying, "Fuck all Crips; shoot the motherfuckers." One of the men then fired a single round in the air, prompting all the men to run off and loiter at a nearby intersection. Charles said he and Willie ran in-side their home and their houseguests fled in their cars. Within seconds of entering his house, Charles said that he heard "80 gunshots" coming from the corner where the men had been standing. When the gunfire ended, the suspects ran south and entered at least two vehicles and then drove off at a high rate of speed. Several additional rounds were fired into the air from the cars as they traveled.

Charles showed the detectives where one of the shots fired had entered a window air conditioner of his home. The bullet was too fragmented to be collected as evidence.

When the detectives checked the area where the shooting had occurred, they located 23 expended 9-millimeter shell casings as well as a live .38-caliber wad cutter round. The casing brands for both the 9-millimeter rounds and the .38-caliber bullet were identical to those found at the murder scene.

When they returned to the police station, Detectives Korpal and Robert Uribe checked the records section for "Charles's" address and located a police report in which a resident of the address had been arrested. His booking photo was of "Charles," but he, in actuality was Willie McFee. McFee feared retribution from the P-9 gang members for talking to the police about the events of Halloween night.

On November 11, based on information provided by an informant, Detectives Korpal and Tom Delgado and Officer Carter interviewed a "John Doe" witness, who wished to remain anonymous, about an unreported shooting that occurred on Halloween near the witness's residence. The witness said he looked out of his second-story window after hearing several shots being fired, and he could see several shadows of people. The witness immediately telephoned his neighbor and asked if he had seen anyone shooting a gun. The neighbor told the witness that he should watch out for the "P-9s." He further said that the P-9s were mad about what had happened to one of their "homies" and that they had just shot up his house. He said that two men named "Lorenzo" and "Solomon" had driven to his home and had gotten out of their car. Solomon had an unknown type of handgun. Lorenzo told the neighbor they were going to "serve" every Crip they knew in Pasadena and they knew that a Crip lived in a white house that matched his. The John Doe witness denied knowing either Lorenzo or Solomon and said he didn't know why they were targeting him.

On November 12, Detectives Korpal and Uribe were contacted by a police officer who had someone in custody who wanted to discuss the Halloween murder case. The man told the detectives that the day after the murders, he had had a conversation with a member of the P-9 street gang. During the conversation, the gang member told the man in custody that three other P-9 gang members—Solomon Bowen, Aurelius Bailey, and Herbert McClain— were responsible for the murders. The man, now considered to be a confidential informant, said he personally knew that Bailey owned a .38-caliber, six-shot revolver that was in a state of disrepair. Further, he personally knew that Lorenzo Newborn had stolen a 9-millimeter Ruger semiautomatic handgun with two magazines from another gang member within the last month. Newborn's weapon had two magazines: one with a fifteen-round capacity and the other with a thirty-round capacity. The informant provided the name of the man whose Ruger was stolen by Newborn.

On November 17, Sergeant Tim Sweetman and Officer John Luna interviewed the man whose Ruger 9-millimeter pistol was stolen by Newborn. The officers told the "witness," who preferred to remain anonymous, that they had heard from several different sources that a man named "Herb" had stolen his handgun. The witness admitted that about six weeks prior, when he was "hanging" with his "homeboys," he was approached by a group of P-9 gang members, among them Lorenzo Newborn. After seeing the witness with a handgun, Newborn asked if he could see it. The witness said he handed the weapon to Newborn, who immediately pulled back the slide, chambering a round, and then "drew down" on him. The witness said Newborn told him, "Now I'm keeping it." Newborn also stole an additional 25-round magazine the witness had in his pocket.

The next day, Detective Robert Uribe and Officer Carter at the Pasadena Police Department interviewed another witness who, like many others in the community, wished to remain anonymous. The man told them he had information regarding the Halloween shooting. The witness said that during the daylight hours of Halloween, he and some friends were driving in town when another vehicle pulled up beside theirs. The other driver told the witness that Fernando Hodges, another Bloods gang member, had been shot and killed at a local federally funded housing project called the Community Arms. The witness said that after purchasing beer, he then drove to a friend's house to "kick back." While he was drinking beer outside the residence, Lorenzo Newborn and Herbert McClain arrived in one of two vehicles that drove up and parked on the street. Karl "Boom" Holmes and another man were in the second car with another Black man he didn't know, but whom he described as being dark-skinned and balding. Shortly thereafter, a third vehicle drove up and also parked.

As the witness and his friend met with the occupants of the vehicles, Newborn asked them if they knew anything about Fernando Hodges' death. He said he had just heard the news. Newborn told them that they were going to go to the local hospital to see how he was doing. Newborn and Holmes then left, but they returned shortly to announce that Hodges had died. The witness described Newborn as being very angry, with "fire" in his eyes. He said it appeared to him that Newborn was "on a mission." Detective Korpal speculated that this was when the conspiracy to murder rival gang members occurred.

When asked, the witness said that he knew that all the people he had met with at his friend's home carried guns and he knew that Newborn carried a 9-millimeter semiautomatic. He also stated that he knew that Newborn had "taken it (a handgun) off somebody." Later that night, the witness said he saw Newborn at a local mini-mart buying beer. Newborn, the witness said, told him to "lay low for a while; we just got two or three of them, down on Wilson." The witness said he understood that to mean that they had just killed two or three Crips on Wilson Avenue. The witness opined that the shooting was in retaliation against the Crips for the murder of Fernando Hodges earlier in the day. Later that evening, the witness met with his girlfriend, who asked him if he had anything to do with the murder of the boys. She told him that one of the victims was her nephew.

The witness said he next ran into Newborn about November 15 or 16 and he tried to talk to him about the shootings. Newborn, the witness said, told him, "I'm laying low, like you know, they don't got nothing on nobody. They got nothing on nobody so I'm not worried about nothing. Nobody is going to jail because they don't have any evidence or nothing."

The witness also said he knew that Newborn was currently staying at a residence in Highland Park and another P-9 gang member, Karl Holmes, had left the area sometime after Hodges' funeral. He said he knew this because he had received a call from Holmes, who said he knew that the witness's girlfriend was telling people that the police had found Holmes's fingerprints on a piece of fencing at the crime scene. Holmes said he wanted to talk to her to tell her to "keep her mouth shut."

The witness concluded by saying that he had heard from various people that Newborn had been acting strangely since the shooting, that he would confront anyone he knew who had been arrested to ask them if the police had asked them about the murders.

On December 8, Detective Delgado and Officer Carlos Lopez interviewed Detrick Bright, Lorenzo Newborn's girlfriend and the mother of his son. Bright was in Los Angeles Police custody for spousal abuse at the time of the interview.

Bright said that Newborn was a member of the P-9 street gang, and she gave the detectives his address in Highland Park, a portion of Los Angeles. Bright said she also knew "Boom," but she didn't know his true name. She admitted knowing Herbert McClain and several other members of the P-9 gang. Bright said she lived several homes away on the same street as Newborn and she loaned the key to her apartment to members of the P-9 gang so they could hide from the police.

On December 18, Detectives Korpal and Uribe interviewed another anonymous witness who stated that three or four days after Halloween, Herbert McClain and two others drove to his home in a burgundy rental car similar to a Buick. He said that the passengers in the car were laughing about "some type of massacre." McClain told the witness, "boom, boom, pow, pow, pow. I can still hear the noise." McClain told the witness that he, Holmes, and some others had shot three Crips in Pasadena in retaliation for the shooting of Fernando Hodges. McClain further said that they were looking for "Steve" when they shot the Crips. Several days later the witness heard that the murder victims McClain spoke about were children, not full-fledged Crips. The witness said that when McClain heard that the victims were children, he became very nervous, cut his hair short, and immediately made plans to leave Pasadena. He told the witness that he needed to get away because "it was too hot to stay."

When asked, the witness told the detectives he knew that McClain had a .38-caliber handgun, but he had sold it. The detectives knew that a .38-caliber revolver had been used during the shootings, along with a 9-millimeter handgun.

Armed with the informants' identification of the suspects, coupled with the finding of identical spent and live rounds at both the murder scene and the scene of the shooting earlier on Halloween, the detectives sought and received search and arrest warrants for the residences of Solomon Bowen and Aurelius Bailey. Both men were now wanted for the murders.

On December 22 and 23, detectives of the Pasadena Police Department executed the state search warrants in connection with this case. When they arrived at Bowen's residence, he was not there. A search of the premises did not reveal any items of evidentiary value.

Detectives did locate Bowen's girlfriend's home address and went there to interview her. When they found her, she was willing to accompany them to the police department for an interview. According to the girlfriend, she had had several conversations with Bowen concerning the Halloween night murders. She said that Bowen told her about the death of Fernando Hodges and that he had rented a mid-sized white car several days before Halloween and returned it about November 3.

The woman also said that whenever she slept with Bowen after the Halloween murder, he seemed depressed and upset. He would "jump" while he slept. When she asked him about his fitful sleep, Bowen admitted to her that he was present at the time of the murders, but he denied either driving a vehicle or shooting anyone. Bowen did tell her that he knew the shooting was going to occur while he was there. She said that Bowen never told her who was involved in the shootings.

At 3:30 A.M., on December 23, detectives executed the search warrant at the home of Aurelius Bailey. After knocking and announcing their intentions, the detectives and officers forcibly entered the dwelling and found Bailey hiding in a bedroom. He was taken into custody without incident and later booked for the murders. He refused to talk to the detectives.

The search revealed the presence of a rifle round for an AK-47 assault rifle and a receipt for an airplane ticket in Bailey's name.

On December 29, Detective Uribe interviewed a previously unknown eyewitness to the shootings. He was shown several photos of the suspects that were contained in several "six packs" of other similar-looking men. The witness was able to positively identify Herbert McClain as the driver of one of the vehicles. The witness also positively identified Karl "Boom" Holmes as having entered one of the vehicles used in the shootings.

On January 17, 1994, Herbert Charles McClain self-surrendered to Detective Korpal after extensive media coverage identified him as one of the suspects.

Karl Darnell Holmes was taken into custody after police conducted a search warrant at his residence.

Lorenzo Newborn was arrested while he was in custody with the Los Angeles Police Department for spousal abuse.

Pasadena police located Solomon Bowen hiding in his brother's home in Eagle Rock, California.

During the initial interviews of the suspects, only Bailey and Holmes agreed to talk to the detectives, and they only said that Newborn had planned the murders. Neither would elaborate.

The murder weapons were never recovered. Police did find a cylinder to a .38-caliber revolver buried in a yard directly across the street from Bailey's residence. Crime laboratory examination failed to tie it forensically to the murders. An informant did later tell detectives that the cylinder was part of a revolver broken up by Bailey that was used in the murders.

The Los Angeles County District Attorney's Office elected to have witnesses testify before the county grand jury in lieu of a customary preliminary hearing. According to Detective Korpal, the strategy was to memorialize the testimony of the witnesses and to protect them from discovery. One key witness was murdered in his home in Palmdale, California, before he had an opportunity to testify before the grand jury. All of the witnesses had good reason to fear for their lives, and the police lodged many in safe houses for several months to validate their promises that they would be protected.

The district attorney sought and received the death penalty for Newborn, McClain, and Holmes after they were found guilty in superior court. Bailey and Bowen were tried separately for conspiracy to commit murder and attempted murder. After detectives conducted an exhaustive three-month search for an essential witness against the pair, they were dismayed to see his reaction in court when he saw several Black Guerilla Family (BGF) prison gang members seated in the audience. The gang members' mere presence, which was orchestrated by defendant Newborn's brother, a BGF leader, caused the witness to break down on the stand and refuse to testify, despite promises of protection from the police. Even after being jailed for a week for refusing to testify, the witness could not bring himself to testify for fear of his life. As a result, Bailey and Bowen pled guilty to voluntary manslaughter and received credit for time served, plus 20 years of formal probation. Both have since been rearrested for drug trafficking violations.

Pasadena police later learned that McClain and the BGF also targeted detectives Korpal and Uribe; Judge J. D. Smith; and the deputy district attorney, Anthony Myers, for murder. Fortunately, no attempts were ever made against their lives.

The Pasadena police detectives had effectively used conspiracy laws to attach weapons charges against all the conspirators in addition to murder. Through the use of testimonial evidence, coupled with the physical evidence located at the crime scene and the earlier shooting on Halloween, they crafted a credible investigation that led to the convictions of the gang members.

Police Chief Bernard K. Melekian initiated a Prevention, Intervention, and Enforcement program (PIE), promising "No more dead kids" on the streets of Pasadena. The goal of the PIE program has always been a three-pronged attack on gang involvement and youth crime. By combining, enhancing, and establishing community services, including police youth services and various community outreach programs such as Drug Abuse Resistance Education, the Youth Accountability Board, diversion courts, and youth advisors, the prevention-and-intervention aspect of the program has become an effective to way reduce crime.

The department expanded the mission of its Special Enforcement Team to include more targeting of street-level criminals. The agency enhanced partnerships with the probation and parole departments, along with the district attorney, and the police became more proactive in enforcing laws against youth-oriented crime and in jailing those with outstanding warrants for their arrest.

From the program's implementation in 1997 until October 2003, only one homicide in the city was attributed to gang activity. The overall crime rate in the gang-infected community also dropped significantly.

Appendix A

Sample Conspiracy Indictment

1

2   UNITED STATES OF AMERICA,   )   CR 01-<u>79</u>
)

3   Plantiff,   )   I N D I C T M E N T
)

4   vs.   )   [21 U.S.C. § 846: Conspiracy; 21
)   U.S.C. § 841 (a) (1) : Distribution of

5   JOSEPH CHARLES SMITH   )   and Possession with Intent to
          aka Joey,   )   Distribute Cocaine; 18 U.S.C. § 2:

6   JOHN WILLIAM JONES,   )   Aiding and Abetting]
    RICHARD EUGENE RICCO   )

7   aka Ricky,   )
    STEVEN ROBERT STOKES   )

8   aka Stevie,   )
)

9   Defendants.   )
)

10   _____)

11   The Grand Jury charges:

12

13   COUNT ONE

14   [21 U.S.C. § 846]

15

16   A.   OBJECTS OF THE CONSPIRACY

17   Beginning on a date unkown to the Grand Jury and countinuing to on or

18   about January 22, 2004, in Los Angeles County, within the Central District of

19   California, and elsewhere, defendants JOSEPH SMITH, aka Joey ("SMITH"), JOHN

20   JONES ("JONES"), RICHARD RICCO, aka Ricky ("RICCO"), STEVEN ROBERT STOKES,

21   aka Stevie ("STOKES"), and others unknown to the Grand Jury,

22   knowingly and intentionally conspired and agreed with each other to commit

23   the following offenses:

24   1.   To distribute at least 5 kilograms of a mixture or substance

25   containing a detectable amount of cocaine, a schedule II narcotic drug

1

2   controlled substance, in violation of Title 21, United States Code, Section

3   841(a) (1).

4   2.   To possess with the intent to distribute at least 5 kilograms of

5   a mixture or substance containing a detectable amount of cocaine, a schedule

6   II narcotic drug controlled substance, in violation of Title 21 United States

7   Code, Section 841(a) (1).

8   B.   MEANS BY WHICH THE OBJECTS OF THE CONSPIRACY WERE TO BE ACCOMPLISHED

9   The objects of the conspiracy were to be accomplished in substance as

10   follows:

11   1.   Defendant SMITH would arrange for the importation of narcotics

12   into the United States for the purpose of distribution.

13   2.   Defendant RICCO would distribute narcotics for SMITH in the New

14   York City, New York, area.

15   3.   Defendant STOKES would transport narcotics from Los Angeles,

16   California, to New York City, New York, for defendants SMITH and RICCO.

17   4.   Defendant JONES would create a hidden storage compartment in a

18   vehicle for defendants SMITH and JONES for the purpose of hiding narcotics.

19   C.   OVERT ACTS

20   In furtherance of the conspiracy and to accomplish the objectives of

21   the conspiracy, on or about the following dates, defendants SMITH, JONES,

22   RICCO, STOKES, and other coconspirators known and unknown to the Grand Jury,

23   committed various overt acts within the Central District of California and

24   elsewhere, including but not limited to the following:

25

1   1.   On January 4, 2004, by telephone, defendant SMITH and an

2   unindicted coconspirator agreed to have defendant RICCO distribute cocaine

3   in New York City, New York.

4   2.   On January 4, 2004, in person, defendant RICCO agreed to

5   distribute 5 kilograms of cocaine for defendant SMITH and an unindicted

6   coconspirator.

7   3.   On January 6, 2004, by telephone, defendant SMITH offered to pay

8   defendant STOKES $5,000 to transport cocaine from Los Angeles, California, to

9   New York City, New York.

10   4.   On January 6, 2004, by telephone, defendant STOKES agreed to

11   transport cocaine for defendant SMITH and an unindicted coconspirator from

12   Los Angeles, California, to New York City, New York, for $5,000.

13   5.   On January 6, 2004, by telephone, defendant SMITH agreed to wire

14   money to defendant JONES to create a hidden storage compartment within a

15   vehicle to be used by STOKES to transport cocaine from Los Angeles,

16   California, to New York City, New York.

17   6.   On January 6, 2004, by telephone, defendant STOKES told defendant

18   SMITH that he would arrive in Los Angeles, California, on January 10, 2004.

19   7.   On January 10, 2004, defendant RICCO arrived in Los Angeles,

20   California, and met with defendant JONES to pay him for creating a hidden

21   storage compartment within a vehicle.

22   8.   On January 11, 2004, STOKES received $5,000 by wire from

23   defendant SMITH for payment to transport cocaine from Los Angeles, California,

24   to New York City, New York.

25   9.   Sometime after January 6, 2004, defendant JONES created a hidden

      storage compartment in a gray 1999 Chrysler LHS ("LHS").

1   10. On January 12, 2004, by telephone, defendants JONES and STOKES

2   discussed the hidden storage compartment in the LHS.

3   11. On January 15, 2004, defendant JONES drove defendant STOKES to a

4   location where the LHS, loaded with approximately 4,995 grams of cocaine, was

5   parked, and provided him with the keys to the vehicle.

6   12. Between January 15, 2004, and January 21, 2004, defendant STOKES

7   drove the LHS, which contained approximately 4,995 grams of cocaine, from Los

8   Angeles, California, to New York City, New York.

9   13. On January 22, 2004, defendant RICCO attempted to sell

10   approximately 4,995 grams of cocaine to an undercover agent of the Drug

11   Enforcement Administration.

12

13   COUNT TWO

14   [21 U.S.C. § 841 (a) (1); 18 U.S.C. § 2 (a)]

15

16   On or about January 15, 2004, in Los Angeles County, within the Central

17   District of California, defendants SMITH, JONES, RICCO, and STOKES knowingly

18   and intentionally distributed, and aided, abetted, counseled, commanded,

19   induced, and procured the distribution of, with intent to distribute, more

20   than 500 grams, that is approximately 4,995 grams, of a mixture or substance

21   containing a detectable amount of cocaine, a schedule II narcotic drug

22   controlled substance.

23

24   A TRUE BILL

25   _____

1   Foreperson

2
    ABRAHAM LINCOLN
3   United States Attorney

4

5   JOHN PAUL JONES
    Assistant United States Attorney
6   Chief, Criminal Division

7

8   MICHAEL ANGELO
    Assistant United States Attorney
9   Chief, Major Narcotics

10

11

12

13

14

15

16

17

18

19

20

21

22

23

24

25

Appendix B

The Zacarias Moussaoui Indictment

IN THE UNITED STATES DISTRICT COURT

FOR THE EASTERN DISTRICT OF VIRGINIA

ALEXANDRIA DIVISION

UNITED STATES OF AMERICA	)	CRIMINAL NO:
	)	
	)	Conspiracy to Commit Acts of Terrorism
-v-	)	Transcending National Boundaries
	)	(18 U.S.C. §§ 2332b(a)(2) & (c))
	)	(Count One)
ZACARIAS MOUSSAOUI,	)	
a/k/a "Shaqil,"	)	Conspiracy to Commit Aircraft Piracy
a/k/a "Abu Khalid al Sahrawi"	)	(49 U.S.C. §§ 46502(a)(1)(A) and (a)(2)(B))
	)	(Count Two)
Defendant.	)	
	)	Conspiracy to Destroy Aircraft
	)	(18 U.S.C. §§ 32(a)(7) & 34)
	)	(Count Three)
	)	
	)	Conspiracy to Use Weapons of Mass
	)	Destruction
	)	(18 U.S.C. § 2332a(a))
	)	(Count Four)
	)	
	)	Conspiracy to Murder United States
	)	Employees
	)	(18 U.S.C. §§ 1114 & 1117)
	)	(Count Five)
	)	
	)	Conspiracy to Destroy Property
	)	(18 U.S.C. §§ 844(1), (i), (n))
	)	(Count Six)

DECEMBER 2001 TERM—AT ALEXANDRIA INDICTMENT

THE GRAND JURY CHARGES THAT:

COUNT ONE

(Conspiracy to Commit Acts of Terrorism Transcending National Boundaries)

Background: al Qaeda

1.   At all relevant times from in or about 1989 until the date of the filing of this Indictment, an international terrorist group existed which was dedicated to opposing non-Islamic governments with force and violence. This organization grew out of the "mekhtab al khidemat" (the "Services

Office") organization which had maintained offices in various parts of the world, including Afghanistan, Pakistan (particularly in Peshawar), and the United States. The group was founded by Usama Bin Laden and Muhammad Atef, a/k/a "Abu Hafs al Masry," together with "Abu Ubaidah al Banshiri," and others. From in or about 1989 until the present, the group called itself "al Qaeda" ("the Base"). From 1989 until in or about 1991, the group (hereafter referred to as "al Qaeda") was headquartered in Afghanistan and Peshawar, Pakistan. In or about 1991, the leadership of al Qaeda, including its "emir" (or prince) Usama Bin Laden, relocated to the Sudan. Al Qaeda was headquartered in the Sudan from approximately 1991 until approximately 1996 but still maintained offices in various parts of the world. In 1996, Usama Bin Laden and other members of al Qaeda relocated to Afghanistan. At all relevant times, al Qaeda was led by its <u>emir</u>, Usama Bin Laden. Members of al Qaeda pledged an oath of allegiance (called a "<u>bayat</u>") to Usama Bin Laden and al Qaeda. Those who were suspected of collaborating against al Qaeda were to be identified and killed.

2.   Bin Laden and al Qaeda violently opposed the United States for several reasons. First, the United States was regarded as an "infidel" because it was not governed in a manner consistent with the group's extremist interpretation of Islam. Second, the United States was viewed as providing essential support for other "infidel" governments and institutions, particularly the governments of Saudi Arabia and Egypt, the nation of Israel, and the United Nations organization, which were regarded as enemies of the group. Third, al Qaeda opposed the involvement of the United States armed forces in the Gulf War in 1991 and in Operation Restore Hope in Somalia in 1992 and 1993. In particular, al Qaeda opposed the continued presence of American military forces in Saudi Arabia (and elsewhere on the Saudi Arabian peninsula) following the Gulf War. Fourth, al Qaeda opposed the United States Government because of the arrest, and conviction and imprisonment of persons belonging to al Qaeda or its affiliated terrorist groups or those with whom it worked. For these and other reasons, Bin Laden declared a jihad, or holy war, against the United States, which he has carried out through al Qaeda and its affiliated organizations.

3.   One of the principal goals of al Qaeda was to drive the United States armed forces out of Saudi Arabia (and elsewhere on the Saudi Arabian peninsula) and Somalia by violence. Members of al Qaeda issued <u>fatwahs</u> (rulings on Islamic law) indicating that such attacks were both proper and necessary.

4.   Al Qaeda functioned both on its own and through some of the terrorist organizations that operated under its umbrella, including: Egyptian Islamic Jihad, which was led by Ayman al-Zawahiri, and at times, the Islamic Group (also known as "el Gamaa Islamia" or simply "Gamaa't"), and a number of jihad groups in other countries, including the Sudan, Egypt, Saudi Arabia, Yemen, Somalia, Eritrea, Djibouti, Afghanistan, Pakistan, Bosnia, Croatia, Albania, Algeria, Tunisia, Lebanon, the Philippines, Tajikistan, Azerbaijan, and the Kashmiri region of India and the Chechnyan region of

Russia. Al Qaeda also maintained cells and personnel in a number of countries to facilitate its activities, including in Kenya, Tanzania, the United Kingdom, Germany, Canada, Malaysia, and the United States.

5.   Al Qaeda had a command and control structure which included a <u>majlis al shura</u> (or consultation council) which discussed and approved major undertakings, including terrorist operations. Al Qaeda also had a "military committee" which considered and approved "military" matters.

6.   Usama Bin Laden and al Qaeda also forged alliances with the National Islamic Front in the Sudan and with representatives of the government of Iran, and its associated terrorist group Hezballah, for the purpose of working together against their perceived common enemies in the West, particularly the United States.

7.   Since at least 1989, until the filing of this Indictment, Usama Bin Laden and the terrorist group al Qaeda sponsored, managed, and/or financially supported training camps in Afghanistan, which camps were used to instruct members and associates of al Qaeda and its affiliated terrorist groups in the use of firearms, explosives, chemical weapons, and other weapons of mass destruction. In addition to providing training in the use of various weapons, these camps were used to conduct operational planning against United States targets around the world and experiments in the use of chemical and biological weapons. These camps were also used to train others in security and counterintelligence methods, such as the use of codes and passwords, and to teach members and associates of al Qaeda about traveling to perform operations. For example, al Qaeda instructed its members and associates to dress in "Western" attire and to use other methods to avoid detection by security officials. The group also taught its members and associates to monitor media reporting of its operations to determine the effectiveness of their terrorist activities.

8.   Since in or about 1996, Usama Bin Laden and others operated al Qaeda from their headquarters in Afghanistan. During this time, Bin Laden and others forged close relations with the Taliban in Afghanistan. To that end, Bin Laden informed other al Qaeda members and associates outside Afghanistan of their support of, and alliance with, the Taliban. Bin Laden also endorsed a declaration of jihad (holy war) issued by the "Ulema Union of Afghanistan."

The September 11 Hijackers

9.   On September 11, 2001, co-conspirators Mohammad Atta, Abdul Alomari, Wail al-Shehri, Waleed al-Shehri, and Satam al-Suqami hijacked American Airlines Flight 11, bound from Boston to Los Angeles, and crashed it into the North Tower of the World Trade Center in New York. (In this Indictment, each hijacker will be identified with the flight number of the plane he hijacked.)

10.   On September 11, 2001, co-conspirators Marwan al-Shehhi, Fayez Ahmed, a/k/a "Banihammad Fayez," Ahmed al-Ghamdi, Hamza al-Ghamdi, and Mohald al-Shehri hijacked United

Airlines Flight 175, bound from Boston to Los Angeles, and crashed it into the South Tower of the World Trade Center in New York.

11.   On September 11, 2001, co-conspirators Khalid al-Midhar, Nawaf al-Hazmi, Hani Hanjour, Salem al-Hamzi, and Majed Moqed hijacked American Airlines Flight 77, bound from Virginia to Los Angeles, and crashed into the Pentagon.

12.   On September 11, 2001, co-conspirators Ziad Jarrah, Ahmed al-Haznawi, Saaed al-Ghamdi, and Ahmed al-Nami hijacked United Airlines Flight 93, bound from Newark to San Francisco, and crashed it in Pennsylvania.

The Defendant

13.   ZACARIAS MOUSSAOUI, a/k/a "Shaqil," a/k/a "Abu Khalid al Sahrawi," was born in France of Moroccan descent on May 30, 1968. Before 2001 he was a resident of the United Kingdom. MOUSSAOUI held a masters degree from Southbank University in the United Kingdom and traveled widely.

MOUSSAOUI's Supporting Conspirators

14.   Ramzi Bin al-Shibh, a/k/a "Ahad Sabet," a/k/a "Ramzi Mohamed Abdellah Omar," was born in Yemen on May 1, 1972. He entered Germany in or about 1995 and afterwards lived in Hamburg, where he shared an apartment with hijacker Mohammed Atta (#11) in 1998 and 1999. Bin al-Shibh also was employed with Atta as a warehouse worker at a computer company in Hamburg.

15.   Mustafa Ahmed al-Hawsawi, a/k/a "Mustafa Ahmed," was born in Jeddah, Saudi Arabia, on August 5, 1968.

The Charge

16.   From in or about 1989 until the date of the filing of this Indictment, in the Eastern District of Virginia, the Southern District of New York, and elsewhere, the defendant, ZACARIAS MOUSSAOUI, a/k/a "Shaqil," a/k/a "Abu Khalid al Sahrawi," with other members and associates of al Qaeda and others known and unknown to the Grand Jury, unlawfully, willfully, and knowingly combined, conspired, confederated, and agreed to kill and maim persons within the United States, and to create a substantial risk of serious bodily injury to other persons by destroying and damaging structures, conveyances, and other real and personal property within the United States, in violation of the laws of States and the United States, in circumstances involving conduct transcending national boundaries, and in which facilities of interstate and foreign commerce were used in furtherance of the offense, the offense obstructed, delayed, and affected interstate and foreign commerce, the victim was the United States Government, members of the uniformed services, and officials, officers, employees, and agents of the governmental branches, departments, and agencies of the United States, and the structures, conveyances, and other real and personal property were, in whole or in

part, owned, possessed, and leased to the United States and its departments and agencies, resulting in the deaths of thousands of persons on September 11, 2001.

Overt Acts

In furtherance of the conspiracy, and to effect its objects, the defendant, and others known and unknown to the Grand Jury, committed the following overt acts:

The Provision of Guesthouses and Training Camps

1.   At various times from at least as early as 1989, Usama Bin Laden, and others known and unknown, provided training camps and guesthouses in Afghanistan, including camps known as Khalden, Derunta, Khost, Siddiq, and Jihad Wal, for the use of al Qaeda and its affiliated groups.

The Training

2.   At various times from at least as early as 1990, unindicted co-conspirators, known and unknown, provided military and intelligence training in various areas, including Afghanistan, Pakistan, and the Sudan, for the use of al Qaeda and its affiliated groups, including the Egyptian Islamic Jihad.

Financial and Business Dealings

3.   At various times from at least as early as 1989 until the date of the filing of this Indictment, Usama Bin Laden, and others known and unknown, engaged in financial and business transactions on behalf of al Qaeda, including, but not limited to: purchasing land for training camps; purchasing warehouses for storage of items, including explosives; purchasing communications and electronics equipment; transferring funds between corporate accounts; and transporting currency and weapons to members of al Qaeda and its associated terrorist organizations in various countries throughout the world.

The Efforts to Obtain Nuclear Weapons and Their Components

4.   At various times from at least as early as 1992, Usama Bin Laden, and others known and unknown, made efforts to obtain the components of nuclear weapons.

The Fatwahs Against American Troops in Saudi Arabia and Yemen

5.   At various times from in or about 1992 until the date of the filing of this Indictment, Usama Bin Laden, working together with members of the fatwah committee of al Qaeda, disseminated fatwahs to other members and associates of al Qaeda that the United States forces stationed on the Saudi Arabian peninsula, including both Saudi Arabia and Yemen, should be attacked.

The Fatwah Against American Troops in Somalia

6.   At various times from in or about 1992 until in or about 1993, Usama Bin Laden, working together with members of the fatwah committee of al Qaeda, disseminated fatwahs to other members

and associates of al Qaeda that the United States forces stationed in the Horn of Africa, including Somalia, should be attacked.

The Fatwah Regarding Deaths of Nonbelievers

7.   On various occasions, an unindicted co-conspirator advised other members of al Qaeda that it was Islamically proper to engage in violent actions against "infidels" (nonbelievers), even if others might be killed by such actions, because if the others were "innocent," they would go to paradise, and if they were not "innocent," they deserved to die.

The August 1996 Declaration of War

8.   On or about August 23, 1996, a Declaration of Jihad indicating that it was from the Hindu Kush mountains in Afghanistan entitled, "Message from Usamah Bin-Muhammad Bin-Laden to His Muslim Brothers in the Whole World and Especially in the Arabian Peninsula: Declaration of Jihad Against the Americans Occupying the Land of the Two Holy Mosques; Expel the Heretics from the Arabian Peninsula" was disseminated.

The February 1998 Fatwah Against American Civilians

9.   In February 1998, Usama Bin Laden endorsed a fatwah under the banner of the "International Islamic Front for Jihad on the Jews and Crusaders." This fatwah, published in the publication Al-Quds al-'Arabi on February 23, 1998, stated that Muslims should kill Americans— including civilians—anywhere in the world where they can be found.

10.   In an address in or about 1998, Usama Bin Laden cited American aggression against Islam and encouraged a jihad that would eliminate the Americans from the Arabian Peninsula.

Bin Laden Endorses the Nuclear Bomb of Islam

11.   On or about May 29, 1998, Usama Bin Laden issued a statement entitled "The Nuclear Bomb of Islam," under the banner of the "International Islamic Front for Fighting the Jews and the Crusaders," in which he stated that "it is the duty of the Muslims to prepare as much force as possible to terrorize the enemies of God."

Usama Bin Laden Issues Further Threats in June 1999

12.   In or about June 1999, in an interview with an Arabic-language television station, Usama Bin Laden issued a further threat indicating that all American males should be killed.

Usama Bin Laden Calls for "Jihad" to Free Imprisoned Terrorists

13.   In or about September 2000, in an interview with an Arabic-language television station, Usama Bin Laden called for a "jihad" to release the "brothers" in jail "everywhere."

MOUSSAOUI Trains at Al Qaeda Training Camp

14.   In or about April 1998, ZACARIAS MOUSSAOUI was present at the al Qaeda–affiliated Khalden Camp in Afghanistan.

The German Cell

15. Beginning in and about 1998, Ramzi Bin al-Shibh, Mohammed Atta (#11), Marwan al-Shehhi (#175), and Ziad Jarrah (#93), and others, formed and maintained an al Qaeda terrorist cell in Germany.

Hijackers Travel to the United States

16. On or about January 15, 2000, Khalid al-Midhar (#77) and Nawaf al-Hazmi (#77) traveled from Bangkok, Thailand, to Los Angeles, California.

Atta (#11) Inquires About Aerial Application of Pesticides

17. At various times in 2000 and 2001, in Florida, Mohammed Atta (#11) made inquiries regarding starting a crop dusting company.

Hijackers Receive Flight Training

18. On or about June 2, 2000, Mohammed Atta (#11) traveled to the United States from Prague, Czech Republic.

19. In or about early July 2000, Mohammed Atta (#11) and Marwan al-Shehhi (#175) visited the Airman Flight School in Norman, Oklahoma.

20. Between in or about July 2000 and in or about December 2000, Mohammed Atta (#11) and Marwan al-Shehhi (#175) attended flight training classes at Huffman Aviation in Venice, Florida.

Money Is Moved to the Hijackers

21. On or about June 29, 2000, $4,790 was wired from the United Arab Emirates ("UAE") to Marwan al-Shehhi (#175) in Manhattan.

22. On or about July 19, 2000, $9,985 was wired from UAE into a Florida SunTrust bank account in the names of Mohammed Atta (#11) and Marwan al-Shehhi (#175).

23. On or about July 26, 2000, in Germany, Ramzi Bin al-Shibh wired money to Marwan al-Shehhi (#175) in Florida.

24. On or about August 7, 2000, $9,485 was wired from UAE into a Florida SunTrust bank account in the names of Mohammed Atta (#11) and Marwan al-Shehhi (#175).

25. On or about August 30, 2000, $19,985 was wired from UAE into a Florida SunTrust bank account in the names of Mohammed Atta (#11) and Marwan al-Shehhi (#175).

26. On or about September 18, 2000, $69,985 was wired from UAE into a Florida SunTrust bank account in the names of Mohammed Atta (#11) and Marwan al-Shehhi (#175).

Jarrah (#93) Attempts to Enroll Bin al-Shibh in Flight Training Courses

27. In or about August 2000, Ziad Jarrah (#93) attempted to enroll Ramzi Bin al-Shibh in a flight school in Florida.

28.   On or about May 17, 2000, in Germany, Ramzi Bin al-Shibh applied for a visa to travel to the United States, listing a German telephone number ("German Telephone #1"). This visa application was denied.

29.   On or about June 15, 2000, in Germany, Ramzi Bin al-Shibh applied for a visa to travel to the United States. This visa application was denied.

30.   On or about August 14, 2000, in Yemen, Ramzi Bin al-Shibh arranged to wire money from his account in Germany to the account of a flight training school in Florida.

31.   On or about September 15, 2000, in Yemen, Ramzi Bin al-Shibh applied for a visa to travel to the United States, listing a residence in Hamburg, Germany. This visa application was denied in September 2000.

32.   On or about October 25, 2000, in Germany, Ramzi Bin al-Shibh applied for a visa to travel to the United States. This visa application was denied.

Bin al-Shibh Sends Money to al-Shehhi (#175)

33.   On or about September 25, 2000, in Hamburg, Germany, Ramzi Bin al-Shibh sent money via wire transfer to Marwan al-Shehhi (#175) in Florida.

MOUSSAOUI Inquires About Flight Training

34.   On or about September 29, 2000, ZACARIAS MOUSSAOUI contacted Airman Flight School in Norman, Oklahoma, using an e-mail account he set up on September 6 with an Internet service provider in Malaysia.

35.   In or about October 2000, ZACARIAS MOUSSAOUI received letters from Infocus Tech, a Malaysian company, stating that MOUSSAOUI was appointed Infocus Tech's marketing consultant in the United States, the United Kingdom, and Europe, and that he would receive among other things, an allowance of $2,500 per month.

Atta (#11) Purchases Flight Training Equipment

36.   On or about November 5, 2000, Mohammed Atta (#11) purchased flight deck videos for the Boeing 747 Model 200, Boeing 757 Model 200, and other items from a pilot store in Ohio ("Ohio Pilot Store").

Bin al-Shibh Travels to London

37.   Between on or about December 2 and December 9, 2000, Ramzi Bin al-Shibh traveled from Hamburg, Germany to London, England.

MOUSSAOUI Travels from London to Pakistan

38.   On or about December 9, 2000, ZACARIAS MOUSSAOUI flew from London, England to Pakistan.

Atta (#11) Purchases More Flight Training Equipment

39.   On or about December 11, 2000, Mohammed Atta (#11) purchased flight deck videos for the Boeing 767 Model 300ER and the Airbus A320 Model 200 from the Ohio Pilot Store.

Flight Training and Exercise

40.   Between in or about January 2001 and March 2001, Hani Hanjour (#77) attended pilot training courses in Phoenix, Arizona, including at Pan Am International Flight Academy.

41.   Between on or about February 1, 2001, and on or about February 15, 2001, Mohammed Atta (#11) and Marwan al-Shehhi (#175) took a flight check ride around Decatur, Georgia.

42.   In or about February 2001, Mohammed Atta (#11) and Marwan al-Shehhi (#175) attended a health club in Decatur, Georgia.

MOUSSAOUI Comes to the United States

43.   On or about February 7, 2001, ZACARIAS MOUSSAOUI flew from Pakistan to London, England.

44.   On or about February 23, 2001, ZACARIAS MOUSSAOUI flew from London, England to Chicago, Illinois, declaring at least $35,000 cash on his Customs declaration, and then from Chicago to Oklahoma City, Oklahoma.

45.   On or about February 26, 2001, ZACARIAS MOUSSAOUI opened a bank account in Norman, Oklahoma, depositing approximately $32,000 cash.

46.   Between on or about February 26, 2001, and on or about May 29, 2001, ZACARIAS MOUSSAOUI attended the Airman Flight School in Norman, Oklahoma, ending his classes early.

Nawaf al-Hazmi (#77) Purchases Flight Training Equipment

47.   On or about March 19, 2001, Nawaf al-Hazmi (#77) purchased flight deck videos for the Boeing 747 Model 400, the Boeing 747 Model 200, and the Boeing 777 Model 200, and another video from the Ohio Pilot Store.

MOUSSAOUI Joins a Gym

48.   In or about March 2001, ZACARIAS MOUSSAOUI joined a gym in Norman, Oklahoma.

Hijackers Travel to and Within the United States

49.   On or about April 1, 2001, Nawaf al-Hazmi (#77) was in Oklahoma.

50.   Between on or about April 23, 2001, and on or about June 29, 2001, Satam al-Suqami (#11), Waleed al-Shehri (#11), Ahmed al-Ghamdi (#175), Majed Moqed (#77), Marwan al-Shehhi (#175), Mohammed Atta (#11), Ahmed al-Nami (#93), Hamza al-Ghamdi (#175), Mohald al-Shehri (#175), Wail al-Shehri (#11), Ahmed al-Haznawi (#93), Fayez Ahmed (#175), and Salem al-Hazmi (#77) traveled from various points in the world to the United States.

<u>MOUSSAOUI Contacts a Commercial Flight School</u>

51.   On or about May 23, 2001, ZACARIAS MOUSSAOUI contacted an office of the Pan Am International Flight Academy in Miami, Florida, via e-mail.

<u>Hijackers Open Bank Accounts</u>

52.   In Summer 2001, Fayez Ahmed (#175), Saeed al-Ghamdi (#93), Hamza al-Ghamdi (#175), Waleed al-Shehri (#11), Ziad Jarrah (#93), Satam al-Suqami (#11), Mohald al-Shehri (#175), Ahmed al-Nami (#93), and Ahmed al-Haznawi (#93) each opened a Florida SunTrust bank account with a cash deposit.

<u>MOUSSAOUI Inquiries About Aerial Application of Pesticides</u>

53.   In or about June 2001, in Norman, Oklahoma, ZACARIAS MOUSSAOUI made inquiries about starting a crop dusting company.

<u>Other Hijackers Attend Gym Training</u>

54.   Between May and July 2001, in Florida, Ziad Jarrah (#93) joined a gym and took martial arts lessons, which included instruction in kickboxing and knife fighting.

55.   In or about June 2001, in Florida, Waleed al-Shehri (#11), Marwan al-Shehhi (#175) and Satam al-Suqami (#11) joined a gym.

<u>MOUSSAOUI Purchases Flight Training Equipment</u>

56.   On or about June 20, 2001, ZACARIAS MOUSSAOUI purchased flight deck videos for the Boeing 747 Model 400 and the Boeing 747 Model 200 from the Ohio Pilot Store.

<u>Al-Hawsawi and Fayez Ahmed (#175) Open UAE Bank Accounts</u>

57.   On June 25, 2001, Mustafa Ahmed al-Hawsawi used a cash deposit to open a checking account at a Standard Chartered Bank branch in Dubai, UAE.

58.   On June 25, 2001, at the same Standard Chartered Bank branch in Dubai, UAE, Fayez Ahmed (#175) used a cash deposit to open a savings account and also opened a checking account.

<u>Atta (#11) and al-Shehhi (#175) Purchase a Knife</u>

59.   On or about July 8, 2001, Mohammed Atta (#11) purchased a knife in Zurich, Switzerland.

<u>MOUSSAOUI Pays for Flight Lessons</u>

60.   On or about July 10 and July 11, 2001, ZACARIAS MOUSSAOUI made credit card payments to the Pan Am International Flight Academy for a simulator course in commercial flight training.

<u>Fayez Ahmed (#175) Gives al-Hawsawi Control Over UAE Account</u>

61.   On July 18, 2001, Fayez Ahmed (#175) gave power of attorney to Mustafa Ahmed al-Hawsawi for Fayez Ahmed's Standard Chartered Bank accounts in UAE.

62.   On July 18, 2001, using his power of attorney, al-Hawsawi picked up Fayez Ahmed's VISA and ATM cards in UAE.

63.   Between July 18 and August 1, 2001, Mustafa Ahmed al-Hawsawi caused Fayez Ahmed's VISA and ATM cards to be shipped from UAE to Fayez Ahmed in Florida. (The VISA card was then used for the first time on August 1, 2001, in Florida.)

Jarrah (#93) Travels to Germany

64.   On or about July 25, 2001, Ziad Jarrah (#93) traveled from the United States to Germany.

Bin al-Shibh Moves Money to MOUSSAOUI from UAE

65.   Between on or about July 29 and August 2, 2001, in Norman, Oklahoma, ZACARIAS MOUSSAOUI made several telephone calls from public telephones to a number in Duesseldorf, Germany ("German Telephone #2").

66.   On or about July 30 and 31, 2001, in Hamburg, Germany, Ramzi Bin al-Shibh, using the name "Ahad Sabet," received two wire transfers, totaling approximately $15,000, from "Hashim Abdulrahman" in UAE.

67.   On or about August 1 and 3, 2001, Ramzi Bin al-Shabh, using the name "Ahad Sabet," wired approximately $14,000 in money orders to ZACARIAS MOUSSAOUI in Oklahoma from train stations in Dusseldorf and Hamburg, Germany.

MOUSSAOUI Purchases Knives

68.   On or about August 3, 2001, ZACARIAS MOUSSAOUI purchased two knives in Oklahoma City, Oklahoma.

Jarrah (#93) Returns to the United States from Germany

69.   On or about August 4, 2001, Ziad Jarrah (#93) traveled from Germany to the United States.

MOUSSAOUI Travels from Oklahoma to Minnesota

70.   On or about August 9 and August 10, 2001, ZACARIAS MOUSSAOUI was driven from Oklahoma to Minnesota.

MOUSSAOUI Takes Commercial Flying Lessons in Minnesota

71.   On or about August 10, 2001, in Minneapolis, Minnesota, ZACARIAS MOUSSAOUI paid approximately $6,300 in cash to the Pan Am International Flight Academy.

72.   Between August 13 and August 15, 2001, ZACARIAS MOUSSAOUI attended the Pan Am International Flight Academy in Minneapolis, Minnesota, for simulator training on the Boeing 747 Model 400.

MOUSSAOUI Possesses Knives and Other Items

73.   On or about August 16, 2001, ZACARIAS MOUSSAOUI possessed, among other things:
- two knives;
- a pair of binoculars;
- flight manuals for the Boeing 747 Model 400;
- a flight simulator computer program;
- fighting gloves and shin guards;
- a piece of paper referring to a handheld Global Positioning System received and a camcorder;
- software that could be used to review pilot procedures for the Boeing 747 Model 400;
- a notebook listing German Telephone #1, German Telephone #2, and the name "Ahad Sabet;"
- letters indicating that MOUSSAOUI is a marketing consultant in the United States for Infocus Tech;
- a computer disk containing information related to the aerial application of pesticides; and
- a hand-held aviation radio.

MOUSSAOUI Lies TO Federal Agents

74.   On or about August 17, 2001, ZACARIAS MOUSSAOUI, while being interviewed by federal agents in Minneapolis, attempted to explain his presence in the United States by falsely stating that he was simply interested in learning to fly.

Jarrah (#93) Undertakes "Check Ride" At Flight School

75.   On or about August 17, 2001, Ziad Jarrah (#93) undertook a "check ride" at a flight school in Fort Lauderdale, Florida.

Final Preparations for the Coordinated Air Attack

76.   On or about August 22, 2001, Fayez Ahmed (#175) used his VISA card in Florida to obtain approximately $4,900 cash, which had been deposited into his Standard Chartered Bank account in UAE the day before.

77.   On or about August 22, 2001, in Miami, Florida, Ziad Jarrah (#93) purchased an antenna for a Global Positioning System ("GPS"), other GPS related equipment, and schematics for 757 cockpit instrument diagrams. (GPS allows an individual to navigate to a position using coordinates preprogrammed into the GPS unit.)

78.   On or about August 25, 2001, Khalid al-Midhar and Majed Moqed purchased with cash tickets for American Airlines Flight 77, from Virginia to Los Angeles, California, scheduled for September 11, 2001.

79.   On or about August 26, 2001, Waleed al-Shehri and Wail al-Shehri made reservations on American Airlines Flight 11, from Boston, Massachusetts, to Los Angeles, California, scheduled for September 11, 2001, listing a telephone number in Florida ("Florida Telephone #1") as a contact number.

80.   On or about August 27, 2001, reservations for electronic, one-way tickets were made for Fayez Ahmed and Mohald al-Shehri, for United Airlines Flight 175, from Boston, Massachusetts, to Los Angeles, California, scheduled for September 11, 2001, listing Florida Telephone Number #1 as a contact number.

81.   On or about August 27, 2001, Nawaf al-Hazmi and Salem al-Hazmi booked flights on American Airlines Flight 77.

82.   On or about August 28, 2001, Satam al-Suqami purchased a ticket with cash for American Airlines Flight 11.

83.   On or about August 28, 2001, Mohammed Atta and Abdulaziz Alomari reserved two seats on American Airlines Flight 11, listing Florida Telephone #1 as a contact number.

84.   On or about August 29, 2001, Ahmed al-Ghamdi and Hamza al-Ghamdi reserved electronic, one-way tickets for United Airlines Flight 175.

85.   On or about August 29, 2001, Amhed al-Haznawi purchased a ticket on United Airlines Flight 93 from Newark, New Jersey, to San Francisco, California, scheduled for September 11, 2001

86.   On or about August 30, 2001, Mohammed Atta (#11) purchased a utility tool that contained a knife.

87.   On or about September 3, 2001, in Hamburg, Germany, Ramzi Bin al-Shibh, using the name "Ahad Sabet," received approximately $1,500 by wire transfer from "Hashim Ahmed" in UAE.

88.   On or about September 4, 2001, Mohammed Atta (#11) sent a FedEx package from Florida to UAE.

89.   On or about September 5, 2001, Ramzi Bin al-Shibh traveled from Dusseldorf, Germany, to Madrid, Spain, and did not return to Germany.

90.   On or about September 6, 2001, Satam al-Suqami (#11) and Abdulaziz Alomari (#11) flew from Florida to Boston.

The Hijackers Return Excess Money to Al-Hawsawi in UAE

91.   On or about September 6, 2001, approximately $8,055 was wired from Fayez Ahmed's (#175) Florida SunTrust account to the Standard Chartered Bank account over which al-Hawsawi had power of attorney.

92.   On or about September 8, 2001, an Arab male retrieved the package from Mohammed Atta (#11) at FedEx in Dubai, UAE.

93.   On September 8, 2001, Mohammed Atta (#11) wired $2,860 to "Mustafa Ahmed" in UAE.

94.   On September 8, 2001, Mohammed Atta (#11) wired $5,000 to "Mustafa Ahmed" in UAE.

95.   On September 9, 2001, Waleed M. al-Shehri (#11) wired $5,000 to "Ahamad Mustafa" in UAE.

96.   On September 10, 2001, Marwan al-Shehhi (#175) wired $5,400 to "Mustafa Ahmad" in UAE.

97.   On September 11, 2001, in UAE, approximately $16,348 was deposited into al-Hawsawi's Standard Chartered Bank account.

98.   On September 11, 2001, in UAE, at about 9:22 a.m. local time (the early morning hours Eastern Daylight Time), Mustafa Ahmed al-Hawsawi moved approximately $6,534 from the $8,055 in Fayez Ahmed's (#175) Standard Chartered Bank account into his own account, using a check dated September 10, 2001, and signed by Fayez Ahmed; al-Hawsawi then withdrew approximately $1,361, nearly all the remaining balance in Ahmed's account, by ATM cash withdrawal.

99.   On September 11, 2001, in UAE, approximately $40,871 was prepaid to a VISA card connected to al-Hawsawi's Standard Chartered Bank account.

<u>The September 11, 2001, Terrorist Attacks</u>

100.   On or about September 11, 2001, the hijackers possessed a handwritten set of final instructions for a martyrdom operation on an airplane using knives.

101.   On or about September 11, 2001, Mohammed Atta (#11) and Abdulaziz Alomari (#11) flew from Portland, Maine to Boston, Massachusetts.

102.   On or about September 11, 2001, Mohammed Atta (#11) possessed operating manuals for the Boeing 757 and 767, pepper spray, knives, and German travel visas.

103.   On or about September 11, 2001, Ziad Jarrah (#93) possessed flight manuals for Boeing 757 and 767 aircraft.

104.   On or about September 11, 2001, Mohammed Atta, Abdul Aziz Alomari, Satam al-Suqami, Waleed M. al-Shehri, and Waleed al-Shehri hijacked American Airlines Flight 11, a Boeing 767, which had departed Boston at approximately 7:55 a.m. They flew Flight 11 into the North Tower of the World Trade Center in Manhattan at approximately 8:45 a.m., causing the collapse of the tower and the deaths of thousands of persons.

105.   On or about September 11, 2001, Hamza al-Ghamdi, Fayez Ahmed, Mohald al-Shehri, Ahmed al-Ghamdi, and Marwanal-Shehhi hijacked United Airlines Flight 175, a Boeing 767, which had departed from Boston at approximately 8:15 a.m. They flew Flight 175 into the South Tower of the World Trade Center in Manhattan at approximately 9:05 a.m., causing the collapse of the tower and the deaths of thousands of people.

106.   On or about September 11, 2001, Khalid al-Midhar, Majed Moqed, Nawaf al-Hazmi, Salem al-Hazmi, and Hani Hanjour hijacked American Airlines Flight 77, a Boeing 757, which had departed

Virginia bound for Los Angeles, at approximately 8:10 a.m. They flew Flight 77 into the Pentagon in Virginia at approximately 9:40 a.m., causing the deaths of 189 persons.

107. On or about September 11, 2001, Saeed al-Ghamdi, Ahmed al-Nami, Ahmed al-Haznawi, and Ziad Jarrah hijacked United Airlines Flight 93, a Boeing 757, which had departed from Newark, New Jersey, bound for San Francisco at approximately 8:00 a.m. After resistance by the passengers, Flight 93 crashed in Somerset County, Pennsylvania, at approximately 10:10 a.m., killing all on board.

Al-Hawsawi Flees the UAE for Pakistan

108. On September 11, 2001, Mustafa Ahmed al-Hawsawi left the UAE for Pakistan.

109. On September 13, 2001, the VISA card connected to Al-Hawsawi's account was used to make six ATM withdrawals in Karachi, Pakistan.

A Co-Conspirator Calls on Muslims to Fight the United States

110. On or about October 7, 2001, in Afghanistan, Ayman al-Zawahiri called on Muslims to join the battle against the United States.

Bin Laden Praises the September 11 Attack and Threatens More Attacks

111. On or about October 7, 2001, in Afghanistan, Usama Bin Laden praised the September 11 attack, and vowed that the United States would not "enjoy security" before "infidel armies leave" the Saudi Gulf.

A Co-Conspirator Solicits Violence Against United States Nationals

112. On or about October 10, 2001, Sulieman Abu Ghaith announced, on behalf of al Qaeda, that all Muslims had a duty to attack United States targets around the world. (In violation of Title 18, United States Code, Sections 2332b(a)(2) and 2332b(c).)

COUNT TWO

(Conspiracy to Commit Aircraft Piracy)

1.   The allegations contained in Count One are repeated.

2.   From in or about 1989 until the date of the filing of this Indictment, in the Eastern District of Virginia, the Southern District of New York, and elsewhere, the defendant, ZACARIAS MOUSSAOUI, a/k/a "Shaqil," a/k/a "Abu Khalid al Sahrawi," and other members and associates of al Qaeda and others known and unknown to the Grand Jury, unlawfully, willfully, and knowingly combined, conspired, confederated, and agreed to commit aircraft piracy, by seizing and exercising control of aircraft in the special aircraft jurisdiction of the United States by force, violence, threat of force and violence, and intimidation, and with wrongful intent, with the result that thousands of people died on September 11, 2001.

Overt Acts

3.   In furtherance of the conspiracy, and to effect its illegal objects, the defendant, and others known and unknown to the Grand Jury, committed the overt acts set forth in Count One of this Indictment, which are fully incorporated by reference.

(In violation of Title 49, United States Code, Sections 46502(a)(1)(A) and (a)(2)(B).)

COUNT THREE

(Conspiracy to Destroy Aircraft)

1.   The allegations contained in Count One are repeated.

2.   From in or about 1989 until the date of the filing of this Indictment, in the Eastern District of Virginia, the Southern District of New York, and elsewhere, the defendant, ZACARIAS MOUSSAOUI, a/k/a "Shaqil," a/k/a "Abu Khalid al Sahrawi," and other members and associates of al Qaeda and others known and unknown to the Grand Jury, unlawfully, willfully, and knowingly combined, conspired, confederated, and agreed to willfully destroy and wreck aircraft in the special aircraft jurisdiction of the United States, and to willfully perform acts of violence against and incapacitate individuals on such aircraft, so as likely to endanger the safety of such aircraft, resulting in the deaths of thousands of persons on September 11, 2001.

Overt Acts

3.   In furtherance of the conspiracy, and to effect its illegal objects, the defendant, and others known and unknown to the Grand Jury, committed the overt acts set forth in Count One of this Indictment, which are fully incorporated by reference. (In violation of Title 18, United States Code, Sections 32(a)(7) and 34.)

COUNT FOUR

(Conspiracy to Use Weapons of Mass Destruction)

1.   The allegations contained in Count One are repeated.

2.   From in or about 1989 until the date of the filing of this Indictment, in the Eastern District of Virginia, the Southern District of New York, and elsewhere, the defendant, ZACARIAS MOUSSAOUI, a/k/a "Shaqil," a/k/a "Abu Khalid al Sahrawi," and other members and associates of al Qaeda and others known and unknown to the Grand Jury, unlawfully, willfully, and knowingly combined, conspired, confederated, and agreed to use weapons of mass destruction, namely, airplanes intended for use as missiles, bombs, and similar devices, without lawful authority against persons within the United States, with the results of such use affecting interstate and foreign commerce, and against property that was owned, leased, and used by the United States and by departments and agencies of the United States, with the result that thousands of people died on September 11, 2001.

Overt Acts

3.   In furtherance of the conspiracy, and to effect its illegal objects, the defendant, and others known and unknown to the Grand Jury, committed the overt acts set forth in Count One of this Indictment, which are fully incorporated by reference. (In violation of Title 18, United States Code, Section 2332a(a).)

COUNT FIVE

(Conspiracy to Murder United States Employees)

1.   The allegations contained in Count One are repeated.

2.   From in or about 1989 until the date of the filing of this Indictment, in the Eastern District of Virginia, the Southern District of New York, and elsewhere, the defendant, ZACARIAS MOUSSAOUI, a/k/a "Shaqil," a/k/a "Abu Khalid al Sahrawi," and other members and associates of al Qaeda and others known and unknown to the Grand Jury, unlawfully, willfully, and knowingly combined, conspired, confederated, and agreed to kill officers and employees of the United States and agencies and branches thereof, while such officers and employees were engaged in, and on account of, the performance of their official duties, and persons assisting such employees in the performance of their duties, in violation of Section 1114 of Title 18, United States Code, including members of the Department of Defense stationed at the Pentagon.

Overt Acts

3.   In furtherance of the conspiracy, and to effect its illegal objects, the defendant, and others known and unknown to the Grand Jury, committed the overt acts set forth in Count One of this Indictment, which are fully incorporated by reference. (In violation of Title 18, United States Code, Sections 1114 and 1117.)

COUNT SIX

(Conspiracy to Destroy Property of the United States)

1.   The allegations contained in Count One are repeated.

2.   From in or about 1989 until the date of the filing of this Indictment, in the Eastern District of Virginia, the Southern District of New York, and elsewhere, the defendant, ZACARIAS MOUSSAOUI, a/k/a "Shaqil," a/k/a "Abu Khalid al Sahrawi," and other members and associates of al Qaeda and others known and unknown to the Grand Jury, unlawfully, willfully, and knowingly combined, conspired, confederated, and agreed to maliciously damage and destroy, by means of fire and explosives, buildings, vehicles, and other real and personal property used in interstate and foreign commerce and in activities affecting interstate and foreign commerce, and buildings, vehicles, and other personal and real property in whole and in part owned and possessed by, and leased to, the United States and its departments and agencies, and as a result of such conduct directly and proximately caused the deaths of thousands of persons on September 11, 2001, including hundreds

of public safety officers performing duties as a direct and proximate result of the said damage and destruction.

Overt Acts

3.   In furtherance of the conspiracy, and to effect its illegal objects, the defendant, and others known and unknown to the Grand Jury, committed the overt acts set forth in Count One of this Indictment, which are fully incorporated by reference. (In violation of Title 18, United States Code, Sections 844(f), (i), and (n).)

                                _____

                                  FOREPERSON

_____

MICHAEL CHERTOFF
ASSISTANT ATTORNEY GENERAL

_____

PAUL J. McNULTY
UNITED STATES ATTORNEY
EASTERN DISTRICT OF VIRGINIA

_____

MARY JO WHITE
UNITED STATES ATTORNEY
SOUTHERN DISTRICT OF NEW YORK

Appendix C

Supreme Court of the United States

SUPREME COURT OF THE UNITED STATES

Syllabus

UNITED STATES *v.* ALVAREZ MACHAIN

certiorari to the united states court of appeals for the ninth circuit

No. 91-712. Argued April 1, 1992—Decided June 15, 1992

Respondent, a citizen and resident of Mexico, was forcibly kidnapped from his home and flown by private plane to Texas, where he was arrested for his participation in the kidnapping and murder of a Drug Enforcement Administration (DEA) agent and the agent's pilot. After concluding that DEA agents were responsible for the abduction, the District Court dismissed the indictment on the ground that it violated the Extradition Treaty between the United States and Mexico (Extradition Treaty or Treaty), and ordered respondent's repatriation. The Court of Appeals affirmed. Based on one of its prior decisions, the court found that, since the United States had authorized the abduction and since the Mexican government had protested the Treaty violation, jurisdiction was improper.

Held: The fact of respondent's forcible abduction does not prohibit his trial in a United States court for violations of this country's criminal laws. Pp. 3–15.

(a) A defendant may not be prosecuted in violation of the terms of an extradition treaty. *United States v. Rauscher,* 119 U.S. 407. However, when a treaty has not been invoked, a court may properly exercise jurisdiction even though the defendant's presence is procured by means of a forcible abduction. *Ker v. Illinois,* 119 U.S. 436. Thus, if the Extradition Treaty does not prohibit respondent's abduction, the rule of *Ker* applies and jurisdiction was proper. Pp. 3–7.

(b) Neither the Treaty's language nor the history of negotiations and practice under it supports the proposition that it prohibits abductions outside of its terms. The Treaty says nothing about either country refraining from forcibly abducting people from the other's territory or the consequences if an abduction occurs. In addition, although the Mexican government was made aware of the *Ker* doctrine as early as 1906, and language to curtail *Ker* was drafted as early as 1935, the Treaty's current version contains no such clause. Pp. 7–11.

(c) General principles of international law provide no basis for interpreting the Treaty to include an implied term prohibiting international abductions. It would go beyond established precedent and practice to draw such an inference from the Treaty based on respondent's argument that abductions are so clearly prohibited in international law that there was no reason to include the prohibition in the Treaty itself. It was the practice of nations with regard to extradition treaties that formed the basis for this Court's decision in *Rauscher, supra,* to imply a term in the extradition treaty between the United States and England. Respondent's argument, however, would require a much larger inferential leap with only the most general of international law principles to support it. While respondent may be correct that his abduction was "shocking" and in violation of general international law principles, the decision whether he should be returned to Mexico, as a matter outside the Treaty, is a matter for the Executive Branch. Pp. 11–15.

946 F. 2d 1466, reversed and remanded.

Rehnquist, C. J., delivered the opinion of the Court, in which White, Scalia, Kennedy, Souter, and Thomas, JJ., joined. Stevens, J., filed a dissenting opinion, in which Blackmun and O'Connor, JJ., joined.

Appendix D

Osama bin Laden Conspiracy Indictment

[Original date unknown; unsealed 4 November 1998]

UNITED STATES DISTRICT COURT
SOUTHERN DISTRICT OF NEW YORK

UNITED STATES OF AMERICA	)
	)
-v-	)
	)
USAMA BIN LADEN,	) **INDICTMENT**
a/k/a "Usamah Bin-Muhammad	)
Bin-Ladin,"	) 98 Cr.
a/k/a "Shaykh Usamah Bin-Ladin,"	)
a/k/a "Mujahid Shaykh,"	)
a/k/a "Abu Abdullah"	)
a/k/a "Qa Qa,"	)
	)
Defendant.	)
_____	)

COUNT ONE

Conspiracy to Attack Defense Utilities of the United States

The Grand Jury Charges:

Background: Al Qaeda

1.   At all relevant times from in or about 1989 until the date of the filing of this Indictment, an international terrorist group existed which was dedicated to opposing non-Islamic governments with force and violence. This organization grew out of the "mekhtab al khidemat" (the "Services Office") organization which had maintained (and continues to maintain) offices in various parts of the world, including Afghanistan, Pakistan (particularly in Peshawar), and the United States, particularly at the Alkifah Refugee Center in Brooklyn. From in or about 1989 until the present, the group called itself "Al Qaeda" ("the Base"). From 1989 until in or about 1991, the group was headquartered in Afghanistan and Peshawar, Pakistan. In or about 1992, the leadership of Al Qaeda, including its "emir" (or prince) USAMA BIN LADEN, the defendant, and its military command relocated to the Sudan. From in or about 1991 until the present, the group also called itself the "Islamic Army." The international terrorist group (hereafter referred to as "Al Qaeda") was headquartered in the Sudan from approximately 1992 until approximately 1996 but still maintained offices in various parts of the world. In 1996, USAMA BIN LADEN and Al Qaeda relocated to Afghanistan. At all relevant times, Al

Qaeda was led by its "emir," USAMA BIN LADEN. Members of Al Qaeda pledged an oath of allegiance to USAMA BIN LADEN and Al Qaeda.

    2.   Al Qaeda opposed the United States for several reasons. First, the United States was regarded as "infidel" because it was not governed in a manner consistent with the group's extremist interpretation of Islam. Second, the United States was viewed as providing essential support for other "infidel" governments and institutions, particularly the governments of Saudi Arabia and Egypt, the nation of Israel, and the United Nations, which were regarded as enemies of the group. Third, Al Qaeda opposed the involvement of the United States armed forces in the Gulf War in 1991 and in Operation Restore Hope in Somalia in 1992 and 1993. In particular, Al Qaeda opposed the continued presence of American military forces in Saudi Arabia (and elsewhere on the Saudi Arabian peninsula) following the Gulf War. Fourth, Al Qaeda opposed the United States Government because of the arrest, conviction, and imprisonment of persons belonging to Al Qaeda or its affiliated terrorist groups, including Sheik Omar Abdel Rahman.

    3.   Al Qaeda has functioned both on its own and through some of the terrorist organizations that have operated under its umbrella, including: the Islamic Group (also known as "al Gamaa Islamia" or simply "Gamaa't"), led by co-conspirator Sheik Omar Abdel Rahman; the al Jihad group based in Egypt; the "Talah e Fatah" ("Vanguards of Conquest") faction of al Jihad, which was also based in Egypt, which faction was led by co-conspirator Ayman al Zawahiri ("al Jihad"); Palestinian Islamic Jihad; and a number of jihad groups in other countries, including Egypt, the Sudan, Saudi Arabia, Yemen, Somalia, Eritrea, Kenya, Pakistan, Bosnia, Croatia, Algeria, Tunisia, Lebanon, the Philippines, Tajikistan, Chechnya, Bangladesh, Kashmir, and Azerbaijan. In February 1998, Al Qaeda joined forces with Gamaa't, Al Jihad, the Jihad Movement in Bangladesh and the "Jamaat ul Ulema e Pakistan" to issue a *fatwah* (an Islamic religious ruling) declaring war against American civilians worldwide under the banner of the "International Islamic Front for Jihad on the Jews and Crusaders."

    4.   Al Qaeda also forged alliances with the National Islamic Front in the Sudan and with the government of Iran and its associated terrorist group Hezballah for the purpose of working together against their perceived common enemies in the West, particularly the United States. In addition, al Qaeda reached an understanding with the government of Iraq that al Qaeda would not work against that government and that on particular projects, specifically including weapons development, al Qaeda would work cooperatively with the Government of Iraq.

    5.   Al Qaeda had a command and control structure which included a *majlis al shura* (or consultation council) which discussed and approved major undertakings, including terrorist operations.

    6.   Al Qaeda also conducted internal investigations of its members and their associates in an effort to detect informants and killed those suspected of collaborating with enemies of Al Qaeda.

7.   From at least 1991 until the date of the filing of this Indictment, in the Sudan, Afghanistan, and elsewhere out of the jurisdiction of any particular state or district, USAMA BIN LADEN, a/k/a "Usamah Bin-Muhammad Bin-Laden," a/k/a "Shaykh Usamah Bin-Laden," a/k/a "Mujahid Shaykh," a/k/a "Abu Abdallah," a/k/a "Qa Qa," the defendant, and a co-conspirator not named as a defendant herein (hereafter "Co-conspirator") who was first brought to and arrested in the Southern District of New York, and others known and unknown to the grand jury, unlawfully, willfully, and knowingly combined, conspired, confederated, and agreed together and with each other to injure and destroy, and attempt to injure and destroy, national-defense material, national-defense premises and national-defense utilities of the United States with the intent to injure, interfere with, and obstruct the national defense of the United States.

Overt Acts

8.   In furtherance of the said conspiracy, and to effect the illegal object thereof, the following overt acts, among others, were committed:

a.   At various times from at least as early as 1991 until at least in or about February 1998, USAMA BIN LADEN, the defendant, met with Co-conspirator and other members of Al Qaeda in the Sudan, Afghanistan, and elsewhere;

b.   At various times from at least as early as 1991, USAMA BIN LADEN, and others known and unknown, made efforts to obtain weapons, including firearms and explosives, for Al Qaeda and its affiliated terrorist groups;

c.   At various times from at least as early as 1991, USAMA BIN LADEN, and others known and unknown, provided training camps and guesthouses in various areas, including Afghanistan and the Sudan, for the use of Al Qaeda and its affiliated terrorist groups;

d.   At various times from at least as early as 1991, USAMA BIN LADEN, and others known and unknown, made efforts to produce counterfeit passports purporting to be issued by various countries and also obtained official passports from the Government of the Sudan for use by Al Qaeda and its affiliated groups;

e.   At various times from at least as early as 1991, USAMA BIN LADEN, and others known and unknown, made efforts to recruit United States citizens to Al Qaeda in order to utilize the American citizens for travel throughout the Western world to deliver messages and engage in financial transactions for the benefit of Al Qaeda and its affiliated groups;

f.   At various times from at least as early as 1991, USAMA BIN LADEN, and others known and unknown, made efforts to utilize non-Government organizations which purported to be engaged in humanitarian work as conduits for transmitting funds for the benefit of Al Qaeda and its affiliated groups;

g.   At various times from at least as early as 1991, Co-conspirator and others known and unknown to the grand jury engaged in financial and business transactions on behalf of defendant USAMA BIN LADEN and Al Qaeda, including, but not limited to: purchasing land for training camps; purchasing warehouses for storage of items, including explosives; transferring funds between bank accounts opened in various names; obtaining various communications equipment, including satellite telephones; and transporting currency and weapons to members of Al Qaeda and its associated terrorist organizations in various countries throughout the world;

h.   At various times from in or about 1992 until the date of the filing of this Indictment, USAMA BIN LADEN and other ranking members of Al Qaeda stated privately to other members of Al Qaeda that Al Qaeda should put aside its differences with Shiite Muslim terrorist organizations, including the Government of Iran and its affiliated terrorist group Hezballah, to cooperate against the perceived common enemy, the United States and its allies;

i.   At various times from in or about 1992 until the date of the filing of this Indictment, USAMA BIN LADEN and other ranking members of Al Qaeda stated privately to other members of Al Qaeda that the United States forces stationed on the Saudi Arabian peninsula, including both Saudi Arabia and Yemen, should be attacked;

j.   At various times from in or about 1992 until the date of the filing of this Indictment, USAMA BIN LADEN and other ranking members of Al Qaeda stated privately to other members of Al Qaeda that the United States forces stationed in the Horn of Africa, including Somalia, should be attacked;

k.   Beginning in or about early spring 1993, Al Qaeda members began to provide training and assistance to Somali tribes opposed to the United Nations' intervention in Somalia;

l.   On October 3 and 4, 1993, members of Al Qaeda participated with Somali tribesmen in an attack on United States military personnel serving in Somalia as part of Operation Restore Hope, which attack killed a total of 18 United States soldiers and wounded 73 others in Mogadishu;

m.   On two occasions in the period from in or about 1992 until in or about 1995, Co-conspirator helped transport weapons and explosives from Khartoum to Port Sudan for transshipment to the Saudi Arabian peninsula;

n.   At various times from at least as early as 1993, USAMA BIN LADEN and others known and unknown, made efforts to obtain the components of nuclear weapons;

o.   At various times from at least as early as 1993, USAMA BIN LADEN and others known and unknown, made efforts to produce chemical weapons;

p.   On or about August 23, 1996, USAMA BIN LADEN signed and issued a Declaration of Jihad entitled "Message from Usamah Bin-Muhammad Bin-Laden to His Muslim Brothers in the

Whole World and Especially in the Arabian Peninsula: Declaration of Jihad Against the Americans Occupying the Land of the Two Holy Mosques; Expel the Heretics from the Arabian Peninsula" (hereafter the "Declaration of Jihad") from the Hindu Kush mountains in Afghanistan. The Declaration of Jihad included statements that efforts should be pooled to kill Americans and encouraged other persons to join the jihad against the American "enemy";

      q.   In or about late August 1996, USAMA BIN LADEN read aloud the Declaration of Jihad and made an audiotape recording of such reading for worldwide distribution; and

      r.   In February 1998, USAMA BIN LADEN issued a joint declaration in the name of Gamaa't, Al Jihad, the Jihad Movement in Bangladesh, and the "Jamaat ul Ulema e Pakistan" under the banner of the "International Islamic Front for Jihad on the Jews and Crusaders," which stated that Muslims should kill Americans—including civilians—anywhere in the world where they can be found.

      (Title 18, United States Code, Section 2155(b).)

[Blank]   [Signature]

_____   _____
FOREPERSON   MARY JO WHITE
                                          United States Attorney

Index